FROM ATHENS TO GORDION

Rodney S. Young at Gordion, 1955

UNIVERSITY MUSEUM PAPERS 1

FROM ATHENS TO GORDION

THE PAPERS OF A MEMORIAL SYMPOSIUM
FOR
RODNEY S. YOUNG

Held at The University Museum
the third of May, 1975

Edited by
Keith DeVries

Published by
THE UNIVERSITY MUSEUM
University of Pennsylvania
Philadelphia

Publication Funding
Gifts made through the Gordion Fund, administered by the Mediterranean Section of The University Museum, University of Pennsylvania, have made possible the publication of this volume of symposium papers honoring the late Rodney S. Young.

Illustrations
Unless noted in the captions, all photographs, maps, plans, and drawings are reproduced courtesy of the excavation projects of the Athenian Agora, Hasanlu, Gordion, and Sardis.

Design, editing, production
Publication Services Division, The University Museum

Book colophon
Elizabeth Simpson

Typesetting
Deputy Crown Inc., Camden, N.J.

Printing
Lithographic Publications Incorporated, Philadelphia

Library of Congress Cataloging in Publication Data

Main entry under title:
From Athens to Gordion.

    (University Museum papers ; v. 1)
    Includes bibliographical references.
    "Publications by Rodney S. Young": p. xviii
    CONTENTS: Thompson, M. Introduction to the symposium.—Thompson, H. A. The tomb of Clytemnestra revisited.—Vanderpool, E. The State prison of ancient Athens. [etc.]
    1. Greece—Antiquities—Congresses. 2. Asia Minor—Antiquities—Congresses. 3. Young, Rodney Stuart, 1907– —Congresses. I. Young, Rodney Stuart, 1907– II. DeVries, Keith. III. Series: Pennsylvania. University. University Museum. University Museum papers ; v. 1.
DF13.F76   938   80-18220
ISBN 0-934718-35-0

CONTENTS

CONTENTS

ILLUSTRATIONS

Frontispiece. Rodney S. Young at Gordion, 1955

VII.   ARCHAIC WALL PAINTINGS FROM GORDION

VIII. ON LYDIAN SARDIS

IX. LYDIAN TEXTILES

X. THE QUESTION OF BALCONIES AT HASANLU

XI. POSTSCRIPT

ABBREVIATIONS

AA   *Archäologischer Anzeiger*
AAA   *Athens Annals of Archaeology*
AJA   *American Journal of Archaeology*
AnatSt   *Anatolian Studies*
AntJ   *Antiquaries' Journal*
AntK   *Antike Kunst*
ArchEph   *Archaiologike Ephemeris*
AthMitt   *Mitteilungen des deutschen archäologischen Instituts, Athenische Abteilung*
BASOR   *Bulletin of the American Schools of Oriental Research*
BCH   *Bulletin de correspondance hellénique*
Belleten   *Belleten Türk Tarih Kurumu*
BSA   *Annual of the British School at Athens*
CVA   *Corpus Vasorum Antiquorum*
FGrHist   F. Jacoby, *Fragmente der griechischen Historiker* (Leiden 1923-1958)
FHG   K. Müller, *Fragmenta Historicorum Graecorum* (Paris 1853-1867)
HSCP   *Harvard Studies in Classical Philology*
ILN   *Illustrated London News*
IstMitt   *Mitteilungen des deutschen archäologischen Instituts, Abteilung Istanbul*
JCS   *Journal of Cuneiform Studies*
JdI   *Jahrbuch des deutschen archäologischen Instituts*
JHS   *Journal of Hellenic Studies*
JNES   *Journal of Near Eastern Studies*
MonAnt   *Monumenti Antichi*
MusHelv   *Museum Helveticum*
OIP   *Oriental Institute Publications*
OJh   *Jahreshefte des österreichischen archäologischen Instituts*
P. Oxy.   Papyrus Oxyrhyncus
Praktika   *Praktika tes en Athenais Archaiologikes Hetairias*
ProcPhilSoc   *Proceedings of the American Philosophical Society*
RE   G. Wissowa *et al.*, eds. *Paulys Realencyclopädie der classischen Altertumswissenschaft* (Stuttgart 1893-1967)
RendLinc   *Rendiconti della Accademia dei Lincei*
RHA   *Revue hittite et asianique*
SMEA   *Studi Micenei ed Egeo-Anatolici*
TürkArkDerg   *Türk Tarih, Arkeologya ve Etnografya Dergisi*
UMB   *University Museum Bulletin*
WVDOG   *Wissenschaftliche Veröffentlichungen der deutschen Orient-Gesellschaft*

PREFACE

"From Athens to Gordion." The phrase sums up the career of Rodney S. Young, and the symposium that was held in his honor in the spring following his death was organized around his interests in the Bronze Age to Classical archaeology of the two lands in which he worked, Greece and Anatolia, and in the archaeology of the further Near East that had bearing on those places and periods.

Much appreciation is owed to the University Museum and its director, Martin Biddle, for taking on the publication of the papers as part of its revived publications program and thus enabling the articles to appear in print together in the same circumstances in which they were presented in their first form—as part of a tribute to Young. The volume follows the program of that spring day, but one should note that beyond the people who took part in it, there are many others, too, who had worked closely or had studied with Young and who held him in high regard.

Some of the papers have been supplemented by addenda, and some footnote references have been updated, but the time elapsed between the composition of the papers and their publication has meant that the authors have not been able to take into full consideration the most recent relevant scholarship that may have appeared in their fields.

KEITH DeVRIES

RODNEY STUART YOUNG

1907 - 1974

Professor Rodney Stuart Young died tragically in an automobile accident on the way to his home from the University of Pennsylvania campus on October 25, 1974. One of the foremost Classical archaeologists of his generation, he played an important role in the Museum, the University, and the Archaeological Institute of America.

He was born on August 1, 1907, in Bernardsville, New Jersey, outside of Newark. His father long served as head of the Newark Board of Education; on his mother's side he was an offspring of the Newark Ballantine dynasty. A conspicuous family house, his Ballantine grandfather's, still stands as a splendid example of Victorian architecture and serves as an annex of the Newark Museum.

After completing school at St. Paul's in New Hampshire, he attended Princeton University, from which he received his B.A. degree in 1929. The fall of that same year he first came to the American School of Classical Studies at Athens, with which he was to maintain a long, close association. He took part in the standard year program of the school, and with his interests in Greek archaeology fully aroused, he entered Columbia to begin archaeological graduate work. Studying with the late William Dinsmoor, Sr., the leading authority on ancient Greek architecture, he received his M.A. degree in 1932. The next year saw his return to Greece and to the American School, where he joined the newly formed staff that was to undertake the excavation of the Athenian Agora. While participating in each of the annual excavation seasons down to the war,

he was able to continue pursuing his formal archaeological studies and took his Ph.D. from Princeton in 1940.

The Athenian Agora proved to be, as expected, a site of outstanding importance, but scarcely anywhere was it more rewarding than in Young's trenches. A rich group of graves of the Geometric period, the ninth and eighth centuries B.C., stimulated in him a long-enduring absorption in that then little understood era; that the time is now much better comprehended is due in part to his own careful, influential studies. For the Classical era, too, of the fifth and fourth centuries B.C., much illumination came from his excavation and publication of a district of houses and sculptors' workshops, a vivid remnant of the neighborhoods of ancient Athens.

With the annual Agora season running only part of the year, he was able to serve as codirector of excavations in a small sanctuary of Zeus near the summit of Mt. Hymettos, overlooking Athens. From this vantage point Young and his workmen watched as a squadron of Italian planes flew over Athens on October 28, 1940. The Second World War had come to Greece.

The war brought for him a whole new life. In the time before the Germans, too, invaded Greece, he raised money for an ambulance, which was presented in the name of the School to the Greek Red Cross. There was even an additional gift: Young came with the ambulance! Serving as its driver on the Albanian front he was severely wounded and was judged, in fact, near death. A long convalescence followed in an Athenian hospital, and while there he received the Greek

Croix de Guerre. In gratitude for his recovery his family dedicated a processional cross in the Episcopalian Cathedral in Newark and set up a replica in stone near where his grave now lies.

Leaving Athens only shortly before the full-scale German occupation, Young became, in recognition of his knowledge of the country, the head of the Greek OSS desk in Cairo. It was his job to coordinate operations during the confused and desperate time of a brutally enforced occupation and of open hostilities between rightist and leftist partisans.

In October 1944, upon the withdrawal of the Germans, he returned to Athens and until 1946 worked as special assistant in the UNRRA food relief project. A perilous time in Greece during which an uprising by the far left was only barely suppressed, it was also a period in which Young himself once more narrowly escaped death when an overloaded island steamer sank in the Aegean.

At the time the Agora excavations resumed in 1947, Young rejoined the staff but is reported to have looked into the possibility of new opportunities. Such there were, and a life which had already been eventful and productive took once more a radical shift that led to his greatest achievements.

In Philadelphia, Prof. J. F. Daniel, Curator of the Mediterranean Section of the University Museum and part-time lecturer in the Classics Department of the University of Pennsylvania, had conceived of two major goals: the creation of a graduate academic program for Classical Archaeology and the undertaking for the Museum of a large-scale excavation at a Classical or related site. The man he soon settled upon to assist him in realizing these plans was Young. The projects and the appointment won approval from the University and the Museum in February 1948. The only remaining matter to settle at that point was the selection of a site, and this turned out to be none too difficult. During a trip through Turkey in the summer of 1948, Daniel and Young were both strongly attracted by the mound identified as Gordion, the capital of the little-known Phrygians. It and its surroundings had previously been touched in only very limited excavations, but what had been found gave promise of much more of value to come, as did its traditional association with King Midas, a figure of considerable power in Assyrian records and of

great wealth in Greek legend. Just, though, as the last bit of Daniel's plans was crystallizing, a grim tragedy intervened. He suffered an attack of pancreatitis, and death followed while he was still in Turkey. His projected new academic program and new excavation now fell upon Young to shape. The challenge was taken up, the two projects became his, and he was to be occupied with them and to be directing them for the rest of his life.

Gordion became the ultimate choice, Turkish approval was obtained, and the excavations got underway in the spring of 1950. They proved to be outstandingly successful. Like the Geometric Greeks with whom Young was previously occupied, the Phrygians as a result of his work lost much of their obscurity. To the earlier none too satisfactory material about them—passing references in Greek literature, a few monuments surviving above ground, the relatively few finds from limited excavations—there now has been added a wealth of evidence. It is the material culture which is, of course, most vividly documented and in fact is represented at Gordion in forms that normally tend not to survive: textile scraps, wooden furniture, and quantities of foodstuffs. In addition, the number of known early Phrygian inscriptions has now more than tripled, giving rise to hopes that progress can be made in understanding the language. This rescuing of an important people of antiquity from oblivion has been among the most significant achievements of postwar archaeology.

Considerable fame came to Young and to Gordion, particularly as a result of the 1957 season when he excavated an intact, very rich royal tomb. The discovery received wide attention in popular and archaeological journals alike.

The other of Daniel's projects, the graduate teaching of Classical archaeology, was launched in the fall of 1949. Just as with Gordion, Young made an impressive success of the undertaking. Progress at first was slow, with no Ph.D. degree awarded until 1961, but by the late fifties an increasing number of students, undoubtedly attracted by the renown of Gordion and its excavator, were entering the program. As numbers continued to swell in the sixties and into the seventies, it came to be a preeminent training ground in the country for the subject.

By the time of Young's death, there was a

whole new rising generation of archaeologists who had been graduate students in the program and who had worked with him. Their positions and ultimate interests vary widely: some are active excavators while others deliberately confine themselves to the classroom and library, and their periods of specialization range from the beginnings of agriculture to the most flourishing periods of Classical civilization. Some, too, have branched out into art historical research or into ancient technological studies. What they do tend to have in common is a pattern of high achievement and, even more consistently, the strongly held, fond memories they have of him.

He himself maintained a high output of scholarly writing, and his long list of publications is characterized, naturally enough, by reports on the sites at which he worked and studies of the material from them. In addition, he undertook the publication of certain finds from the American excavations at Corinth and of material in the University Museum. His written work always tended to be definitive, and it was marked by a grasp of Greek, Anatolian, and Near Eastern archaeology alike.

His outstanding record as excavator, archaeological scholar, and teacher made him a natural choice as president of the Archaeological Institute of America, a post he held with distinction from 1968 until 1972.

Great as were his many accomplishments, perhaps equally memorable were his own highly individual person and character. His imposing physical bulk combined with something imposing in his manner to produce an awe in many who encountered him. As was once aptly put in reference to his conduct of archaeological meetings, "When he presides, he presides." Other characteristics, though, were more conspicuous to those better acquainted with him. Among the most remarkable of the traits was a highly idiosyncratic sense of humor, and notable, too, was his combination of blunt outspokenness with great consideration and kindness.

He was for plain ways, decidedly against intellectual and social affectation, and nothing was as sure to earn his scorn as the excessively theoretical or the dogmatic. An outlook of unpretentious pragmatism is what he consistently brought to his excavations, his writings, and his teaching.

PUBLICATIONS

BY

RODNEY S. YOUNG

1935 "A Black Figure Deinos," *Hesperia* 4 (1935) 430-441.

1938 "Ceramic Evidence for the Introduction of the Greek Alphabet," paper read at the general meeting of the Archaeological Institute of America in Philadelphia, December 28-30, 1937; abstract in *AJA* 42 (1938) 124-125.
"Pottery from a Seventh Century Well," *Hesperia* 7 (1938) 412-428.

1939 *Late Geometric Graves and a Seventh Century Well in the Agora* (*Hesperia* Supplement II, 1939; Ph.D. dissertation, Princeton 1939).

1940 "Excavation on Mount Hymettos," *AJA* 44 (1940) 1-9.

1941 "ΑΝΤΙΠΗΞ: A Note on the *Ion* of Euripides" *Hesperia* 10 (1941) 138-142.

1942 "The Early Alphabet in Attica," paper read at the general meeting of the Archaeological Institute of America at Hartford, December 29-31, 1941; abstract in *AJA* 46 (1942) 124-125.
"Graves from the Phaleron Cemetery," *AJA* 46 (1942) 23-57.

1949 "An Early Amulet Found in Athens," in *Commemorative Studies in Honor of Theodore Leslie Shear* (*Hesperia* Supplement VIII, 1949) 427-433.
"An Early Geometric Grave near the Athenian Agora," *Hesperia* 18 (1949) 275-297.

1950 "Excavations at Yassihuyuk-Gordion 1950," *Archaeology* 3 (1950) 196-201.

1951 "Gordion 1950," *UMB* 16,1 (1951) 2-20.
"Sepulturae Intra Urbem," *Hesperia* 20 (1951) 67-134.
"An Industrial District of Ancient Athens," *Hesperia* 20 (1951) 135-288.

1952 "Progress at Gordion," *UMB* 17,4 (1952) 2-39.

1953 "Making History at Gordion," *Archaeology* 6 (1953) 159-166.
"Where Alexander the Great Cut the Gordian Knot," *ILN*, Jan. 3, 1953, 20-23.

1955 "Gordion, Preliminary Report 1953," *AJA* 59 (1955) 1-18.
"Grave Robbers' Leavings," *Archaeology* 8 (1955) 191-197.
"The South Wall of Balkh-Bactra," *AJA* 59 (1955) 267-276.

1956 "The Campaign of 1955 at Gordion," *AJA* 60 (1956) 249-266.
"Discoveries at Gordion 1956," *Archaeology* 9 (1956) 263-267.
"Grave Of A Princely Child," *ILN*, Nov. 10, 1956, 797-799.
"King Midas' Kitchen," *ILN*, Nov. 17, 1966, 857-859.

1957 "Gordion Excavations, 1956," *TürkArkDerg* 7 (1957) 26-38.
"Gordion 1956: Preliminary Report," *AJA* 61 (1957) 319-331.
"Bronzes from Gordion's Royal Tomb," *Archaeology* 11 (1957) 227-231.

1958 *From The City of King Midas: Phrygian Art*, exhibition catalogue of the University Museum, 1958-59 (Philadelphia 1958) 1-23.

"Gordion Campaign of 1957: Preliminary Report," *AJA* 62 (1958) 139-154.

"Gordion Report, 1957," *TürkArkDerg* 8 (1958) 34-44.

"The Gordion Tomb," *Expedition* 1,1 (1958) 3-13.

"Tomb of a King of Phrygia," *ILN,* May 17, 1958, 828-831.

1960 "The Gordion Campaign of 1959: Preliminary Report," *AJA* 64 (1960) 227-244.

"Gordion 1959," *TürkArkDerg* 10 (1960) 3-6.

"Phrygian Architecture and Construction," *Expedition* 2, 2 (1960) 2-9.

Review of T. J. Dunbabin, *The Greeks and Their Eastern Neighbours* in *AJA* 64 (1960) 385-387.

1961 "Footnote on Griffins," *Expedition* 3,2 (1961) 12-14.

1962 "Phrygian Construction and Architecture: II," *Expedition* 4,4 (1962) 2-12.

"The 1961 Campaign at Gordion," *AJA* 66 (1962) 153-168.

1963 "Gordion on the Royal Road," *ProcPhilSoc* 107 (1963) 348-364.

1964 "The 1963 Campaign at Gordion," *AJA* 68 (1964) 279-292.

"The Geometric Period" and "The Protocorinthian Period" in C. W. Blegen, H. Palmer, R. S. Young, *The North Cemetery* (Corinth XIII; Princeton 1964) 13-52.

Review of E. Akurgal, *Die Kunst Anatoliens von Homer bis Alexander* in *AJA* 68 (1964) 73-75.

"The Nomadic Impact: Gordion" in M. J. Mellink, ed., *Dark Ages and Nomads c. 1000, Studies in Iranian and Anatolian Archaeology*

(Istanbul, Nederlands Historisch-Archaeologisch Instituut, 1964) 52-57.

1965 "Early Mosaics at Gordion," *Expedition* 7,3 (1965) 4-13.

"Gordion: Problems of Western Anatolia" in *Le rayonnement des civilisations grecque et romaine sur les cultures périphériques* (Huitième congrès international d'archéologie classique [Paris 1963]; Paris 1965) 481-485.

1966 "The Gordion Campaign of 1965," *AJA* 70 (1966) 267-278.

"Early Iron Age, Classical, and Roman Empire" in *Art Treasures of Turkey*, exhibition catalogue circulated by the Smithsonian Institution (Washington, D.C., 1966) 21-35.

1967 "A Bronze Bowl in Philadelphia," *JNES* 26 (1967) 145-154.

1968 "The Gordion Campaign of 1967," *AJA* 72 (1968) 231-241.

Gordion, A Guide to the Excavations and Museum (Ankara, Archaeological Museum, 1968; 2nd ed. with unchanged text 1975).

"Operation Gordion," *Expedition* 11,1 (1968) 16-19.

1969 "Old Phrygian Inscriptions from Gordion," *Hesperia* 38 (1969) 252-296.

"Doodling at Gordion," *Archaeology* 22 (1969) 270-275.

1972 Review of C. H. Emilie Haspels, *The Highlands of Phrygia* in *AJA* 16 (1972) 444-447.

1974 "Phrygian Furniture from Gordion," *Expedition* 16,3 (1974) 2-13.

1978 "The Phrygian Contribution" in *The Proceedings of the Xth International Congress of Classical Archaeology, Ankara-Izmir . . . 1973* I (Ankara 1978) 9-24.

I. INTRODUCTION TO THE SYMPOSIUM*

Margaret Thompson

Today's symposium in memory of Rodney Stuart Young brings together a cross section of those who knew him best—relatives, colleagues, students, and friends. Many others, here and abroad, are surely present in thought if not in person. The program which follows is also a cross section, designed to point up major areas of Rodney's scholarly career and concerns.

Rodney was fortunate in knowing from the beginning exactly what he wanted to do and in having the opportunity and ability to pursue his goal to splendid fruition. Training was gained in Greece at the American School of Classical Studies and at the Athenian Agora, where he made important contributions to our knowledge of that ancient site. Those years were, I venture to say, his happiest. He had a deep affection for Greece and the Greek people, and that affection influenced his decision to stay on and volunteer for hospital service when the Italians invaded Epirus. It was service that brought him decorations for valor from the United States and Greek governments and almost cost him his life.

The true fulfillment of Rodney's scholarly career came in the postwar years during which he taught at the University of Pennsylvania, served as curator at the University Museum, and directed the Gordion excavations. The spectacular results of his work in Turkey have been par-

tially recorded in preliminary reports and lectures. That we shall never have his final account is a great loss, but it is good to know that he had finished over half of the volume on the tumuli and that there are notes indicating his analysis and interpretation of the site with which his name will always be linked.

In addition to his responsibilities as teacher and excavator, Rodney found time for peripheral concerns. He was a founding father of the American Research Institute in Turkey, serving on its board of directors and following with keen interest the growth of its archaeological branch in Ankara. He was a mainstay of the Archaeological Institute of America, a member of its various governing bodies and for four years its president. The AIA is immeasurably indebted to him for devoted service, wise guidance, and generous contributions of time, effort, and financial support.

It is easy to describe the distinguished scholar, far harder to take the measure of the man. Rodney's priorities were as simple and uncluttered as his way of life. One felt that he cared little or nothing for material possessions, and that left him free for essential commitments. About people he cared a great deal. His students respected the depth and breadth of his learning, the clarity of his teaching, and the firm but gentle quality of his supervision; they responded even more to his obvious concern for their welfare and his interest in them as individuals. The same bond of mutual understanding and affection was apparent at Gordion. As one member of the staff put it, "By his personality alone, Rodney created a

---

*At the symposium the paper was read for Miss Thompson by Evelyn B. Harrison, of the Institute of Fine Arts, New York University, who also filled in for Miss Thompson by presiding over the program.

warm, homelike atmosphere, which compensated for the lack of physical comforts and made us reluctant to leave even for vacations."

We all have our special memories. Mine go back nearly forty years to 1937 when I first went to the Agora, and I shall never forget how kind he was to a bewildered novice, trying to get her bearings in a strange new environment. Years later, we were closely associated in the affairs of the AIA and it was then that I realized more than ever before the extent to which one could count on Rodney. Whatever the need—for advice, support, service—there was never any hesitation or reservation about his response. Other memories, which we all share, are of Rodney at his informal best. Any gathering was the livelier for his presence. He had a talent for hospitality, for putting one at ease, for cheerful and witty conversation. His sense of humor was irrepressible, and if his sallies were at times disconcerting, they were always amusing. Our meetings in the future will be duller without his quips and infectious chuckle.

Last December the Council of the AIA recorded its tribute in the following memorial:

Fate was cruel, one feels, to snatch Rodney Young before he had finished his life's work. But fate cannot rob us of the contributions that Rodney had already made to the cause of human studies. For four years (1968-1972) he guided the affairs of this Institute with devotion, good judgment and fairness. The establishment of the American Research Institute in Turkey is due largely to his energetic support. Through active participation in major excavations in both Greece (the Athenian Agora) and Turkey (Gordion) he made substantial additions to the knowledge of the early history of these areas. In doing so he retained the respect, and indeed the affection, of the living people of both lands. As a teacher in both the formal and informal sense of the word he attracted many students of outstanding quality. This younger generation may be counted on to complete the publication of Gordion, a worthy memorial of one who was to them a great teacher and to all of us a warmhearted friend.

II. THE TOMB OF CLYTEMNESTRA REVISITED*

Homer A. Thompson

I am glad to be here to join in honoring the memory of Rodney Young, one of my oldest friends and earliest professional colleagues. He and I found ourselves together in Athens, both for the first time, in the fall of 1929. Later on we were colleagues on the staff of the Agora excavations from the time he became a member in 1934 until he forsook Greece for Turkey in 1950.

Today I am thinking especially of Young's first major study in the Agora. It was based mainly on the contents of a score of graves dating from the second half of the eighth century B.C. which he had excavated near the Tholos.[1] In working up his finds for publication Young was quick to realize their importance for the study of the beginnings of Classical Greek civilization, and he gave much thought to sorting out the elements that went into the new amalgam. The indigenous strain was, of course, dominant, especially in the pottery with its long continuity from Mycenaean through Protogeometric and Geometric. But from the late eighth century onward Near Eastern influence became apparent in both subject matter and style. A third element, and the one in which I am most interested at this moment, derived from a conscious harking back to the heroic age of Greece. This tendency was illustrated in various ways by the finds from the Tholos Cemetery: by the picture of a chariot race on a funerary urn,[2] probably an echo of Homer's account of the funeral of Patroklos (*Iliad* XXXIII, 362 ff.), and again by the representation of Siamese twins on a curious wine jug; these are now generally accepted as the Molione or Aktorione with whom Nestor strove in the *Iliad* (XI, 750 ff; XXIII, 638 ff.).[3] The jug dates from the latter part of the eighth century, and the picture is to be ranked among the very earliest representations of an epic theme in Greek art. The depiction of epic themes was, of course, to be a major component of Greek art for centuries thereafter. For the rest of his life Young continued to take an active interest in the problems relating to the origins of Classical Greek civilization.

I wish now to invite your attention to another

*Since this paper was delivered on May 3, 1975 I have profited from reading several more recent studies and from talking with a number of colleagues, among them Sinclair Hood, Sarah Immerwahr, Günter Kopcke, and John Sakellarakis, none of whom, however, is to be held responsible for such errors as may remain. Edwin M. Schorr has made helpful comments.

[1] R. S. Young, *Late Geometric Graves and a Seventh Century Well in the Agora* (*Hesperia* Supplement II, 1939); E. T. H. Brann, *Late Geometric and Protoattic Pottery* (The Athenian Agora VIII; Princeton 1962) 111f.; H. A. Thompson and R. E. Wycherley, *The Agora of Athens* (The Athenian Agora XIV; Princeton 1972) 10-15.

[2] Agora Inv. P 4990, discussed by R. S. Young (*supra* n. 1) 55-57.

[3] Agora Inv. P 4885, discussed by R. S. Young (*supra* no. 1) 68-71. The identification has not been accepted by all scholars. For subsequent discussion cf. G. Ahlberg, *Fighting on Land and Sea in Greek Geometric Art* (Stockholm 1971) 12f., 56, 109; J. Carter, "Narrative Art in the Geometric Period," *BSA* 67 (1972) 52f. I am informed by Lilly Kahil that the forthcoming first volume of the *Lexicon Iconographicum Mythologiae Classicae* will contain a detailed study of the Molione by Roland Hampe, who first proposed the identification of the scene on the oinochoe from the Agora.

example of how a conscious revival of interest in the heroic age may have influenced the formation of what was to become another very characteristic element in Greek art of Classical times, *viz.,* the Doric column. For this illustration we go to a place that was much more redolent than Athens of heroic legend, *viz.,* Mycenae.

Most scholars have long been inclined to believe that the principal source of inspiration for the Doric column is to be sought in the architecture of the Minoan-Mycenaean world. The evidence has been examined thoroughly in recent years, especially by Professor Heinrich Drerup of Marburg and his pupils. Their conclusions have been presented lucidly and convincingly by Burkhardt Wesenberg in his recent book *Kapitelle und Basen.*[4] Today I should like to add just a footnote to their findings.

According to Vitruvius (IV, 1, 3) the first temple to be built in the Doric order was one erected by King Dorus in the Argive Heraion. This ancient tradition connecting the origin of the Doric order with the Argolid is supported by the archaeological evidence. A preponderant proportion of the earliest Doric columns of stone, as also of representations of such columns, have come to light in the Argolid, in the adjacent Corinthia, and in the Corinthian colony of Kerkyra.[5] But none of the Doric columns or drawings of such columns yet known can be shown to antedate the second half of the seventh century B.C., i.e., a time four or five centuries after the collapse of Mycenaean civilization. How then did knowledge of the Mycenaean prototypes become known to the early Greek builders?

Theoretically we may consider the possibility that the inspiration came through minor works of art such as carved ivories, metal reliefs and seal stones on which columns or half columns of typical Minoan-Mycenaean type were commonly represented.[6] Many such objects have been found in modern times, notably in the tombs and great houses of Mycenae, and there is no reason why similar discoveries should not have been made in the critical period of antiquity. Without ruling out the possibility of some role having been played by the minor arts let us turn to major monuments.

In the Mycenaean palaces columns were freely used in the interior of megara, in their porches, and in propylaia. We are all familiar with the massive stone bases of such columns, but there can be no doubt that in normal architectural usage where freestanding columns were employed the shafts, capitals, and entablature were all of wood. This woodwork perished in the destruction of the palaces at the end of the Bronze Age.[7] A limited number of monuments on the Greek mainland did, however, have attached columns of

---

[4] *Kapitelle und Basen: Beobachtungen zur Entstehung der griechischen Säulenformen* (Düsseldorf 1971); see also H. Drerup, *Griechische Baukunst im geometrischer Zeit* (Archaeologia Homerica II; Göttingen 1969). To the bibliography of earlier observations given by Wesenberg, *supra* 62, add R. Martin, *Recherches sur l'agora grecque* (Paris 1951) 121-123, H. Plommer, *Ancient and Classical Architecture,* (London 1956) 84, and J. L. Benson, *Horse, Bird and Man* (Amherst 1970) especially chap. V: "Tradition and its Transmission."

The purpose of the present paper is to recall a particular instance of a possible relationship between a Classical architectural form and a prototype of the Bronze Age in the light of our increasing knowledge of the phenomenon in general.

[5] The importance of the role played by the Argolid and Corinthia in the cultural development of Greece in the eighth and seventh centuries B.C. becomes increasingly apparent. Cf. in general C. G. Starr, *The Origins of Greek Civilization 1100-650 B.C.* (New York 1961) 245-252; T. Kelly, *A History of Argos to 500 B.C.* (Minneapolis 1976) chap. IV, esp. p. 52; J. N. Coldstream, *Geometric Greece* (London 1977) 140-156 (Argolid), 167-190 (Corinth and West Greece). For the role of this region in the origin of monumental Greek architecture, cf. C. Weickert, *Typen der archaischen Architektur in Griechenland und Kleinasien* (Augs-

burg 1929) 42-44; K. Schefold, *MusHelv* 3 (1946) 88f.; Martin (*supra* n. 4) 121-123; R. M. Cook, *BSA* 46 (1951), 50-52; P. Amandry, *Hesperia* 21 (1952) 274; G. Gruben, *Die Tempel der Griechen,* 2nd ed. (Darmstadt 1976) 105-108; J. J. Coulton, *The Architectural Development of the Greek Stoa* (Oxford 1976) 27-30, 215.

[6] Wesenberg (*supra* n. 4) has listed representations of Minoan-Mycenaean columns in ivory (pp. 4f.), gold relief (pp. 5f.), wall paintings (p. 13), seals (pp. 17f.). For the possible importance of the ivory miniatures in particular cf. Drerup (*supra* n. 4) 112-116.

[7] On the mainland of Greece there appear to be no certainly identifiable parts of stone columns of Mycenaean date in the round and intended for architectural use. J. Sakellarakis has drawn my attention to some small stone capitals in the round from Mycenae, comparable with one from Zakros on Crete, but these all appear to have formed parts of tables of offering: *SMEA* 17 (1976) 185f. The richly carved abacus found in the palace at Mycenae is also more probably from a stand or table than from a freestanding column: J. Papadimitriou, *Praktika* 1955, 230, pl. 79a; H. Plommer, *BSA* 60 (1965) 207ff., pls. 56f.; Wesenberg (*supra* n. 4) 4, 12f., fig. 8.

stone. The most familiar is the Lion Gate at Mycenae.[8] The gateway and the relief above it are fully visible today. They were seen and mentioned by Pausanias (II, 16, 5) in the second century after Christ, and there is no reason to doubt that they were equally accessible in the eighth and seventh centuries before Christ. In view of the great prominence of the monument, in view also of the obvious similarity between this column and the Doric columns of the Archaic period, it would be foolish to deny the possibility of influence from this quarter. But the column of the Lion Gate could not have been the sole model. In the first place it served no structural function; its purpose would appear rather to have been sacred, magical, or, more probably, heraldic. Secondly, the shaft is smooth and lacks the vertical fluting so characteristic of the Doric column even in its earliest history.

The other major structures that we must take into account are the tholos tombs. Of the nine tombs of this type known at Mycenae only two included columns in their design: the so-called Treasury of Atreus and the Tomb of Clytemnestra. These were the most developed, most monumental, and probably the latest tombs of the series. In each case the doorway was flanked by a pair of attached half columns. Such columns appear in no other known tholos tomb whether of the Argolid or elsewhere in the Minoan-Mycenaean world. Their presence at Mycenae is due in all likelihood to Cretan influence. Some at least of the material, particularly the alabaster for the columns of the Tomb of Clytemnestra, is of Cretan origin, and some of the elaborately carved stonework is identical in design and execution with that found at Knossos and Phaistos.

Let us look first at the Treasury of Atreus (fig. 1). We are all familiar with the design of the façade as it has been recovered through the labors of successive generations of scholars on the basis of the *disiecta membra* now scattered among Athens, London, Nauplia, Karlsruhe, and Berlin.[9]

Some uncertainty still exists, and always will exist, about the exact disposition of the various elements in the veneer of carved stone slabs that concealed the massive masonry of the upper storey. But it is with the columns that we are primarily concerned, and here, fortunately, the evidence permits a reasonably certain restoration. Parts remain of both the shafts and the capitals of both orders. Note the striking disparity in scale between the columns of the lower and upper storeys.

Here again the Mycenaean column is similar enough to the early Doric to leave little doubt as to their kinship, but direct descent of one from the other is ruled out by the striking difference in surface treatment. In place of the vertical fluting and plain echinus of early Doric, the Mycenaean column is richly carved in angular designs on both shaft and echinus. There is the further problem of accessibility. It is now well established that the tholos tombs—dromoi, doorways, and all—were covered with earth after each burial. In the case of the Atreus tomb we know very little about its later history, and there is no certainty that its façade was visible in the early Archaic period.[10]

We come, finally, to the so-called Tomb of Clytemnestra (fig. 2).[11] Set into the steep hillslope 130 m. west of the Lion Gate, the round chamber of this tomb cut through the edge of the Second Grave Circle.[12] In retribution, so to speak, the dromos of the tomb was overlaid in the Hellenistic period by the *prohedria* of a

[8]A. J. B. Wace, *BSA* 25 (1921-23) 9-38; *idem, Mycenae, An Architectural History and Guide* (Princeton 1949) 51-54; G. E. Mylonas, *Mycenae and the Mycenaean Age* (Princeton 1966) 17f., 173-176; Wesenberg (*supra* n. 4) 4, 9; S. E. Iakovidis, *Mycenae-Epidaurus, Argos-Tiryns-Nauplion* (Athens 1978) 30-32.

[9]A. J. B. Wace, *BSA* 25 (1921-23) 342-349; *idem, Mycenae, An Architectural History and Guide* (Prince-

ton 1949) 28-31; Mylonas (*supra* n. 8) 121; Iakovidis (*supra* n. 8) 51f. An extensive bibliography, especially for the capitals, is given by Wesenberg (*supra* n. 4) 3f.

[10]The only post-Mycenaean object that may be associated with the Treasury of Atreus appears to be a bronze pin of Geometric type reported to have been found in a pit in the dromos: *JHS* 96 (1976) 9, n. 12.

[11]G. Perrot and C. Chipiez, *Histoire de l'art dans l'antiquité* VI (Paris 1894) 593-608, 641-647 (especially valuable for drawings by W. Dörpfeld); A. J. B. Wace, *BSA* 25 (1921-23), 357-376 (description and catalogue of finds); *idem, Mycenae, An Architectural History and Guide* (Princeton 1949) 35-38; *idem, BSA* 50 (1955) 194-198 (notes on construction); G. E. Mylonas, *Ancient Mycenae* (Princeton 1957) 91-96; *idem* (*supra* n. 8) 122-125; Iakovidis (*supra* n. 8) 46-49.

[12]G. E. Mylonas, Ὁ ταφικὸς κύκλος Β τῶν Μυκηνῶν (Library of the Archaeological Society in Athens 73; Athens 1973) 18.

theater.[13] Here we see the entrance to the tomb as it appears after the work of conservation carried out by the Greek authorities in 1951.[14] Their attention was confined to straightening the east wall of the dromos and to restoring the upper part of the dome through which Veli, Pasha of Nauplia, had entered on a pillaging expedition at the beginning of the nineteenth century. The façade of the tomb, with which we are principally concerned, remains virtually as it was found by the excavators.

Let me remind you briefly of the circumstances of the excavations (fig. 3). The intruders from Nauplia had broken through the top of the vault and had ransacked the tomb chamber. It was left to the Schliemanns to begin the systematic exploration of the monument.[15] Work was begun in the autumn of 1876 under the supervision of Mrs. Schliemann and with the help of thirty laborers and two horse carts. It was a difficult operation. Schliemann writes feelingly of "the scorching sun and incessant tempest," of the hundreds of huge stones fallen from the vault, and of the intransigence of the Greek authorities in forbidding the removal of the remains of an "Hellenic house" (actually the scene building of the theater) from above the lower part of the dromos. There were also some distractions: a visit from the Emperor of Brazil and the discovery of the shaft graves inside the Lion Gate. As a result, Mrs. Schliemann was unable to finish her job. The tomb chamber proper was rendered accessible, and the actual doorway (*stomion*) was cleared, but masses of stone and earth remained in the dromos to a depth of nine feet. The final clearance was made by Professor Chr. Tsountas in the 1890's.[16]

With respect to the façade chance has been relatively kind. The scheme was basically like that of the Atreus tomb. The massive conglomerate masonry was enlivened by a purely decorative architectural arrangement in fine stone applied in much the same spirit as in the great buildings of Minoan Crete and of imperial Rome. Half columns of gypsum flanked the doorway of the tomb. The semicircular bases of both columns were found in place, and the lower part of the shaft proper had survived on the left side. These remains were fortunately recorded soon after their discovery in excellent drawings by Wilhelm Dörpfeld (fig. 4). The shafts were slender with a gentle downward taper. They were carved with simple vertical fluting, thirteen flutes to the half column.[17]

On turning to the upper storey of the façade, we need not linger over the veneer in colored stone, of which several beautiful fragments have been found. More relevant to our present purpose is the question whether or not the upper space was flanked, like the lower, with half columns. Before the recognition of an upper storey in the Atreus façade Wace had been inclined to believe that the line of the columns flanking the doorway in the Tomb of Clytemnestra had been continued upward only by the slightly projecting pilasters at the upper level.[18] But in 1951 Professor Marinatos observed the outline for the base of an upper half column on top of the plinth above the certainly attested lower columns.[19] This called for the restoration of an upper storey on the Clytemnestra façade like that already established for the sister tomb. To one of these upper columns may be assigned a much weathered fragment of a capital with a ring of leaves below the echinus which came to light in Tsountas' excavation of 1892 and which is now in the National Museum in Athens (fig.

[13]For the remains of the theater see especially A. J. B. Wace, *BSA* 50 (1955) 196f., pls. 35, 36 (plan); G. E. Mylonas, *Ancient Mycenae* (Princeton 1957) fig. 28 (photograph).

[14]J. Padadimitriou, *ArchEph* 1938-49 (published 1951) 43-48; Wace (*supra* n. 13) 194-198; Mylonas (*supra* n. 13) 92, figs. 28-36.

[15]H. Schliemann, *Mycenae: a Narrative of Researches and Discoveries at Mycenae and Tiryns* (New York 1878) 102-105, 118-121, 139-141; C. Schuchhardt, *Schliemann's Excavations* (London 1891) 148-151.

[16]*Praktika* 1891, 19; 1892, 57; 1897, 25; Chr. Tsountas and J. L. Manatt, *The Mycenaean Age* (London 1897) 122-124; 139-143.

[17]Wace reported the discovery during the work of conservation carried out in 1913 of "a fragment of gypsum carved with a spiral pattern with the angles filled in with a plaited design, perhaps from the capitals of the engaged columns": *BSA* 25 (1921-23) 366f. I have not seen this piece. For another fragment of a capital found earlier, see below.

[18]Wace (*supra* n. 17) 360.

[19]*ArchEph* 1953-54, A, 12f. Marinatos' re-examination of the Clytemnestra façade was inspired by his recent recognition of fragments from the upper half columns of the Atreus façade.

5).[20] The diameter of the shaft on which this capital rested is estimated as ca. 0.40 m. This is much too small for the lower columns, which had a lower diameter of 0.395 m. and consequently an upper diameter considerably greater. No part of the shafts of the upper columns is recorded so that their design is uncertain; on the analogy of the Atreus façade they may be assumed to have been basically similar to the lower.

In the half columns of the Clytemnestra tomb we have, I believe, one possible source of inspiration for the earliest Doric column. Some of the essential elements are here: a slender shaft standing on a very inconspicuous base, simple vertical fluting, a ring of leaves below a well-curved echinus. But is there any possibility that this façade was accessible in the critical period of the eighth and seventh centuries before Christ? There can be no doubt that this tholos, like the Treasury of Atreus, was covered after the burial by a huge mound of earth, large enough to fill the dromos and high enough to conceal even the lofty façade.[21] The construction of a theater above the dromos in the Hellenistic period may be taken to imply ignorance of the existence of the tomb at that time. But the excavation of 1876 produced evidence which at least opens up the possibility that the dromos was partly accessible in the late eighth century and for some time thereafter.

In the dromos, and exclusively in the dromos, Mrs. Schliemann found quantities of fine pottery that are now readily recognizable as Late Geometric Argive, datable to the latter part of the eighth century. Some of the sherds were illustrated by Schliemann in his book *Mycenae* (fig. 6),[22] and many were listed by Wace in his dis-

cussion of the tomb.[23] According to Wace the non-Mycenaean pottery also included Late Corinthian (fig. 7) and even some Attic red-figure. In assessing the significance of this material one should admit the possibility that some of the Geometric sherds came from graves of that period; Geometric graves were in fact found quite close to the tomb by the Greek authorities engaged in drainage operations in 1909.[24]

This post-Mycenaean pottery, however, is regarded by most scholars, and I think rightly, as evidence for a hero cult. This view is strengthened by the discovery, along with the pottery, of archaic terracotta figurines, notably horses and riders, of types not found in graves but commonly found in the votive deposits of hero shrines in various parts of Greece.

The group of material from the dromos of our tomb is best paralleled, in fact, by that recovered from the shrine of Agamemnon explored by John Cook in 1950 at a point about one kilometer SSW of the acropolis of Mycenae.[25] There too the earliest offerings consist of Late Geometric

---

[20]Perrot and Chipiez (*supra* n. 11) 629, fig. 278; Wace (*supra* n. 17) 360; Wesenberg (*supra* n. 4) 4, no. 4. I am most grateful to Dr. John Sakellarakis for having the fragment photographed and for calculating its lower diameter. Perrot and Chipiez, 642, had already recognized that this capital was too small for the lower columns which alone were known at the time; they suggested that it might have come from some other structure.

[21]W. Taylour, *BSA* 50 (1955) 209-223. A poros retaining wall laid out on the arc of a circle with a radius of ca. 36 m. has been traced over a length of some 50 m. to the east of the tholos; this appears to have supported the mound on its lower side.

[22](*Supra* n. 15) figs. 157, 158, pls. XX, XXI. A. Furtwängler and G. Loeschke (*Mykenische Vasen* [Berlin 1886] 52) report fragments of at least twenty-five gen-

erally very large Dipylon vases and also Attic red-figure found to a depth of 5 meters. For Argive Geometric cf. P. Courbin, *La céramique géométrique de l'Argolide* (Paris 1966) 557-566 (dating); J. N. Coldstream, *Greek Geometric Pottery* (London 1968) 112-147, 330, 406.

[23](*Supra* n. 17) 363-374. The post-Mycenaean material from Mrs. Schliemann's excavation seen by Professor Wace in the National Museum comprised 95 fragments of developed Geometric pottery, a small Corinthian aryballos, 4 Classical Greek pieces including 2 Corinthian and 1 red-figured, small fragments of moulded Hellenistic ware, 12 archaic terracotta figures including animals, probably horses, and a lead figurine of a woman (0.05 m. high) of archaic date. In 1975 only the small Corinthian aryballos (fig. 7) could be identified by Dr. John Sakellarakis to whom I am greatly indebted for the report.

[24]*ArchEph* 1912, 127-141. The amount of Geometric pottery found on the site of the temple on top of the acropolis of Mycenae prompted Wace to suspect the existence of a shrine on that site already in the ninth to eighth centuries B.C. For references to other finds of Geometric pottery at Mycenae see the Site Index in Coldstream (*supra* n. 22) 406. Some of the sherds from the dromos of the Tomb of Clytemnestra derive from large, figured vases of a size and quality more commonly found in grave offerings than in votives. But J. R. Cook in publishing the Late Geometric pottery from the Sanctuary of Agamemnon at Mycenae commented on the large size of many of the vases: *BSA* 48 (1953) 34f.

[25]*BSA* 48 (1953) 30-68: "The Agamemnoneion." Cook has given a more general discussion of the historical implications of this discovery in Γέρας 'Αντωνίου Κεραμοπούλου (Athens 1953) 112-118.

pottery of the end of the eighth century; the cult flourished into the early fifth century, then languished until the temenos was rehabilitated in the Hellenistic period.

Material, especially pottery, of the Late Geometric period has been reported from all the tholos tombs and from several of the chamber tombs at Mycenae.[26] In most cases these finds probably represent chance intrusions and cannot be regarded as proof of the existence of post-Mycenaean cults. The example that has perhaps the strongest claim to be a votive deposit related to an early tomb came to light within a few meters of the Tomb of Clytemnestra in the form of a large deposit of Late Geometric pottery centered about a round structure, apparently an altar, immediately above a Mycenaean chamber tomb beneath the edge of the Second Grave Circle.[27] One is reminded also of the discovery of a sherd of the early fifth century B.C. inscribed "I belong to the hero" that was found within Grave Circle A: a small but telling piece of evidence for the existence of a hero cult above another venerable burial place of the Bronze Age.[28]

Outside of Mycenae the occurrence of votive deposits of the Late Geometric period in tombs of the Bronze Age is now recognized as a widespread phenomenon; it is attested throughout much of the Peloponnese, in Attica and Boeotia, on Delos and on Kephallenia. This efflorescence of hero cults has been attributed at least in part to the impact of the Homeric poems. The popularity of the poems and such gestures of veneration toward the dead of an earlier age are both to be regarded, of course, as manifestations of the "Greek Renaissance" that came about in the eighth century with the recovery of prosperity and with the growth of national self-consciousness centered about a common participation in the exploits of the heroic age.[29]

The establishment of a cult in the dromos of the Clytemnestra tomb ca. 700 B.C. would therefore have been a normal phenomenon. We need not concern ourselves with the question of who was believed to be the occupant of the tomb and so the object of worship. Having in mind the confused state of the local tradition as recorded by Pausanias in his account of Mycenae (II, 16, 4-7), we may be sure only that this tomb would have been regarded as the burial place of some member of the royal family.

For a tomb to be recognized as such in the Geometric period some part of its structure must have been exposed and visible. This may well have come about through natural erosion. Unfortunately we do not know the exact depth at which Mrs. Schliemann found the Geometric pottery. The cross section published by her spouse shows in a general way, however, the level which she had reached in the autumn of 1876 (fig. 8).[30] It is clear that she stopped well above the floor of the dromos except in the area immediately in front of the doorway. No Geometric pottery is reported from the subsequent clearing of the lower levels in the dromos. But now that the existence of an upper order of half columns is established we realize that the ancient façade exposed even to this extent might well have made a great impression on people whose minds were becoming attuned to reverence for the distant past.

The timing is significant. If we may trust the evidence of the recorded pottery we may assume that the façade was partially accessible from the turn of the eighth to seventh centuries until at least some time in the period of Attic red-figure. The destruction of Mycenae by the Argives ca. 468 B.C. may have put an end to the cult, as the outbreak of the Peloponnesian War appears to have terminated the cult in the dromos of the Mycenaean tomb at Menidi in Attica.[31] In the

[26]Mylonas (*supra* n. 8) 176-186; J. N. Coldstream, *JHS* 96 (1976) 9f.

[27]*Praktika* 1952, 470; 1953, 208, n. 1; Mylonas (*supra* n. 12), 18, pls. 1, 5.

[28]L. H. Jeffery, *The Local Scripts of Archaic Greece* (Oxford 1961) 174, no. 6, pl. 31; Coldstream (*supra* n. 26) 9f.

[29]For the phenomenon in general cf. J. N. Cook, Γέρας Ἀντωνίου Κεραμοπούλου (Athens 1953) 112, 118; A. M. Snodgrass, *The Dark Age of Greece*, (Edinburgh 1971) 190-194, 416-436; T. Hadzisteliou Price, "Hero Cult

and Homer," *Historia* 22 (1973) 129-144; Coldstream (*supra* n. 26) 8-17.

[30]Schliemann (*supra* n. 15) plan E.

[31]H. Lolling and R. Bohn, *Das Kuppelgrab bei Menidi* (Athens 1880); P. Wolters, *JdI* 13 (1898) 13-28; 14 (1899) 103-135, especially 115-118; Mylonas (*supra* n. 8) 181-184. In the Menidi tomb there was an abundant votive deposit ranging in date from the Late Geometric period to the time of the Peloponnesian War. The earliest of this material lay at a level little lower than the lintel of the door.

subsequent long period of semidesolation the dromos may again have become filled with down-washed earth so that by the third century B.C. the builders of the theater were oblivious to its existence.

If this reconstruction is sound, the façade of our tomb, as well, of course, as the relief above the Lion Gate, would have been before men's eyes at a time when some of the earliest temples involving substantial stone masonry were being erected in Greece, most of them within the Argolid and Corinthia. Among these early buildings were the temple attested by the limestone reliefs found on the acropolis of Mycenae,[32] the temple on the acropolis of Tiryns of which we have a stone capital, some terracotta roof tiles and probably the foundation set down in the ruins of the Mycenaean megaron,[33] the early

Temple of Hera at the Argive Heraion,[34] the Temple of Apollo at Corinth,[35] and the Temple of Poseidon on the Isthmus of Corinth.[36]

Attractive as this "scenario" may seem it is admittedly in large part hypothetical. Nevertheless I believe we should seriously consider the possibility that the Tomb of Clytemnestra may have played a small but direct role in bridging the long gap between the Bronze Age and the Classical period of Greece.

---

[32]A. J. B. Wace, *Mycenae, An Architectural History and Guide,* (Princeton 1949) 84-86; F. Harl-Schaller, *ÖJh* 50 (1972/73) 94-116.

[33]*Tiryns* I (Athens 1912) 2-13; H. Sulze, *AA* 1936 cols. 14-36; Wesenberg (*supra* n. 4) 53, no. 20; Iakovidis (*supra* n. 8) 100f.

[34]H. Lauter, "Zur frühklassischer Neuplanung des Heraions von Argos," *AthMitt* 88 (1973) 175-183; Gruben (*supra* n. 5) 105-108; Iakovidis (*supra* n. 8) 80f.

[35]H. S. Robinson, *Hesperia* 45 (1976) 224-235.

[36]O. Broneer, *Temple of Poseidon* (Isthmia I; Princeton 1971); rev. by W. Koenigs, *Gnomon* 47 (1975) 402-406. Is it possible that the regular ashlar masonry which is such a striking feature of the early temples at the Isthmus and at Corinth was inspired by the magnificent stonework in the dromoi of the Atreus and Clytemnestra tombs? There were few other sources of inspiration in this part of Greece.

Figure 1. Treasury of Atreus: façade (ca. 1:50). Restoration by Wace and Mari-
natos. From A. J. B. Wace, *Mycenae: An Archaeological History and
Guide* (copyright 1949 © 1977 by Princeton University Press) fig. 51.
Reprinted by permission of Princeton University Press.

Figure 2. Tomb of Clytemnestra: entrance as cleared. From George E. Mylonas, *Mycenae and the Mycenaean Age* (copyright © 1966 by Princeton University Press) fig. 115. Reprinted by permission of Princeton University Press.

Figure 3. Tomb of Clytemnestra during excavation of 1876. From H. Schliemann, *Mycenae* (New York 1878) frontispiece.

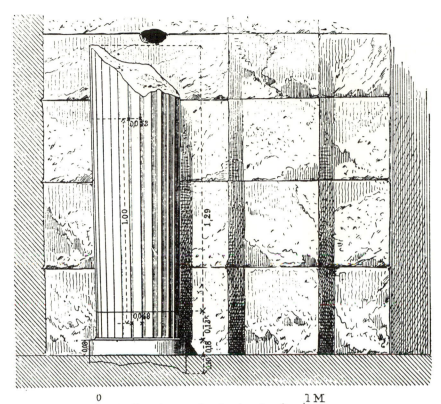

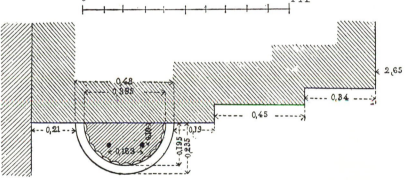

0   1 M

Figure 4. Tomb of Clytemnestra: attached
column to left of doorway, drawn
by W. Dörpfeld. From G. Perrot
and C. Chipiez, *Histoire de l'Art*
VI (Paris 1894) fig. 201.

Figure 5. Fragment of alabaster capital
from Tomb of Clytemnestra.
Max. dim. 0.525 m.; D. of top of
column shaft ca. 0.40 m. National Museum, Athens, 1487.
Photo: National Museum.

No. 192. (5 M.)

No. 193. (5 M.)

No. 194. (5 M.)

No. 195. (5 M.)

No. 196. (6 M.)

No. 197. (3 M.)

Figure 6. Geometric sherds from dromos of Tomb of Clytemnestra. From H. Schliemann, *Mycenae,* pl. XX.

Figure 7. Late Corinthian aryballos from dromos of Tomb of Clytemnestra (ca. 1:1). National Museum, Athens, 1422. Photo: National Museum.

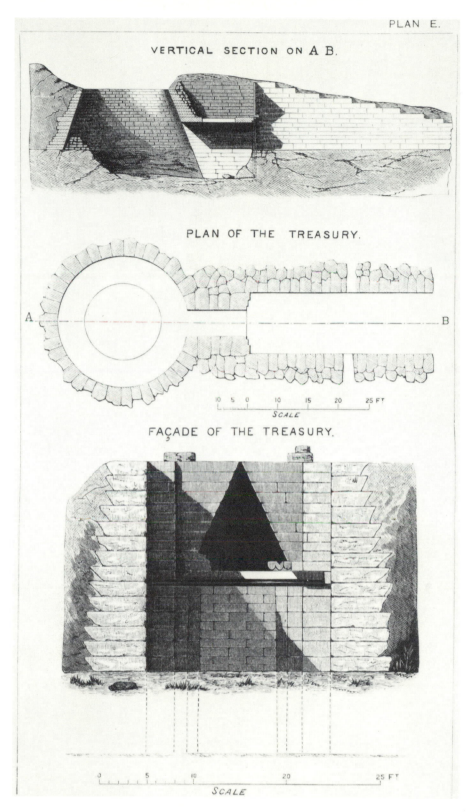

Figure 8. Tomb of Clytemnestra: plan and section after excavation of 1876. From H. Schliemann, *Mycenae,* plan E.

III. THE STATE PRISON OF ANCIENT ATHENS*

Eugene Vanderpool

RODNEY STUART YOUNG *IN MEMORIAM*

Rodney Young excavated in the Athenian Agora for eleven seasons, from 1934 through 1940 and from 1946 through 1949. Most of his work was in the southwest area, a large tract extending from the Tholos up into the deep valley between the Areopagus and the Hill of the Nymphs (fig. 1). He found many interesting and important things, some of which he studied and published himself, thereby establishing areas of interest which were to continue to hold his attention throughout his life. Thus the Geometric cemetery south of the Tholos and the nearby seventh century well gave him a thesis topic at the start of his career and led to his interest in the Phrygian pottery from Gordion with Geometric and Orientalizing decoration. And again, the graffito inscriptions from his area of excavation with their examples of early alphabetic writing gave him a chance to make a contribution of his own to a subject in which his interest had already been aroused by the lectures and articles of Rhys Carpenter. He pursued this interest further on his own in an excavation on top of Mt. Hymettos, which produced numerous examples of early writing, and finally one of the last articles he published was on early Phrygian inscriptions from Gordion written in alphabetic script resembling early Greek.

Farther up the valley southwest of the Tholos he cleared and carefully studied a residential and industrial district, which gave us for the first time ground plans of Athenian houses and small workshops of Classical times. In the midst of this residential and industrial area he discovered and did the initial clearing of a building larger and more solidly constructed than other buildings in the area, with some large squared blocks of poros in its foundations. This came to be known as the Poros Building and was recognized from the start as a public building rather than a private one from its size and its heavier construction. After the initial clearing by Rodney Young the building was more thoroughly explored by the late Margaret Crosby, and she wrote a detailed account of it which was published as a separate chapter in Rodney Young's study of the district as a whole.[1] Throughout the excavation the two archaeologists were aided by the architect John Travlos, who drew the plan of the building (fig. 2). Travlos has continued his interest in the building, and for the present study he has revised the plan and provided two perspective views as his contribution to this memorial symposium (figs. 3 and 4).

It is this Poros Building that I wish to discuss, and I begin with a description of its location and remains. But lest I deceive the expectations of my audience, I must say at the start that the building has been very badly destroyed right down to its foundations, and the poros blocks which are its characteristic feature are preserved at only a few points; elsewhere nothing but the pillaged foundation trench has survived. The site

---

*At the symposium the paper was read for Mr. Vanderpool by Dorothy Burr Thompson of Princeton.

[1]Rodney S. Young, "An Industrial District of Ancient Athens," *Hesperia* 20 (1951) 135-288. Margaret Crosby, "The Poros Building," *ibid*. 168-187. The reader is referred to Miss Crosby's chapter for fuller details of construction, chronological evidence, and the like.

was built over in Roman times, and many of the Roman walls and mosaic floors are still standing to obscure the outline of the original building, so that the visitor to the site sees little or nothing unless he has a detailed plan of the ruins in hand.

The building is a large one, its north to south length being 37.56 m. and its width at the south 16.50 m. It is located about a hundred meters outside the southwest corner of the Agora and lies in the bottom of the valley, with its west wall along the Great Drain and its east side set back deeply into the hillside. It is of irregular shape and consists of three main parts, a central section with rooms on either side of a corridor, a large open-air courtyard at the south enclosed by a high wall, and a sort of annex at the northeast with four rooms set at an odd angle corresponding to the bend in the street outside. This annex was probably a two-storey structure as its walls are slightly thicker than those of the main complex, and there seems to have been a stair in the narrow space between the two southern rooms. The entrance to the complex was from the north where the building faces on an important east-west street which the excavators have named "Piraeus Street" since it comes in from the Piraeus Gate. The entrance leads into an irregular open area and then on into a corridor which divides this section of the building longitudinally. This corridor was unroofed and there was a drain running the length of it. The corridor widens from 3.00 m. at the north to 4.50 m. at the south because the outer walls of the building are not quite parallel with each other. Opening off this passage are eight rooms, five on the right and three on the left, each about 4.50 m. square. These, of course, were roofed, and fragments of the Laconian tiles that covered them were found.

There was little in the way of furnishings in any part of the building. We may note, however, that the northwest room of the main complex had some simple arrangements for bathing (figs. 5-9). A basin was found in the northwest corner of the room, set down into the ground with its rim flush with the floor, an arrangement which recalls that found in bathing establishments.[2] A

pithos[3] set deeply into the floor near the center of the room probably held a supply of fresh water. An attempt had even been made to provide water directly from a well dug in the room itself, but the sides collapsed and the attempt was given up as unsuccessful. The supply of water for the annex was provided in Hellenistic times by a cistern complex consisting of a cistern proper outside the annex to the south connected by underground passages to draw shafts in the two northern rooms of the annex.

The building was originally constructed about the middle of the fifth century B.C., as shown by the pottery found beneath the earliest floors of hard-packed clay. There is evidence of remodeling in the late fifth or perhaps the early fourth century when the floor levels were raised considerably and the floors surfaced with marble chips to give a clean surface on which to walk. In the late fourth century the floor level was again raised slightly and surfaced with a rough pebble mosaic, fragments of which were found here and there. The building continued in use through the Hellenistic period with minor changes in plan until it was destroyed in Sulla's sack of the city in 86 B.C. When the area was rebuilt in Augustan times two private houses replaced the Poros Building.

The identification of the Poros Building has aroused considerable discussion, for it was recognized from the start that a building of such size and construction, of fifth century B.C. date, and located so near the Agora should be a public building. The most favored suggestion was that it was a law court, but this idea had to be given up because the form of the building did not suit the functions of a law court as we know them. The idea that it was a *synoikia,* or apartment building, found even less favor, and it was finally concluded in a general sort of way that the building housed civic offices for some of the many city officials and commissions, without specifying which.[4]

---

[2]The basin: Inv. P 19423. *Hesperia* 20 (1951) 180 fig. 6a. Brian Sparkes and Lucy Talcott, *Black and Plain Pottery* (The Athenian Agora XII; Princeton 1970) 366, no. 1849. Bathing establishments: R. Ginouvès, *Bala-*

neutiké, Recherches sur le bain dans l'antiquité grecque (Paris 1962) pl. 7, 20-21; pl. 30, 98; pl. 35, 114.

[3]The pithos: Inv. P 19422. *Hesperia* 20 (1951) 180, fig. 6b.

[4]The most recent discussion is to be found in H. A. Thompson and R. E. Wycherley, *The Agora of Athens* (The Athenian Agora XIV; Princeton 1972) 74.

I should like to make a new suggestion as to the identification of the Poros Building, namely, that it is the State Prison of Athens, the Desmoterion.

Now the most famous prisoner of ancient Athens was Socrates, and the Platonic dialogues that describe his last days and hours give us incidentally quite a few bits of information about the location of the prison and about its furnishings. A few more facts can be gleaned from other authors. This evidence is of course well known and has been collected more than once,[5] but the picture that emerges from the literary evidence alone is neither very full nor very precise and does not enable us to say just where the prison should be sought or what sort of building it was. But now that we have postulated a definite location and a particular building, let us see how the literary evidence fits the case.

"We used to meet at daybreak," says Phaedo, "in the court where Socrates' trial took place, for it was near the prison. Every day we used to wait about, talking to each other, until the prison was opened, for it was not opened early. When it was opened we went in to Socrates and passed most of the day with him."[6] It is now well established that there were several law courts in the Agora,[7] including the Heliaia, and it is most probable that Socrates was tried in one of these, perhaps the Heliaia itself. The Poros Building, which is just outside the Agora, could be described as near any law court in the Agora, and the nearest, of course, is the Heliaia. Furthermore, Plato in another passage where he is describing the ideal state says that the general prison for the majority should be near the Agora.[8] Vitruvius likewise says that the prison should adjoin the forum, and the Mamertine Prison in Rome is in fact so located.[9] Finally, when in 403 B.C. Theramenes was taken from the Bouleuterion by the Eleven, he was led by way of the Agora to the place where he was to drink the hemlock, i.e., the prison.[10] Therefore, our building, which is just outside the Agora, meets the requirements of the sources in respect to general location.

The prison must have faced on a wide street, for in May of 318 B.C., when the Athenian general Phocion and four others were drinking the hemlock in the prison, the scene outside is described as follows by Plutarch.[11] "It was the nineteenth day of the month Munychion, and the horsemen conducting the procession in honor of Zeus were passing by the prison. Some of them took off their garlands, and others gazed at the door of the prison with tears in their eyes. And it was thought by all those whose souls were not wholly savage and debauched by rage and jealousy that an impious thing had been done in not waiting over that day and so keeping the city pure from a public execution when it was holding festival." A religious procession conducted by horsemen must have been moving along a wide street, and our "Piraeus Street," on which the prison opens, was one of the principal east-west thoroughfares of the city and could easily have accommodated such a procession.

As to size and form the Poros Building seems suitable also. There would have been no need for a huge prison because prison sentences were not given for any and every kind of offence as they are now.[12] People were held in prison while awaiting trial or sentence, or for failure to pay a fine. Only occasionally was a prison term itself the penalty. The eight rooms on either side of the corridor probably provided enough space for ordinary needs. When it was necessary to round up and hold a large number of people, such as the forty described by Andocides (I, 48), the courtyard at the back could be used. Prisoners of war like the 292 Spartans captured on Sphakteria were probably held elsewhere and not in the State Prison.

Socrates was certainly a very special prisoner, and his wealthy friends were probably able to

---

[5]Curt Wachsmuth, *Die Stadt Athen im Altertum* II (Leipzig 1890) 383-387. R. E. Wycherley, *Literary and Epigraphical Testimonia* (The Athenian Agora III; Princeton 1957) 149-150.

[6]Plato, *Phaedo* 59 D. This and the following quotations from the *Crito* and the *Phaedo* are from the translation by H. N. Fowler in the Loeb Classical Library, though I have occasionally made some small changes.

[7]Thompson and Wycherley (*supra* n. 4) 52-72.

[8]Plato, *Laws* 908 A.

[9]Vitruvius V, 2, 1. For the Mamertine Prison see Ernest Nash, *Pictorial Dictionary of Ancient Rome*, 2nd ed. (New York 1968) 206-208.

[10]Xenophon, *Hellenica* II, 3, 50-56. Diodorus Siculus XIV, 4, 7; 5, 3.

[11]Plutarch, *Life of Phocion* 37.

[12]R. J. Bonner and Gertrude Smith, *The Administration of Justice from Homer to Aristotle* II (Chicago 1938) 275-276.

obtain certain amenities for him. When Crito arrives very early one morning[13] Socrates remarks, "I am surprised that the watchman of the prison was willing to let you in," to which Crito replies, "He is used to me by this time, Socrates, because I come here so often, and besides I have done something for him." Socrates seems to have had a cell to himself; at least we do not hear of any other prisoners sharing it, and this may have been arranged by his friends. The people who came to see him on his last day are named,[14] nine Athenians and five foreigners plus Phaedo himself making fifteen, and there were said to be "some other Athenians" making perhaps twenty or so in all. These would have pretty well filled a room about 4.50 m. on a side which would provide floor space of about twenty square meters. Socrates himself was fettered, so the door could be left open and people could come and go.

The couch on which Socrates lay[15] was perhaps also supplied by his friends. At least it seems unlikely that the state would provide prisoners with more than a straw pallet on the floor. The low stool on which Phaedo sat while Socrates stroked his head[16] was perhaps also an extra.

There were facilities for bathing in the prison. Shortly before the end Socrates interrupts the conversation by saying,[17] "It is about time for me to go to the bath, for I think it is better to bathe before drinking the poison, that the women may not have the trouble of bathing the corpse." Shortly afterwards[18] Socrates got up and went into another room to bathe. He spent a long time, and when he came back it was nearly sunset and he sat down, fresh from the bath. We have seen that the northwest room of the main complex of the Poros Building was arranged at about this time with simple bathing facilities: a small basin set in the floor and a pithos to hold a supply of fresh water.

The annex at the northeast occupies an area of about twelve by eight meters. It is divided into four rooms and probably had an upper storey

reached by a stair in the narrow space between the southern rooms. It probably had a flat roof and could have served as a sort of guard tower, housing the wardens of the prison. The ground floor may have provided offices for the Eleven, the board of commissioners who had general supervision over the prison and related matters.[19]

Two items found in the building may have some connection with its function. A group of thirteen small pots[20] of a sort usually described as medicine pots (fig. 10), each about four centimeters high, was found at the bottom of the cistern in the northwest room of the annex in a context of the third century B.C. This is a remarkable concentration, for these thirteen little pots are a homogeneous lot and they make up about half of the total number of such pots catalogued at the Agora. Of the other half, five are of the same general type as the thirteen, but the remaining nine are heterogeneous, and all come from widely separated areas (fig. 11).[21] There must be some reason for this concentration, and I wonder if these particular pots did not once contain hemlock, each pot a single dose. We know that the amount given was carefully measured because Socrates when he was about to drink his potion asked the man who was administering it whether he might pour a libation to some deity. "No," said the man, "we prepare only as much as we think is enough."[22] And again, when Phocion, Thudippus and others were awaiting execution in 318 B.C., Plutarch[23] reports that "Thudippus on entering the prison and seeing the executioner bruising the hemlock, grew angry and bewailed his hard fate. . . . When all the rest had drunk of the hemlock, the drug ran short, and the executioner refused to bruise another portion unless he were paid twelve drachmas, which was the price of the weight required. However, after a delay of some length, Phocion called one of his friends and, asking if

---

[13]Plato, *Crito* 43 A.

[14]Plato, *Phaedo* 59 B-C.

[15]*Phaedo* 60 B.

[16]*Phaedo* 89 B.

[17]*Phaedo* 115 A.

[18]*Phaedo* 116 A.

[19]Aristotle, *Constitution of the Athenians* 52, 1.

[20]These thirteen pots received collectively a single inventory number, P 20858.

[21]Four of these medicine pots of different shapes are published in Sparkes and Talcott (*supra* n. 2) nos. 2000-2003. The last of these, Inv. P 20137 (fig. 11), is of elongated shape and comes from an early fourth century B.C. layer in the bathroom of the building under discussion.

[22]*Phaedo* 117 B.

[23]*Life of Phocion* 36.

a man could not even die at Athens without paying for the privilege, bade him give the executioner his money."

Finally we may mention a statuette of Pentelic marble (fig. 12)[24] found in the northwest room of the annex in debris of late Hellenistic times, namely, the time of the destruction of the Poros Building. The statuette is broken at the waist and the preserved upper part is about ten centimeters high. The head and face are damaged at the right. We have a representation of a bearded man standing, with a cloak thrown over one shoulder but leaving the chest bare. The cloak was also carried around the waist just below the point of breakage. The statuette represents Socrates, and the type is best known from a statuette in the British Museum.[25] What a statuette of Socrates was doing in the offices of the State Prison of Athens we can only guess. We may recall, however, that the Athenians soon repented of having put Socrates to death and they tried and punished his accusers and later on erected a bronze statue of him in the Pompeion.[26] Perhaps one of the prison officials thought it appropriate to have a small replica of the statue in the place where Socrates was executed.

In conclusion, then, although formal proof of identification is lacking and although the Poros Building has nothing like the dramatic dungeon of the Mamertine Prison in Rome or even rock-cut chambers like those on the Museum Hill in Athens which have long appealed to the public imagination as the "Prison of Socrates," the building does seem to meet in a satisfactory way the known requirements of location, form, and furnishings and may be considered with some assurance to be the State Prison of ancient Athens.

ADDENDA

1. Christian Habicht has called my attention to a Samian decree of the fourth century B.C. which he published some years ago and in which there is mention of the Desmoterion in Athens and of the Eleven (*AthMitt* 72, 1957, 156-165, no. 1). The decree is in honor of one Antileon of Chalkis who ransomed and thus saved from death a group of Samians. These Samians had been arrested by the Athenian general in Samos on the basis of a decree of the Boule of Athens brought over by the state trireme, the Paralos. The general is said to have arrested many good and upright citizens and sent them to Athens where the Athenians locked them up in the Desmoterion and condemned them to death. Just how many people were involved is not known beyond the statement that they were many, but we may imagine that the arrival of such a group probably strained the facilities of the prison. Habicht suggested 321 B.C. as the date of the events recorded, but R. M. Errington has argued for 323 B.C.[27]

2. In Socrates' last hour, when it was nearly sunset the servant of the Eleven came and told him that it was time to drink the poison. Socrates agreed, but Crito protested, "I think, Socrates, the sun is still upon the mountains and has not yet set. Do not hurry, for there is still time."[28] With the prison located in the valley as we have it this detail is seen to be a realistic one. The sun would have dropped behind the Hill of the Nymphs leaving the prison in shadow but would still have been visible shining on the distant mountains.

3. In the summer of 1977 a little work was done in the area of the prison under the supervision of John McK. Camp II. The foundations of two Roman houses which overlay the prison were removed, and the Classical remains were exposed as far as they were preserved. Undisturbed stratification was encountered in a number of rooms, allowing us to check and generally confirm the results of the initial excavation. These suggest that the building was constructed shortly after the middle of the fifth century B.C., was damaged and refurbished in the years around 400 B.C., and then remained in use, with minor alterations, throughout the Hellenistic period, perhaps until the sack of Athens by Sulla in 86 B.C. Following excavation, the lines of the walls were filled out with dry masonry where necessary, the ground level was raised to the floor level of the Greek period, and the plan of the building can now be made out with ease (figs. 13, 14).

---

[24]Inv. S 1413.

[25]G. M. A. Richter, *The Portraits of the Greeks* I (London 1965) 116 and figs. 560-562.

[26]Diogenes Laertius II, 43.

[27]*Chiron* 5 (1975) 51-57.

[28]*Phaedo* 116 B-E.

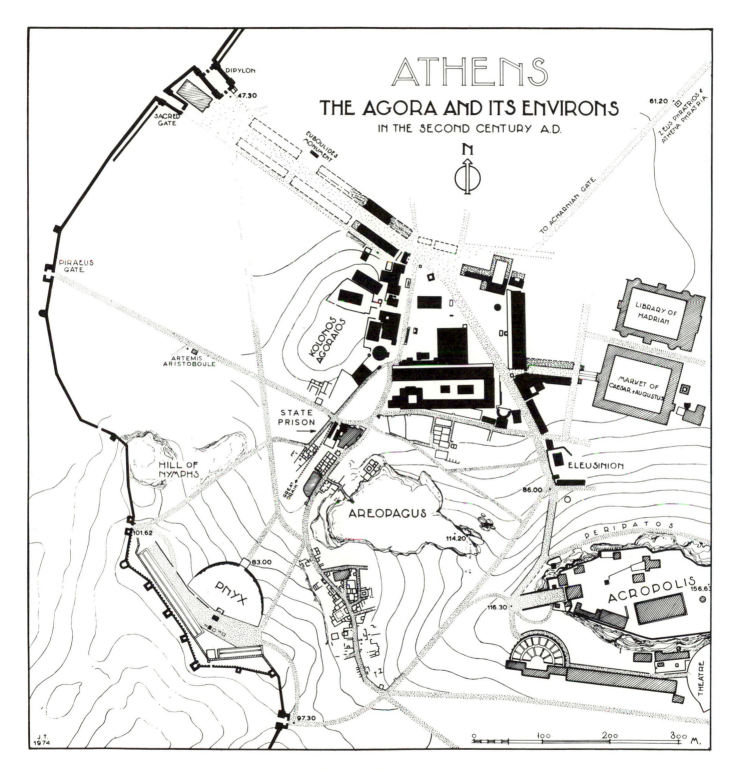

Figure 1. The Athenian Agora and its environs

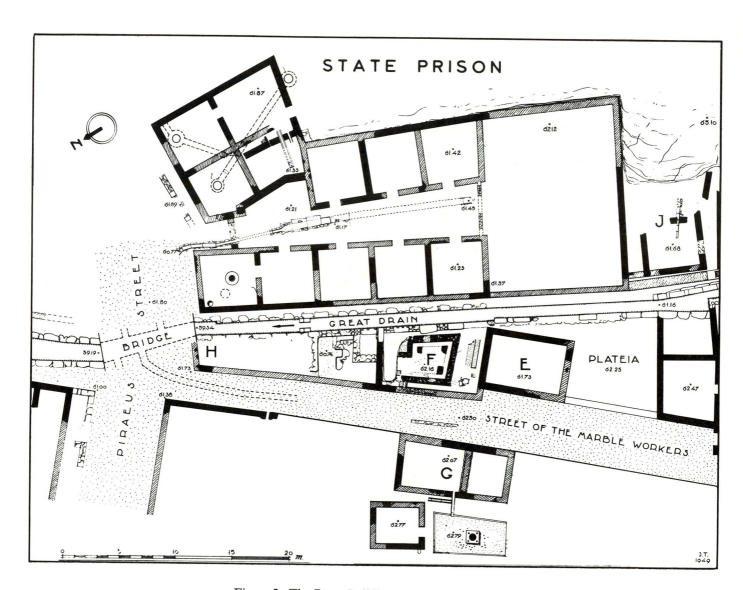

Figure 2. The Poros Building, or State Prison: plan

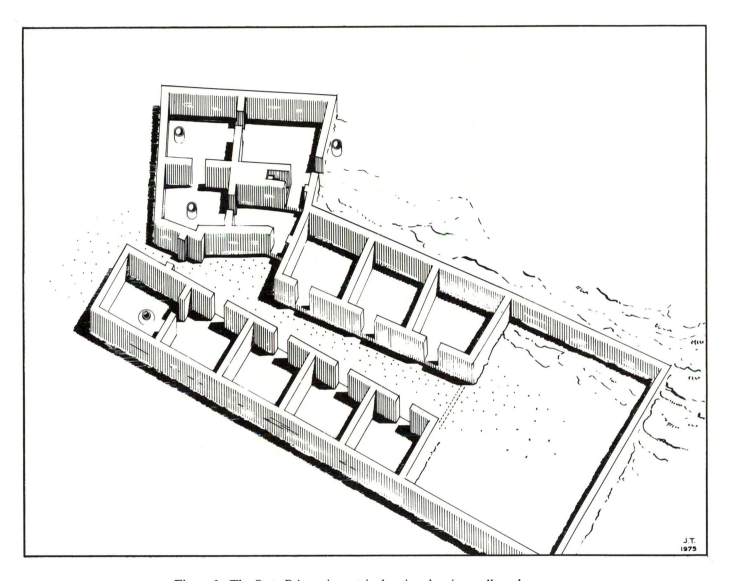

Figure 3. The State Prison: isometric drawing showing walls and rooms

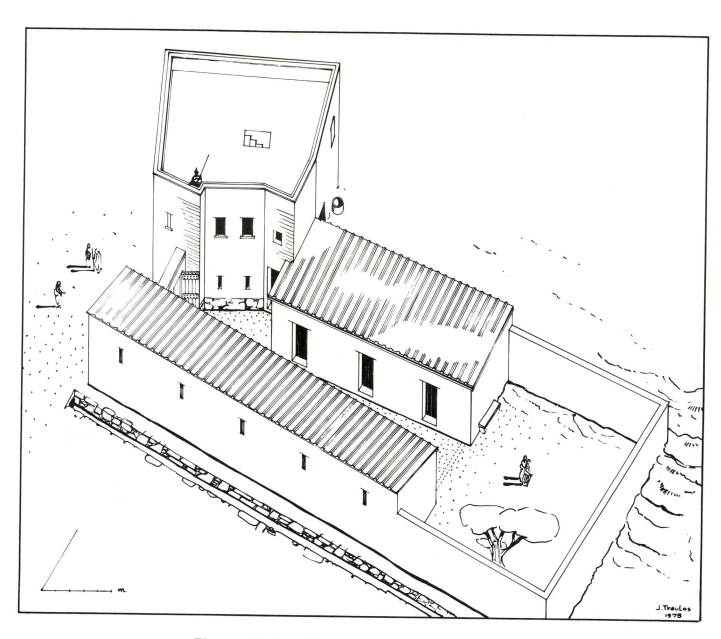

Figure 4. The State Prison: isometric reconstruction drawing

Figure 5. View of the bathroom from west showing basin (center), well (dark hole), and pithos (extreme right)

Figure 6. View of the bathroom from the northeast showing basin, poros wall blocks, and cover slabs of Great Drain

Figure 7. The bathroom: basin *in situ* with mosaic floor

Figure 8. The basin restored. H. 32 cm.

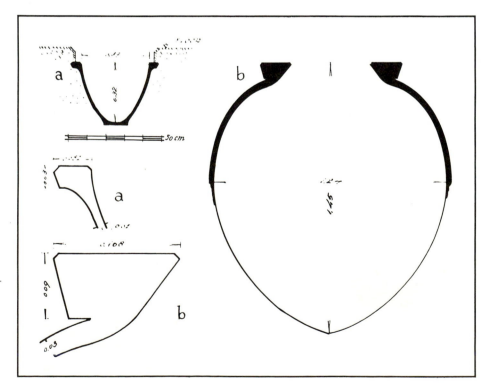

Figure 9. Profiles of basin and pithos

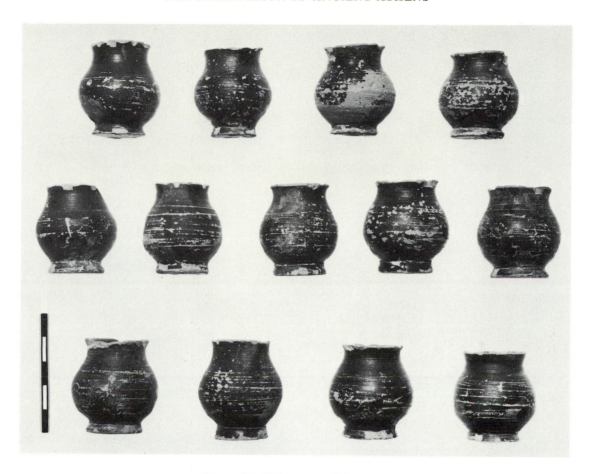

Figure 10. Thirteen medicine pots

Figure 11. Single medicine pot

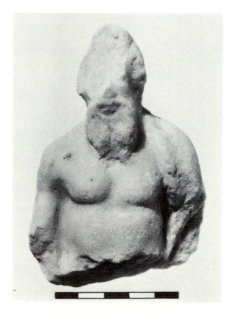

Figure 12. Marble statuette of Socrates

Figure 13. The State Prison from north, as consolidated in 1977

Figure 14. The northern part of the State Prison from west, as consolidated in 1977

Figure 15. The northern part of the State Prison from west, as it appeared in 1949

IV. GREEKS AND PHRYGIANS IN THE EARLY IRON AGE

Keith DeVries

Rodney Young made a profound change in his life in his early forties. In coming to the University of Pennsylvania in 1949 he began museum work and teaching for the first time, and in his archaeological fieldwork he shifted from Greece, where he had excavated over a period of fifteen years, to Turkey, with the new aim of investigating the Phrygians.

In the end, however, the two phases of his scholarly work and excavations seem not to be discordant but instead to form a single whole. During his years in Greece he had concentrated on the emerging Hellenic culture of the early first millennium B.C., especially the eighth and seventh centuries, and his work in Turkey illuminated the same time span for the Phrygians. His investigations into the early history of the alphabet in Greece, partly spurred by his excavations with the late Carl Blegen on Mt. Hymettos, were nicely complemented by his pursuit of the same problem in Phrygia, and his interest in Eastern imports to Greece was rounded out by study of similar goods reaching inland Anatolia and the Phrygians.

In this volume which honors Rodney Young, it seems fitting that we too concern ourselves with the two peoples of his interests, the Greeks and the Phrygians of the early first millennium, and that we seek the common elements that may link them together and give an underlying theme to a lifetime's work.

First of all, it seems probable that the two groups were in fairly close contact with each other. In the fifth century B.C., the historian Herodotos claimed that a splendid wooden throne still on display at Delphi was a gift of Midas,[1] the powerful Phrygian king of the late eighth and early seventh centuries B.C., and stories traceable back to the fourth century had Midas taking a wife from the East Greek city of Kyme.[2] Phrygian fibulae and bronze bowls of eighth to seventh century date have been recovered at sanctuaries in East and mainland Greece,[3] and conversely at Gordion, the Phrygian capital explored by Young, there have been found sherds of six Greek vases dating to the decades just before and after 700 B.C.[4]

Finds from the two regions show as well that the two peoples shared down through the eighth century a common taste for a decoration of densely packed geometric patterning, as evidenced on pottery (figs. 2, 3), woodwork (figs. 4, 5), and in Phrygia, textiles (fig. 6); in both lands a way of achieving a more complex ornamentation was to embed within the overall patterning small panels containing a figure or a geometric motif (as figs. 2, 3). Debate continues on how close specific decorative motifs are in the

---

[1] Herodotos I, 14.

[2] Aristotle fragments 611, 37 Rose. Pollux IX, 83.

[3] J. Birmingham, "The Overland Route Across Anatolia in the Eighth and Seventh Centuries B.C.," *AnatSt* 11 (1961) 186-190. O. Muscarella, *Phrygian Fibulae from Gordion* (London 1967) 59-63.

[4] Unpublished. Gordion inventory numbers P 2984 East Greek Late Geometric oinochoe, P 3241 a, b Early Protocorinthian kotyle, P 3696 a, b Corinthian Late Geometric kotyle, P 4668 Early Protocorinthian kotyle, P 4805 Euboean Late Geometric oinochoe (?), P 4871 Corinthian Late Geometric kotyle.

two regions and whether or not the styles betray direct borrowing from one by the other, but what is unmistakable is the closeness of the overall effect.[5]

Certainly stemming from contact, but with the exact transmission debatable, is the use already in the eighth century by both Greeks and Phrygians of essentially the same script, the Levantine alphabet with some letter forms modified and with certain consonants given the value of vowels.[6]

The most significant correspondences, however, come in the ways of life. For the Phrygian culture, there is now abundant evidence for the eighth to early seventh centuries at the apparent seat of royal power, Gordion.[7] There are two main sources of information: a set of four rich burial tumuli (MM, P, W, and III, the last excavated by the German Körte brothers in 1900) and a level of severe destruction on the main citadel mound of probably the early seventh century and almost certainly wrought by the invading Kimmerians, who in Greek tradition brought to an end Midas's rule. The very thoroughness of the destruction has preserved the level unusually well; many buildings swept by fire still retained large amounts of their goods at the time of excavation. It seems most practicable first to examine the wealth of evidence provided at Gordion for Phrygian life and then to turn to the Greek sphere to see what parallels are there.

One zone of the citadel was in Rodney Young's view the royal residential quarter:[8] the partially excavated area at the east characterized by freestanding megarons (buildings with a deep, main room with a hearth and a shallow foreroom, itself often provided with a hearth; fig. 1) and divided into two courtyards by the wall that lies between the ends of Megarons 2 and 3 and runs between Megarons 10 and 12. Certainly an impression of wealth, luxury, and perhaps power is given by the largest of these megarons, Megaron 3. The main room of this building, found still amply filled with goods, is the most informative unit in the quarter, and a close study of it is helpful in assessing the character of the whole zone.

Within the room there was a small embodiment of the most persuasive symbol of riches, gold, in the form of a pellet, quite possibly a dump: that is, it may have been an unstamped but weight-determined piece that could serve as a pre-coinage type of currency.[9] Other gold was present as foil in combination with another luxury material, ivory, on a small socket or handle carved with leaf patterns, which seems likely to have been imported from the Levant. Ivory in general was well represented in the room, most spectacularly by a set of carved plaques.[10] The majority of these are figured, with such representations as a cavalryman (fig. 7), a foot soldier, and various animals and monsters, and the whole set fitted onto a piece of wooden furniture as part of a scheme of decoration that also in-

[5]E. Akurgal, *Phrygische Kunst* (Ankara 1955) 33-47. T. J. Dunbabin, *The Greeks and Their Eastern Neighbors* (London 1957) 66. J. Boardman, *The Greeks Overseas*, 1st ed. (Harmondsworth 1964) 104-105. E. Akurgal and P. Amandry in *Le rayonnement des civilisations grecque et romaine sur les cultures périphériques* (Paris 1965) 470-471, 485-486. Muscarella (*supra* n. 3) 59-63. J. N. Coldstream, *Greek Geometric Pottery* (London 1968) 378-379. G. K. Sams, "The Phrygian Painted Pottery of Early Iron Age Gordion and its Anatolian Setting" (Dissertation, University of Pennsylvania 1971) 345-355. A. M. Snodgrass, *The Dark Age of Greece* (Edinburgh 1971) 348. G. K. Sams, "Schools of Geometric Painting in Iron Age Anatolia," *AJA* 77 (1973) 226.

[6]R. S. Young, "Gordion on the Royal Road," *ProcPhil Soc* 107, 4 (1963) 362-364. R. S. Young, "Old Phrygian Inscriptions from Gordion," *Hesperia* 38 (1969) 252-257, 262-267. M. Lejeune, "Discussions sur l'alphabet phrygien," *SMEA* 10 (1969) 40-47. M. Lejeune, "Les inscriptions de Gordion et l'alphabet phrygien," *Kadmos* 9 (1970) 51-74.

[7]Gordion is cited as the residence of Midas and of his alleged predecessor and father Gordios in relatively late sources: Strabo XII, 568; Quintius Curtius Rufus, *Life of Alexander* III, 1, 11; Arrian, *Anabasis* II, 3; Plutarch, *Life of Alexander* 18. The last three reports, however, may go back to a statement in an early biography of Alexander, in connection with his visit to Gordion. The tradition of Gordion as a royal capital seems substantiated by the number and size of the surrounding burial tumuli, which are unsurpassed at any other Phrygian site.

[8]R. S. Young, "The Phrygian Contribution," *The Proceedings of the Xth International Congress of Classical Archaeology, Ankara-Izmir . . . 1973* I (Ankara 1978) 9-24.

[9]Gordion inventory number J 126. For a brief discussion of dumps, E. S. G. Robinson, "The Coins from the Ephesian Artemision Reconsidered," *JHS* 71 (1951) 164.

[10]R. S. Young, "The Gordion Campaign of 1959," *AJA* 64 (1960) 240, pl. 60, fig. 25a-c.

cluded strips of wooden inlay and raised bronze studs. The piece would have rivaled the contemporary throne with ivory plaques found at Salamis on Cyprus and the similarly decorated thrones or beds at Nimrud.[11] The Gordion plaques, though, and presumably the entire piece, are Phrygian work.

There was evidence as well for up to five other pieces of furniture in the room, including a table with an inlaid wood mosaic and a piece of uncertain form with delicately carved reliefs depicting a battle scene and animals (fig. 8).[12] The furniture was mostly ranged along the east wall.

Lending its own embellishment was a wealth of textiles. Most ubiquitous in the excavation were scraps of a loosely woven hemp or linen that, to judge from the evidence of the tumuli (below), may have hung on the walls. Other textiles seem to have been laid on furniture; fragments of felt and a fabric with decorative high stitching were picked up with the ivory-inlaid piece, and a textile with a thick fringe seems to have gone with a nearby piece of furniture. In the southeast corner was a pile of elaborately patterned fabrics (fig. 6) associated with burned wood first thought to be the remains of a couch or bed, though that interpretation was later doubted.[13]

Within the richly furnished room, one activity that seems suggested by the finds is drinking, beer drinking perhaps most clearly. Among the pottery are six jugs that are characterized by a spout running out from a perforated area on the wall and by a handle set at right angles to the spout (fig. 9). The type, well known for Phrygia since the excavations of the Körte brothers in 1900, is generally and surely rightly interpreted as a beer mug, with the perforations serving to strain out the barley particles that flecked ancient Anatolian beer, and the position of the handle

being for the ease of a drinker who would hold up the pot and drink from its spout.[14]

Other vessels, though, and ones in other materials, may point to wine drinking as well. A shallow bronze bowl, or phiale, with a raised omphalos dome in its center, is of a type which in the Near East was used for the drinking of a liquid clearer than beer, presumably wine.[15] A plain shallow bronze bowl could have matched the omphalos bowl in function, and so could an indeterminate but large number of handsomely carved wooden ones. In addition, at least two deep, broad bronze bowls (one with a griffin attachment on its shoulder) were present and are of the type called by archaeologists "cauldrons," but in spite of that name they may not have served so much to heat a liquid as to hold an alcoholic one, if they had the functions of similar vessels in eighth-century Assyria and archaic and Classical Greece.[16] The liquid was definitely wine in Greece, probably so in Assyria, and in Greece at least it was mixed with water in the bowl. Finally, the room contained a bronze ladle, an implement that in Greece was used for dipping out the wine from such a bowl or an equivalent.

The drinking looks to have been accompanied by eating, and again there are signs of a certain

---

[11]V. Karageorghis, *Excavations in the Necropolis of Salamis* III, 1 (Salamis 5,1; London 1974) 87-94. M. Mallowan and G. Herrmann, *Furniture from S.W. 7 Fort Shalmaneser* (Ivories from Nimrud [1949-1963] III; London 1974).

[12]Young (*supra* no. 10) 240, pl. 61, figs. 23-24.

[13]Changing interpretation by R. S. Young in the course of excavation as recorded in Gordion Notebook 80, pp. 90, 100. For the textiles of the room (incorrectly identified as having come from a tumulus), L. Bellinger, "Textiles from Gordion," *Bulletin of the Needle and Bobbin Club* 46 (1962) 15-16, pls. 10-16.

[14]G. and A. Körte, *Gordion: Ergebnisse der Ausgrabung im Jahre* 1900 (*JdI*, 5th Ergänzungsheft, 1904) 83-84. G. K. Sams, "Beer in the City of Midas," *Archaeology* 30 (1977) 108-115. Key ancient reference: Xenophon, *Anabasis* IV, 5, 26.

[15]As exemplified by phiales on a relief of Assurbanipal, H. Frankfort, *Art and Architecture of the Ancient Orient* (Harmondsworth 1954) pl. 114, and on ivories from Megiddo, *ibid.* 158-159, figs. 74-75.

[16]Assyria: relief from palace of Sargon at Nimrud, P. E. Botta, *Monuments de Ninive* I (Paris 1849) pl. 76; R. S. Young, "Bronzes from Gordion's Royal Tomb," *Archaeology* 11 (1958) fig. on p. 227.

Greece: Herodotos (IV, 152) refers to a griffin "cauldron" as an Argive "krater," that is, a bowl for the mixing of wine and water. That already by the seventh century the "cauldrons" were used as kraters or at least not heating vessels is suggested by a production of them in fine-ware pottery. For an especially striking example, complete with Near Eastern-derived stand, see J. Boardman, "A Protocorinthian Dinos and Stand," *AntK* 13 (1970) 92-94. A use as kraters is explicit in some Late Archaic and Early Classical representations, e.g., vase paintings by Euphronios and Smikros, E. Vermeule, "Fragments of a Symposion by Euphronios," *AntK* 8 (1965) pls. 11,2 and 14,2, and a relief from Thasos, B. S. Ridgway, *The Severe Style in Greek Sculpture* (Princeton 1970) pl. 63.

luxury. In the southeast of the room were approximately nineteen cornelian cherry pits; the paleobotanist Gordon Hillman was able to determine that at the time of the fire the body of the fruit was already gone, presumably from having been eaten, but it remains uncertain whether the Phrygians of Midas's time ate the cherries raw or after they had been boiled, in the known manner of the Phrygians of Ovid's time and of the modern Turks. A striking aspect of the cornelian cherries is that they could not have grown near Gordion if the environment in ancient times was at all like that today. Hillman suggests that the closest likely source is a range of the Pontus mountains 100 km. north. A further imported food was hazel nuts, perhaps coming from the Black Sea region. A few shells, from which the meat had been shucked before the fire, were recovered from a storage jar, and bits of other hazel nuts, whether shells or meat, came from a small jug with a trefoil lip. A further food product, one likely to be local, was found in another jug of the same type: a mass of seeds of *Ziziphora*, probably *Ziziphora capitata*, a steppe plant growing in the area. Hillman notes that Kurds in northern Syria brew an herbal tea from the flowering heads of a similar species, and while he is not aware of any use for the seeds alone, he supposes that when ground up they might have value as a flavoring.[17]

Incidentally the trefoil jugs containing the food are part of a total of over thirty such vessels in the room. In later Greece, the pot type was used for the pouring of wine, but the very fact that foodstuffs were in two of the pieces here and the wide variety of contents elsewhere in the citadel—including further foodstuffs, needles, and gaming pieces—make one hesitate to suppose a similar, particular function in Phrygia and to add the jugs to the evidence for wine drinking set out above.

A further pleasant aspect of life in the room is indicated by fifteen or sixteen astragals, ancient dice, found together in a mug.

Quite different finds were a number of iron pieces, all with ambiguous or uncertain func-

tions. An iron axe-adze could have served as either a carpenter's tool or a battle axe, the latter being a potential function in the contemporary Near East and one alluded to in the *Iliad*.[18] In the context of this room, with the military themes of the ivory plaques on one furniture piece and of the relief carvings on another, the alternative as a weapon is a tempting one. More baffling are ten iron pieces, nine belonging to a single set, which have paddlelike blades and sockets for the insertion of wooden shafts. Mrs. Joanna McClellan in her doctoral dissertation on the Gordion iron suggests that they may have been hearth tools.[19]

The other buildings in the quarter yielded only limited finds in comparison with Megaron 3. Those on the east escaped burning altogether, with the possible exception of a small part of Megaron 11, and thus did not have their goods trapped inside. Megarons 1 and 2, while burned, had little in their principal rooms, whether due to their not being intensively used or to their being looted before the fire; and Megaron 4, though caught up in the fire and seemingly well provisioned at that moment, looks to have been churned through after the destruction.

Nevertheless, what evidence there is points on the whole to the character of the entire quarter being similar to that of Megaron 3. Comparable rich material there certainly was. A gold plate for a box turned up just outside Megaron 4,[20] and within the building were fragments of an ivory lion figurine and of ivory appliqués depicting horses and riders.[21] More ivory in the form of

---

[17]Report by Dr. Gordon Hillman, November 17, 1977. The Ovid passage is in the *Metamorphoses* VIII, 665; I owe this reference to Prof. Crawford H. Greenewalt, Jr.

[18]In an Assyrian relief, axe-adzes can be seen in a military context, in the demolition of a fortress, A. Perrot, *Assur* (Paris 1961) 39, fig. 46, and in other Assyrian reliefs axes lacking the adze end are among the weapons on war chariots, B. Hrouda, *Die Kulturgeschichte des assyrischen Flachbildes* (Bonn 1965) pls. 61, 3 and 63, 4. *Iliad* XIII, 611-612; XV, 711.

[19]J. McClellan, "The Iron Objects from Gordion" (Dissertation, University of Pennsylvania 1975) 387-391.

[20]R. S. Young, "The 1963 Campaign at Gordion," *AJA* 68 (1964) 287.

[21]Young (*supra* n. 20) 287, pl. 89, fig. 22. Young in that context theorized that the ivories, which were found in a post hole, belonged to fill laid down at the time of the construction of the building. The pieces were burned, however, and thus seem to have been caught up in the destruction of the building, and the excavations of later years turned up many objects in post holes of the destruction level and belonging to

a fragmentary cymbal player was in a small area of burning or of burned dumped debris in Megaron 11.[22] What vessels and implements there are have a similar nature to those noted. In Megaron 4 there was a cauldron of fancy type with bull's head attachments,[23] and two iron axes from the same building along with an iron axe-adze from a storeroom alongside Megaron 1 share with the axe-adzes of Megaron 3 the ambiguity of whether in their contexts they were for carpentry or war. Also, both Megarons 1 and 2 had a set of two iron "paddles." In other parallels, Megaron 4 yielded hazel nuts, and two of the buildings had astragals in quantity: 293 in a trefoil jug by the hearth of Megaron 2 and a grand total of 494 in a pot in a back storeroom of Megaron 1.

In addition, the splendor suggested by the furnishings of Megaron 3 is echoed more structurally in Megarons 1, 2, and 9, where pebbles were laid to create mosaic floors.[24]

Some finds from the quarter, however, present wholly new aspects not documented in Megaron 3. Grain, both wheat and barley, was stored in the rooms to the rear of Megaron 1, and there was some textile equipment. Loom weights characterized as "occasional" in the excavation notebook and a very few spindle whorls, perhaps no more than two, were in the back storerooms of Megaron 1, while about seventy-five loom weights were in a similar rear storeroom of Megaron 4; about twenty spindle whorls were found within the walls of the main room of that building, but as they were in burned debris above the floor the place of their storage or use just before the destruction is not clear.

On the whole then, the character of the quarter that emerges from the finds does seem consistent with Rodney Young's view of it as the royal one; at a minimum it was an exceedingly rich one with its buildings luxuriously fitted out and with dining and drinking provided for in Megaron 3 at least; tempering the overall picture only slightly is the evidence pointing to a limited amount of textile work.

Further information on princely or aristocratic society at Gordion comes from the four rich tumulus burials MM, P, W, and III. The date of W perhaps lies in the first half of the eighth century, that of the others within a range of the second half of the century into the early seventh. P is the tomb of a child, the three others adult burials.[25]

Gratifyingly, the types of goods within the tumuli tend to be like those found in the rich quarter of the citadel. While gold is lacking and ivory scanty, fine furniture is abundant, and the dazzlingly complete state in which some pieces were found, especially in MM, reveals just what luxurious items they could be, with extensive inlays of contrasting wood (fig. 4). Textiles were plentiful, too, with loosely woven linen or hemp, like that of Megaron 3, detected in P, MM, and W. In all three of those tombs it apparently hung on the walls. Thicker and perhaps richer cloths were at the beds: felt in MM and a woven woolen fabric with geometric patterns in P.

Vessels for drinking are as conspicuous in the tomb chambers (Edwards, *infra*, fig. 11) as they were in Megaron 3. Jugs with strainers and spouts and, as noted, suited for beer drinking, are in all four tombs, reaching a maximum of 15 in Tumulus III. They are represented in bronze in MM, but almost all are terracotta in the other three tombs. Even more numerous are the bronze vessels suggested above as going with wine drinking: cauldrons, ladles, and shallow bowls of phiale type (here including a Phrygian variant with movable, horizontal handles). The proportions of these vessels in the four tumuli do tend to bear out such an interpretation for their

---

that level. Young's later opinion concerning such objects in general was that they had once hung on posts. In the original *AJA* report it was further stated that the ivories included unworked but cut pieces along with chips and that this raw material and debris indicated that the whole group stemmed from an ivory-working establishment. However, the pieces of ivory that have been kept and inventoried seem all to be finished goods; the excavation notebook entry (106, p. 63) reads as follows: "In post hole 3 was found a small carved ivory horse(s) and part of its rider. (c. 10 cmt.) burned. Below were numerous fragments of burned ivory—some of them carved. (one a fragment of a Lion figure)."

[22]Unpublished. Gordion inventory number BI 529.

[23]Unpublished. Gordion inventory number B 1440.

[24]R. S. Young, "Early Mosaics at Gordion," *Expedition* 7, 3 (1965) 9-13.

[25]Tumulus III is published in Körte and Körte (*supra* n. 14) 38-98. P, MMT, and W ("Pauline") are the subject of the forthcoming first Gordion volume, largely written by R. S. Young. The preliminary publications, by Young, are in the *AJA* 61 (1957) 325-331; 62 (1958) 147-154; 64 (1960) 227-232.

functions. Thus, in Tumulus W there were 2 large cauldrons, 2 small ones, 2 ladles, and 14 shallow bowls; in III 2 large cauldrons, 4 small ones, 1 ladle, and 28 bowls; in P 2 large cauldrons, 3 small ones, 2 ladles, and 22 bowls (plus 1 glass one); in MM 3 large cauldrons, 10 small ones, 2 ladles, and 115 bowls. It can be seen that the numbers of ladles come close to matching those of the large cauldrons in all cases, as they should if the ladles are wine dippers and the cauldrons the wine holders; the smaller cauldrons whose numbers are more anomalous could conceivably be interpreted as spares or as substitutes for less demanding occasions. And that the shallow bowls are the vessels present in greatest numbers is also fitting, if they would indeed be the cups of the individual drinkers. If it be accepted that such was the use of the latter, then the number they reach in MM, the awesome 115, could imply some staggeringly large gatherings for drinking. Such might, of course, have occurred, and the spacious megarons, like Megaron 3 with a main room of ca. 15 × 19 m. where drinking and dining were certainly done, could have accommodated large companies if not quite such overwhelming crowds.

However, it would probably be simplistic to see such vessels as just the components of functioning wine sets. While the general proportions of the various pieces seem to be consistent with such a use, the specific ratios vary widely from tomb to tomb. Thus, in MM for every large cauldron there are 38.4 shallow bowls, and in III the ratio becomes 1:14, in P 1:11.5, and in W 1:7. Furthermore, the child buried in Tumulus P is unlikely to have entertained guests at wine parties during his lifetime with the vessels deposited in his grave. The shallow bowls, cauldrons, and ladles appear then to have a significance beyond their likely primary functions. The same could be true of the bronze strainer jugs and of still a further class of bronze containers: 29 trefoil jugs in MM, a shape which had, as noted above, a variety of uses. Altogether, the pieces constitute imposing collections of bronzes in the tombs, and one wonders if that was not part of their meaning: if the very amassing of the bronze vessels, apart from consideration of their strict practical uses, may not have been felt desirable and if the bronze vessels, in view

of the absence of gold in the tombs, may not have been an embodiment of wealth.

A curiosity is that four of the bronzes in MM along with one of the pottery vessels bear incised inscriptions, and while C. Brixhe suspects personal names to be embodied in at least four of the graffiti, all of the names are different.[26]

Beyond the bronze pots, the tumuli, like the megarons, contained some iron objects; these, like certain ones of the citadel, may predominantly have had hearth functions. In III were found both a bronze and an iron fire rake, and in P were a pair of iron tongs and a long iron rod with a hook at its end. Simplest of all were two iron ingots in III, of value as the material from which finished products could be made.

In one final correspondence, astragals turned up in a single tumulus, fittingly the child's, where they totalled at least 506. As the majority, though, are reported to have been pierced for bronze rings, it is doubtful whether this particular group would have been gaming pieces.

The tumuli then and the area of freestanding megarons yield evidence for upper-class life that is consistent. Finds pointing to a much different way of life and to a very different class of society come from a zone of the citadel directly to the west of that considered. Separated from the area of the individual buildings by a blank back wall and by indirect passageways are two lines of megarons built up in solid rows and facing each other across a wide street: at the east the row of the Terrace Building, or TB, with eight units and at the west the CC row, which has so far yielded parts of four units and which might well also have had eight in all.

Two of the units, at the south end of TB, are idiosyncratic. Unlike the others they lack all permanent installations of stands, ovens, and hearths. The absence of the last would have made living or working in them difficult during the harsh Anatolian winters, but it would be consistent with their being storage houses, even treasure houses, functions suggested by the nature of the finds from them. In TB 2 there were three separate caches of considerable value: jewelry of electrum, gold, silver, and glass; bronze animal

[26]R. S. Young, "Old Phrygian Inscriptions from Gordion." *Hesperia* 38 (1969) 260-261, nos. 25, 30-33. C. Brixhe in forthcoming first Gordion volume.

figurines; and ivory and iron outfittings for a four-horse chariot team.[27] Going with these were the more pedestrian finds of loom weights (over 300). Next door, TB 1 had even more loom weights, ca. 800, with some 464 heaped up in a single great pile. A few spindle whorls were in the unit, too, and there was a small quantity of grain, but most striking was the presence of at least five bronze cauldrons, one having bull-protome attachments.[28]

The other nine known units are unvaryingly similar in installations, finds, and, it would seem, functions. To an extent, they, too, could serve as storage depots for objects probably unrelated to any activities in them. A number, for example, contained the sorts of iron axes and axe-adzes noted in the freestanding megarons and which here may have hung from posts. Overwhelmingly, though, the units look to have been devoted to the production on a large scale of two types of goods: foodstuffs and textiles.

A production of cereal foods is particularly evident. The basic materials, wheat and barley, which were modestly present in the annex of Megaron 1 and in TB 1, were abundant in both rooms of the standard units of the zone. In the main rooms there took place the grinding down of those grains into flour by means of saddle querns on stands centered against the rear walls (fig. 10); strikingly, wheat still lay on the surface of a quern in TB 5. The number of querns, and thus of grinding places, varies from five to eighteen. Further processes appear to have taken place in the anterooms. Broad, shallow trays of wood or clay may have been for kneading flour, mixed with water, into dough, and presumably the baking of dough into bread would have been done in the invariable one to two ovens of the rooms.[29]

Lentils, requiring cooking, and hazel nuts, needing no preparation, were also in the units, and a meat production is clear in CC 3, where there were the skeletons of two partially butchered calves.

Textile production, like the bread making, involved all stages from initial work with raw materials to finished goods. Some clumps of coarsely twisted fiber in CC 3 may represent rove; the further working into spun thread is attested not by the material itself but by masses of spindle whorls, which are present in the standard units in far greater numbers than they are in Megarons 1 and 4 and in TB 1 (e.g., over 175 in the main room of CC 3; at least 46 in the main room of TB 7; and nearly 90 in its anteroom). Iron knives, often found together with whorls, perhaps served in those pre-scissors days to cut spun thread. Once made, the thread was woven into cloth. Loom weights are plentiful (e.g., nearly 500 in the main room of CC 3, over 450 in the main room of TB 7, and over 150 in its anteroom), being far more numerous than those in the storerooms of Megarons 1 and 4; and unlike the abundant ones in the idiosyncratic units TB 1 and TB 2, it is clear that those of the usual units were put to use in the rooms in which they were found: loom weights in the main room of CC 3 still had traces of thread in their holes and a set of 21 weights in the front room of TB 7 lay in a 1.59 m. line on the floor, in the position of the vertical loom to which they had been attached.

There were a few signs of luxury and of relaxed living in the units. A fine necklace was in TB 4, and a knife in CC 3 as well as another in TB 7 were fitted with ivory handles.[30] Among the large quantities of pottery are a certain number of sieve-spouted jugs, perhaps for beer drinking on the spot, and hazel nuts found together with spindle whorls in a jug in CC 3 suggest that some at least of this imported food would be eaten by people right within the zone. Astragals are numerous and hint at recreation. Nonetheless, in comparison with the zone of freestanding megarons, finds of intrinsic richness are scanty, and the basic character of the quarter, no matter

---

[27]R. S. Young, "The 1961 Campaign at Gordion," *AJA* 66 (1962) 165-167, pls. 46-47, figs. 20-26.

[28]G. R. Edwards, "Gordion: 1962," *Expedition* 5,3 (1963) 45, fig. 22.

[29]The ovens were also used to roast grains, as indicated by a layer, judged to be wheat, up to 10 cm. deep in an oven in the anteroom of CC 1 (Gordion Notebook 91, p. 186).

[30]Necklace of glass beads (Gordion inventory numbers G 264-265) with one bead having the form of a duck's head. The knife and handle of CC 3 were found separately and rejoined (inventory number ILS 711); the handle alone is known from TB 7 (inventory number BI 453).

how tempered, emphatically remains that of a work area.

The number of laborers appears high. As noted, the number of querns on the stands ranges from five to eighteen, thus indicating the number of people that might be grinding at any one time in any one unit. Grinding, of course, was only one of the activities in the units, and it would seem that different jobs were pursued at the same time: in the front room of TB 7 a loom was up and iron tools were lying on a hearth and by an oven, as if fire tending was going on concurrently with weaving just when disaster struck. A further statistical pointer is the twenty-two separate occurrences in the main CC 3 room of one or more knives, which, as noted, appear to be spinners' equipment. While clearly there will have to be pursued a careful, sustained statistical analysis of the TB and CC rooms, a working estimate that could be risked now and that ought to be well on the safe side would be twenty-five people per unit (a figure that could easily be accommodated within the spacious inner dimensions of ca. 11.5 × 21 m. for each). With six units of the TB complex devoted to work and with six hypothesized for the CC, the resulting labor force would be three hundred.

To judge from other ancient societies, the workers are likely to have been women. Among the most telling and full evidence is that from the Aegean where it was precisely the two jobs of textile work and food preparation that were the particular provinces of women from the palaces of the Bronze Age to the middle-class households of Classical times.[31] Similarly in Iron Age Palestine it was the norm for women to do the jobs of spinning, weaving, and grinding within a household, though at least the latter two jobs might be done by men in other settings.[32] Among the Bronze Age Hittites in Central Anatolia itself, women likewise did the grinding and baking; weaving, however, is known as a male profession.[33]

Furthermore, it seems likely that the labor force at Gordion was not free, to judge from what may be a fairly tight enclosure of the work zone within the citadel and from the apparent existence itself of largish work gangs.

When one turns from the evidence for Phrygian life at the time of Midas to that for contemporary Greece, one correspondence is conspicuous. The high esteem given to hearth or fire utensils of iron, as manifested by their being deposited in two of the Gordion tumuli and by their being among the goods of Megaron 3, is matched in Greece by the prizing of iron spits. Sets in multiples of six, once with the fire dogs on which they would lie, have come from two eighth-century graves in Argos,[34] and early dedications of such sets in Greek sanctuaries are known from both archaeological and written sources.[35] It seems clear indeed that spits served as a measure of wealth and as a medium of exchange from the fact that when coinage emerges in archaic Greece there is a small denomination termed an "obelos," or "spit," and six of these have the worth of a higher denomination known as a "drachma," or "spit set."[36]

Other correspondences emerge above all from the Homeric epics, which though having a dramatic setting in the Bronze Age and being the products of a long tradition, are now generally believed to have taken much their present form in the eighth or early seventh century B.C. Thus while a social practice or an object mentioned in

---

[31]M. Ventris and J. Chadwick, *Documents in Mycenaean Greek*, 2nd ed. (Cambridge 1973) 155-162, esp. texts PY 1, 3, 4, 8, 14, 15. *Odyssey* VII, 104-106; XX, 105-119; XIII, 421-423. Xenophon, *Memorabilia* II, 7, 5; *Oikonomikos* VII, 6 and 21; X, 10-11.

[32]Proverbs 31, 10-15. Judges 16, 21. I Samuel 17, 7.

[33]H. A. Hoffner, Jr., *Alimenta Hethaeorum* (New Haven 1974) 133. Hittite Law Code, Paragraphs 176B

---

and 200B, with recent text, F. Imparati, *Le Leggi Ittite* (Incunabula Graeca VII; Rome 1964). I owe these references to Miss Lin Foxhall and Prof. J. D. Muhly.

[34]P. Courbin, "Chronique des fouilles en 1952. Argos," *BCH* 77 (1953) 260. P. Courbin, "Une tombe géométrique d'Argos," *BCH* 81 (1957) 368-370. P. Courbin, "Dans la Grèce antique: Valeur comparée du fer et de l'argent," *Annales: Économies Sociétés Civilisations* 14 (1959) 212.

[35]Herodotos II, 135. L. H. Jeffery, *The Local Scripts of Archaic Greece* (Oxford 1961) 102-103, pl. 12, 7. C. Waldstein, *The Argive Heraeum* I (Cambridge, Mass., 1902) 62, 77. J. N. Svoronos, "Obeloi Sideroi," *Journal international d'archéologie numismatique* 9 (1906) 195-197. H. T. Wade-Gery in H. Payne, *Perachora* I (Oxford 1940) 256-267.

[36]The core meaning of *drachma* is "a handful" (cf. δράσσομαι), but the word had already taken on the meaning of "spit set" (from "handful of spits," cf. Plutarch, *Life of Lysander* 17) in a ca. seventh-century Perachora inscription: Wade-Gery (*supra* n. 35) 257-261, pl. 36c.

them might have been most firmly anchored in a past reality, it still would have been at least artistically current.

In four detailed passages the poems give revealing insights into the material goods valued most highly: the lists of prizes given at Patroklos's funeral games, the gifts bestowed by the Phaeacians on Odysseus, and the offerings made separately to Achilles by Agamemnon and Priam.[37] The kinds of goods cited are consistent among themselves, and they tend to match the very ones prominent in the tombs and megarons of the Gordion rich. Thus, gold is only once present in these contexts as a finished product (a libation bowl); normally, like the probable dump in Megaron 1, the gold is valued simply as a weight of itself. Similarly, iron, too, can be prized in a raw form, as it was in Tumulus III, but it is interesting to find Achilles awarding iron single- and double-edged axes, items comparable to the axes and axe-adzes of the Gordion citadel. Paradoxically, iron spits, or for that matter fire utensils, do not figure at all.

The metal objects most commonly mentioned in the passages are vessels. Only twice are they specified as being of precious metal, the one example being the gold libation bowl and the other a silver krater. Bronze seems implied as the material for the others, and bronze pots would thus be as standard items of value in the Homeric poems as they are at Gordion. Some which are specified as cups would, along with the silver krater, match the interpretation of the Gordion vessels as drinking equipment, but it should be noted that the most conspicuously cited ones would not: tripods and lebes basins, which in part at least were clearly used for heating water or cooking.[38]

Beyond metal, fine fabrics are given. While these are mostly garments, their category is roughly comparable to the textiles that embellished Megaron 3 and the tumuli.

It is significant that we can best estimate the worth assigned to classes of material goods from passages dealing with prizes or outright gifts. Gift-giving itself, apart from the items involved, was a critically important practice in Homeric society; in particular, a gift from a host to a guest was an imperative.[39] Such diverse hosts as Menelaos in Sparta, a Polybos in Egypt, and, mockingly, Polyphemos on his cannibal island were all conceived of as adhering to the practice,[40] and a plausible explanation given for Odysseus's absence was that he was assembling riches through calculated visits.[41] Gifts might pass from person to person over the years, and the pedigrees of the objects were remembered. A silver krater of Menelaos's was traced back through two previous owners and one of Patroklos's through three.[42] A similar system of gift-giving among the Phrygians might account for the vessels' bearing different names in the MM burial.

In other social aspects, banquets are a conspicuous feature of the Homeric poems, in spite of the relatively few vessels suitable for them presented as gifts. With ample supplies of food and wine (but never beer), they are on something of the grand scale that may be indicated for Gordion: thus Menelaos gives a wedding feast for his kinsmen and neighbors, King Alkinoos entertains the whole body of aristocrats of Scheria, and the band of Penelope's suitors dine and drink at Odysseus's palace.[43] The suitors' banquets and apparently those of Alkinoos's group as well are regular occurrences. Interestingly, the setting of the Homeric banquets seems comparable to the Gordion megarons and especially to Megaron 3, where something of the furnishings is known and where food and drink were served: a large hall with a hearth and with furniture ranged along the walls.[44] There is a foreroom to these halls, as at Gordion; in the

---

[37]*Iliad* IX, 121-156; XXIII, 257-897 (especially 262-270, 653-656, 700-705, 740-751, 798-810, 826-827, 850-858, 883-886); XXIV, 229-235. *Odyssey* VIII, 392-393 with XIII, 10-14.

[38]*Iliad* IX, 122; XXIII, 267, 702, 885. *Odyssey* VIII, 433-437; X, 358-361; XII, 237-238. But lebes as basin for sacrificial water: *Odyssey* III, 440; for ordinary water: *Odyssey* I, 137 and recurrences of the formulaic phrase.

[39]M. I. Finley, *The World of Odysseus,* 2nd ed. (London 1977) 64-68.

[40]*Odyssey* IV, 126-129; 589-619; IX, 368-370; XV, 75-130.

[41]*Odyssey* XIX, 282-284.

[42]*Odyssey* IV, 615-619. *Iliad* XXIII, 740-747.

[43]*Odyssey* I, 144-160 and *passim;* IV, 1-16; VII, 136-137 with XIII, 7-9.

[44]*Odyssey* VII, 95-99, 153-154.

poems it is the place where guests sleep, the host and his wife being in the main hall.[45]

Along with domestic entertainment, domestic labor is noted in the epics. Both King Alkinoos's and Odysseus's households were staffed by fifty slave women, who ground grain and did the textile work.[46] The situation described seems strikingly like that at Gordion, with its quarter devoted to just those jobs. But where Alkinoos and Odysseus had fifty women, Midas may have had (conservatively) three hundred. However, the domestic work in the Homeric poems was done by women other than just slaves. Alkinoos's queen Arete, like her servants, spins, Helen has her spinning work brought with her when she joins Menelaos and guests in the banquet hall, and Penelope finds a long-successful ruse in her never-ending work at the loom.[47] Such participation in the making of fabrics by the upper-class women may be relevant on the one hand to the signs of some textile work within the free-standing megaron quarter at Gordion and on the other hand to the occasional jewelry or rich equipment in the workrooms of the TB and CC zone, which otherwise seem lacking in luxury.

The Homeric society, then, and the Phrygian seem to share certain ways of life and certain attitudes as to what was materially valuable and worth accumulating. For Homeric society there has been much debate as to what era in the Aegean, if any, it is most firmly anchored, but what does emerge from the excavations of Rodney Young at Gordion is that at the time the epics were coalescing along the Ionian Greek fringe of Anatolia the society in some of its most striking aspects had a living counterpart in lands not far to the east.

ADDENDUM

Of relevance perhaps for the Gordion bronze vessels (and certainly for those in the Homeric poems) is the use of tripods and lebetes as standard reckonings of value in Gortyn in Crete in archaic times.[48] An item of interest in connection with the Gordion axes and axe-adzes is the citing of weight by "axes" in a Cretan inscription of ca. 500 B.C. and quite likely also in a Cypriote one of the fifth century.[49] While the Gordion pieces are not likely to have been weight determinants, the possibility is raised that they, too, embodied some standard value.

---

[45] *Odyssey* IV, 302-305; VII, 344-347.

[46] *Odyssey* VII, 104-106; XX, 105-119; XXII, 421-423.

[47] *Odyssey* II, 93-110 (with repetitions in XIX, 138-156, and XXIV, 129-146); IV, 131-135; VI, 305-307.

---

[48] M. Guarducci, "Tripodi, lebeti, oboli," *Rivista di Filologia Classica* 72-73 (1944-1945) 171-180. M. Guarducci, *Tituli Gortyni* (Inscriptiones Creticae IV; Rome 1950) 41-42 and texts 1, 5-8, 10-11, 14, 21. C. M. Kraay, *Archaic and Classical Greek Coins* (Berkeley and Los Angeles 1976) 314-315.

[49] C. D. Buck, *The Greek Dialects* (Chicago 1955) 210-213, text 23. L. H. Jeffery and A. Morpurgo-Davies, "ΠΟΙΝΙΚΑΣΤΑΣ and ΠΟΙΝΙΚΑΖΕΝ . . . a New Archaic Inscription from Crete," *Kadmos* 9 (1970) 124 (B 11-12) and 144. Kraay (*supra* n. 48) 315.

GORDION

DESTRUCTION LEVEL

0   100 m.

1973   HEMANS, CUMMER   1:500 SCALE

Figure 1. Gordion: plan of citadel at destruction level, ca. early seventh century B.C.

Figure 2. Phrygian jug from Tumulus P, Gordion, ca. last third of eighth century B.C.   H. 25.5 cm.

Figure 3. Late Geometric Greek pyxis (Argive), ca. 750-730 B.C.   H. 104 cm. Courtesy of École Française d'Athènes.

Figure 4. Phrygian wooden screen with phiale in front, Tumulus MM, Gordion, ca. early seventh century B.C. H. 95 cm.

Figure 5. Reconstruction of Greek wooden stool, ca. 700 B.C., from Samos. H. ca. 23 cm. Reprinted, by permission of Gebr. Mann Verlag, from *AthMitt* 68 (1953) 91, fig. 3.

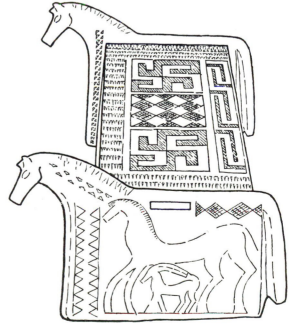

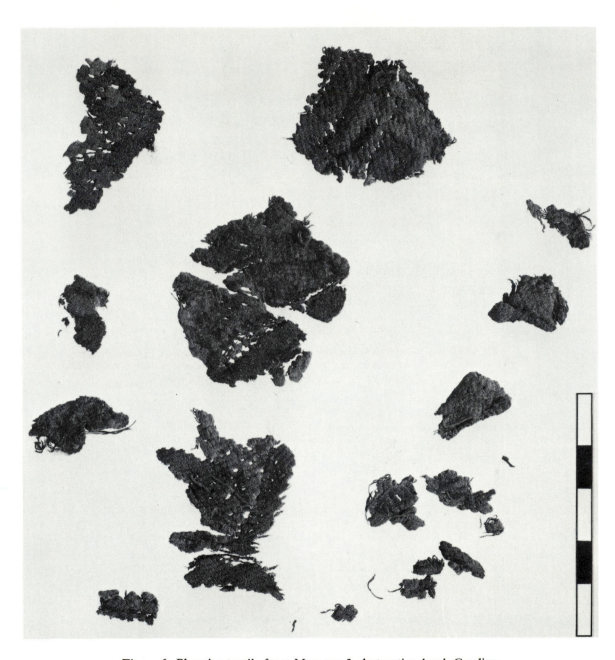

Figure 6. Phrygian textile from Megaron 3, destruction level, Gordion

Figure 7. Ivory furniture inlay with horse and armed rider from Megaron 3. H. 4.6 cm.

Figure 8. Drawing of furniture fragment with battle scene in light relief from Megaron 3. L. 29 cm.

Figure 9. Strainer jug from Megaron 3.   H. 14.6 cm.

Figure 10. Grinding stand in CC 2, destruction level, Gordion

V. SEALS AND SEALING IN HITTITE LANDS*

Hans G. Güterbock

A few Hittite seals were found at Gordion, both on the mound by Professor Young and in the Hittite cemetery by Professor Mellink. Short of cuneiform texts, which may still be waiting somewhere inside the mound, these seals are the most eloquent vestiges of the Hittite settlement on the site. To put them into a wider framework seemed to be a fitting way of honoring the memory of a dear friend.

Before turning to the use of seals it may be useful briefly to review the typology of Anatolian stamp seals. Using the terminology of Hogarth in his book *Hittite Seals*,[1] we may start with two of the most archaic shapes as represented by finds from Gordion: the "stud" (fig. 1) and the stalk (fig. 2), both from burials and published by Professor Mellink in her publication of the cemetery.[2] As she pointed out, the stud seal, made of faience, comes from a child burial and therefore is more likely to have served as an amulet than for actual sealing, while the bronze stalk has a design of concentric circles frequently stamped on vessels of Old Hittite type.

Two examples of pottery stamps on jar handles come from the mound. One (fig. 3), also published by Mellink, has the shape of a naked human foot, for which there exist parallels else-where.[3] The other (fig. 4), published by Professor Young in his report on the campaign of 1965,[4] was made with a regular Hittite stamp seal and has a hieroglyphic inscription which, unfortunately, I am unable to read. Nor am I able to shed light on the meaning and purpose of seal impressions on pottery in general; the problems were well stated by Miss Seidl in her publication of the Boğazköy potmarks. Even the observation made there that impressions produced with the same stamp, showing a human figure and symbols, were found on a handle at Boğazköy and on one at Hüyük[5] allows for more than one explanation.

To continue with the survey of stamp types, the very common so-called "knob," really a knob on top of a cone or many-sided pyramid, is now firmly dated to the period of Karum I B at Kültepe and the corresponding levels at Alishar and Boğazköy.[6] The designs are either geometric or show stylized birds or animals.

A shape developed out of the knob is the "hammer," of which there are two subgroups de-

*The author read a slightly different version of this paper at the symposium held at the Oriental Institute of the University of Chicago in 1976. See M. Gibson and R. D. Biggs, eds., *Seals and Sealings in the Ancient Near East* (Biblioteca Mesopotamica 6; Malibu 1977) 3. For special abbreviations, see p. 57.

[1]*HS* pp. 20-23.

[2]Machteld J. Mellink, *A Hittite Cemetery at Gordion* (Philadelphia 1956) 42, pl. 23 k-n.

[3]Mellink (*supra* n. 2) 41, pl. 23e. Cf. Ursula Seidl, *Gefässmarken von Boğazköy* (Boğazköy-Hattuša VIII = WVDOG 88; Berlin 1972) nos. A 114-115, pp. 72, 75.

[4]Rodney S. Young, "The Gordion Campaign of 1965," *AJA* 70 (1966) 277, pl. 74, 24.

[5]Seidl (*supra* n. 3) no. A 81, p. 71 with n. 68; p. 79.

[6]A good survey of Anatolian seals is by R. M. Boehmer, *PKG* 14, 437-453. For "knob"-handled seals see Nimet Özgüç, *Seals and Seal Impressions of Level Ib From Karum Kanish* (Türk Tarih Kurumu Yayınlarından, V. Seri, no. 25; Ankara 1968) esp. pl. XXXVI; H. H. von der Osten, *The Alishar Hüyük, Seasons of 1930-32* II (OIP 29; Chicago 1937) esp. 212-214, figs. 249, 251; *WVDOG* 76, "Gruppen II-VIII," 19-24, 48-56, pls. 2-8.

pending on whether the body of the seal is four-sided or round. A four-sided hammer in the Ashmolean Museum[7] shows deities and worshippers accompanied by hieroglyphic symbols, which include the *crux ansata* meaning "life" and the triangle, which symbolizes "well-being" or "good luck." Another hammer seal of the same type, found at Bitik west of Ankara,[8] is interesting because of its unfinished state: apparently the name of an owner was going to be added in the central field when the seal was acquired by him.[9]

Of the hammers with round body a good example in the Walters Art Gallery[10] has a name and the title SCRIBE in the middle and a circle of signs (symbols?) whose meaning escapes us.

Another form derived from the knob is the "knob-cylinder." The most famous of the type is the so-called Tyskiewicz seal in Boston.[11]

Whereas the hammers and the knob-cylinders belong to the older Hittite period—and I leave it open, how old!—the New Kingdom or Empire introduces new shapes. One is the tripod, always of metal, mostly a silver alloy. A good example in the Berlin Museum[12] shows a man, the name

Pi-ya-Tarhun-ta, and a symbol which I now take as the late form of the *crux ansata,*[13] together with the triangle. These two symbols also form the outer circle. Also the famous silver seal of a king of Mira, known as the Tarkondemos seal, in the Walters Art Gallery,[14] may have had a tripod handle.

Another metal shape is the signet ring. There are two types: one has a circular bezel, while in the other the sealing surface is a widening of the ring itself, shaped into a pointed oval.[15]

One of the most common shapes of the New Kingdom is the lentoid or biconvex (Hogarth called it "bulla," but we reserve that term for sealed clay lumps!).[16] An example from Ras Shamra shows that the perforation served to hold a metal mounting.[17]

There are also discs, i.e., two-faced flat seals of circular shape as well as "tabloids," flat seals in shapes other than circular.

Finally there are hemispheroids (Hogarth's "semibullae"); fig. 5 shows an example formerly in a private collection in Ankara, which has a metal mounting.

These, then, are the main shapes of Hittite stamp seals. Cylinders exist but are rare and seem to be restricted to the southeast; the impressions of cylinders of the kings of Carchemish[18] are the outstanding examples, and others point to the same general area.

[7]*HS* no. 196; E. Akurgal and M. Hirmer, *The Art of the Hittites* (New York n.d. [1961]) pl. 52; *PKG* 14, pl. 375c. R. L. Alexander, "The Tyskiewicz Group of Stamp-Cylinders," *Anatolica* 5 (1973-1976 [1978]) 141-215, esp. 175ff. with fig. 9, proposes a later date.

[8]Remzi O. Arık, "Bitik Kazısı," *Belleten* 8 (1944) 341-354, pl. LX and drawing on title page.

[9]Cf. one of the hammer seals in the Louvre where hieroglyphs are found inside a frame identical with that on the Bitik seal: Delaporte, *Louvre,* no. A.1029, pl. 101, 4e.

[10]WAG 42.352. Cyrus H. Gordon, "Western Asiatic Seals in the Walters Art Gallery," *Iraq* 6 (1939) 3-34, esp. 24f., no. 70, pl. VIII (also in *HS* 75, fig. 79; H. Th. Bossert, *Altanatolien* [Berlin 1942] no. 679f.; *PKG* 14, pl. 376g). See H. G. Güterbock, in *Journal of the Walters Art Gallery* 36 (1977) 7-16, esp. 8-10, no. 2. Another example: S. Alp, *Athenaeum* n.s. 47 (1969) = *Studi in onore di Piero Meriggi* 1-3 with pl. I.

[11]Boston Museum of Fine Arts, no. 98-706. Henri Frankfort, *Cylinder Seals* (London 1939) 285-287, pls. II n and XLIII n-o; *PKG* 14, pl. 375a. For others see A. Parrot, "Cylindre hittite nouvellement acquis," *Syria* 28 (1951) 180-190, pls. XIII-XIV, and now Alexander (*supra* n. 7). For stamp impressions related to the base of the Boston seal see S. Alp, *Zylinder- und Stempelsiegel aus Karahöyük bei Konya* (Türk Tarih Kurumu Yayınlarından, V. Seri no. 26; Ankara 1968) pls. 49-52, 64-67, 74-75, 80-85.

[12]L. Jakob-Rost, *Die Stempelsiegel im Vorderasiatischen Museum* (Berlin 1975) no. 78; Ed. Meyer, *Reich und*

Kultur der Chetiter (Berlin 1914) 44-45, fig. 35. Cf. Güterbock (*supra* n. 10) 10, no. 3.

[13]Hittite hieroglyphs are here referred to by their number (preceded by "L") in E. Laroche, *Les hiéroglyphes hittites* I: *L'écriture* (Paris 1960). I now take L440 and L441 as more recent forms of the older L369.

[14]WAG 57.1512. Gordon (*supra* n. 10) no. 69. Dorothy K. Hill, "The Rediscovered Seal of Tarqumuwa King of Mera," *Archiv Orientální* 9 (1937) 307-310 (with bibliography), pl. XXVI; *PKG* 14, pl. 376k; Güterbock (*supra* n. 10) 11-16, no. 4.

[15]Both types shown in *HS* p. 22, figs. 21f. The seals are nos. 194 and 195 (p. 38 and pl. VII). The latter also in *PKG* 14, pl. 377e and Akurgal (*supra* n. 7) pl. 52, top; an older bezel ring, *ibid.* pl. 45, bottom.

[16]A good example of this common type is *PKG* 14, pl. 377d.

[17]*Ug.* III 63, fig. 88; also in *PKG* 14, 451, fig. vDcf. For the seal inscriptions, see the section by E. Laroche, *Ug.* III 97-160.

[18]*Ug.* III pp. 22-30, figs. 30-37, and pp. 121-131. Others: Edith Porada, *Corpus of Ancient Near Eastern Seals in North American Collections* I (The Bollingen Series 14; New York 1948) 115f., pl. CXXXVII, no. 909; Th.

Let us now turn to the use of seals.[19] For "seal" the Hittite texts usually write the word sign NA₄.KIŠIB (always with the determinative NA₄ "stone") which stands for the Akkadian *kunukku* "seal." The Hittite word, if correctly reconstructed, is *šiyatar,* literally "pressing"; the Hittite term would refer primarily to the impression in contrast to the Sumerian which is characterized as "stone."

Seals were impressed on tablets. At Kültepe it was only during the period Karum I B that seals were impressed either on the envelope or on the tablet itself, in contrast to Level II, the heyday of the Assyrian merchant colonies, when only the envelopes were sealed. One of the latest examples of a sealed tablet is in the Walters Art Gallery.[20]

From the Old Hittite Kingdom we have land deeds (fig. 6) beginning around 1620 B.C. (middle chronology).[21] These tablets are thick, pillow-shaped, and bear the royal seal in the center of the obverse, which, in contrast to normal usage, is the more convex in these documents. The first line of the text refers to the seal: "Seal of the Tabarna," sometimes but not always adding the individual king's name. These tablets had strings embedded in their clay; in complete tablets only the holes through which the strings emerged are visible in the lower edge, but one fragment (fig. 7) shows the impressions of the strings in the break.[22] They converge toward

a hole in the lower edge of the tablet. We can only speculate about this strange device. Maybe clay bullae with seals of other persons—the recipient of the donation or witnesses—were appended, but we don't know.

We do know that treaties were sealed. Best known is the description of the silver tablet bearing the seals of Hattusili and Pudukhepa as described in the inscriptions of Ramses II.[23] One wonders how a silver tablet could be sealed, even on both sides as the description says! Was there a wax coating on it? Strangely enough hardly any of the treaty tablets found in the Hittite capital are sealed, although the seals are mentioned in the text of some, e.g., the Aleppo Treaty of Mursili II as renewed by his son Muwatalli.[24] In another document of Mursili we read that the tablet was not yet sealed because not all parties were present, but would be sealed after they had been heard.[25] Were the official, sealed copies all of metal like the one described by Ramses?[26] Or did we simply not yet find the "real" archive where the official documents were kept? To be sure, there are just a few fragments of sealed tablets which once contained treaties or similar texts, tantalizingly few and broken.[27] Fig. 8 is one example, with part of the common seal of Suppiluliuma I and his queen.

In contrast to this, many of the documents found at Ugarit are sealed. They emanate from the royal court of Hatti, from the Hittite viceroys at Carchemish, from the neighboring kingdom of Amurru, or from individual officials, and they include not only treaties but also decisions and

Beran, "Hethitische Rollsiegel der Grossreichszeit," *IstMitt* 8 (1958) 137-141, pl. 35; 9/10 (1960) 128-133, pl. 88.

[19]Cf. H. G. Güterbock "Das Siegeln bei den Hethitern," *Symbolae Paulo Koschaker Dedicatae* (Leiden 1939) 26-36.

[20]WAG 48.1464. J. V. Canby, *JNES* 34 (1975) 225ff., figs. 1-8; previously Julius Lewy, "Old Assyrian Documents from Asia Minor," *Archives d'Histoire du Droit Oriental* 1 (1937) 1-18, esp. 16ff. with pl. II. The tablet referred to on p. 17 as "*TC* 94" is illustrated in Delaporte, *Louvre* pl. 123, 9, A.843 (inv. AO 7305). Others: N. Özgüç (*supra* n. 6) pls. V, 1, 3, and VII.

[21]VAT 7463; courtesy Vorderasiatisches Museum, Berlin, DDR. For the land deeds see *SBo* I 47-55; K. K. Riemschneider, "Die hethitischen Landschenkungsurkunden," *Mitteilungen des Instituts für Orientforschung* 6 (1958) 321-381. Fig. 6 is text no. 3 in both publications, with the seal *SBo* I no. 87 (*WVDOG* 76 no. 143).

[22]Fig. 7 is *SBo* I text 15, pl. V; another example is text 13 on p. 81.

[23]See "Description of the Tablet" in John A. Wilson's translation of the treaty in James B. Pritchard, ed., *Ancient Near Eastern Texts Relating to the Old Testament* (Princeton 1950) 201.

[24]E. F. Weidner, *Politische Dokumente aus Kleinasien* (Boghasköi-Studien 8; Leipzig 1923) 80ff., line 5; references to other sealed treaties in lines 26 and 32 of the text.

[25]Horst Klengel, "Der Schiedsspruch des Mursili II . . . ," *Orientalia,* n.s. 32 (1963) pp. 32-55, esp. 44f., col. IV; pp. 53f.

[26]*KBo* 4, no. 10, rev. 21f., seems to indicate that the official copy of the treaty with Ulmi-Teshub of Tarhuntissa was made of iron.

[27]*SBo* I text 1, seal no. 9 (pp. 6f., 73; pl. I); others are *SBo* II text 1, seal no. 5 (pp. 10f., 82); *KBo* 14, 45 with seal of Hattusili and Pudukhepa; *KUB* 31, 103 (seal broken off).

other pronouncements. The material is well known, so a few examples may suffice.

In two cases a common seal of King Hattusili III and Queen Pudukhepa was impressed, strangely, on one corner of the tablet. One is a letter to Niqmepa, king of Ugarit, instructing him how to deal with Hittite merchants, the other a verdict in a case of murder.[28]

Two tablets with the seal of Shaushga-muwa, king of Amurru, concern the extradition of his sister, the divorced former queen of Ugarit.[29] His name appears in hieroglyphs in the stamp impressions which are made with two different seals. In both seals his title is KING'S SON, although he is called "king" in at least one of the two texts. On the top of that tablet is the impression of the cylinder of Aziru, his ancestor, in typical Syrian style. Aziru was the first king of Amurru who concluded a treaty with the Hittites, so he may be considered a dynasty founder, and the use of his seal by a descendant is comparable to the use of the "dynastic seal" of Ugarit, of which the excavators distinguish two versions: impressions made with the original seal, others made with a later replica.[30]

A court order issued against a certain Kumya-ziti, probably a Hittite merchant, by Zuzuli, a representative of the king of Carchemish, bears the round impression of the latter's seal on top, that of the oval ring seal of the former below, both identified by cuneiform adscripts.[31]

Returning to the Hittite capital, we read about sealed documents of various kinds. *The Instruction of Temple Officials*[32] stipulates that gifts received from the king should be sold openly and before witnesses and that this sale should be documented in something called *uṣurtu*, literally "drawing," a term that has been interpreted as referring to hieroglyphic script. This document was to be sealed twice: once at the time of the sale, the second time by the Palace (i.e., "countersigned" by the "fiscus"). In another text[33] the border commander is instructed to decide any lawsuit brought before him on a sealed tablet or a sealed *uṣurtu*. The elaborate court proceedings concerning cases of embezzlement[34] mention various documents that should have been, but were not, sealed. It seems that these were, in part, receipts or inventories. Also sealed containers and the fact that their seals were broken are mentioned.

Of sealed administrative documents from Boğazköy we have two: one is a cult inventory sealed by a high official named Tabrami, who apparently was responsible for the cults of the city of Karahna listed in the text.[35] On the other tablet with the seal of LION-*ziti* (fig. 9) only a few names in connection with a "house" or estate are preserved; presumably the seal belongs to the official responsible for the transfer of an estate with its inhabitants.[36]

As said before, Ras Shamra yielded many sealed tablets, Boğazköy only a few. Most of the seal impressions found in the Hittite capital are on bullae, i.e., lumps of clay that were pressed around the knots of strings or straps, etc., and then sealed to secure the knot. Apart from stray finds they were found in quantity in two spots: at the west end of a corridor in the basement of Building D on Büyükkale and, more recently, in some storerooms on the north side of the Great Temple.[37] All were found baked, but this must have been caused by the destruction fire. Whether the bullae had served to seal packages or written documents, perhaps made of perishable material (the above-mentioned *uṣurtu*?) remains unknown. The accumulation of some 200 of them in one place in Building D seems to indicate that they were kept, perhaps as a record, after having been detached.

---

[28]*Ug.* III 16, fig. 21. For texts of sealed Ras Shamra tablets see *PRU* III and *PRU* IV. The tablets here mentioned are in *PRU* IV 103-106.

[29]*Ug.* III p. 34, figs. 43f., and pp. 131-133; texts: *PRU* IV 139-143.

[30]*Ug.* III 66-77 with figs. 92-99; cf. Schaeffer in *PRU* III xxivf. with pls. XIIf.; Nougayrol, *ibid.* xl-xliii with pls. XVIf.

[31]*Ug.* III 56, figs. 78f.; text: *PRU* IV 202f.

[32]E. H. Sturtevant and G. Bechtel, *A Hittite Chrestomathy* (Philadelphia 1935) 148-167, esp. 155, lines 39-58.

[33]E. von Schuler, *Hethitische Dienstanweisungen* (*Archiv für Orientforschung*, Beiheft 10, 1957) 47f., lines 21-23.

[34]R. Werner, *Hethitische Gerichtsprotokolle* (Studien zu den Boğazköy-Texten 4; Wiesbaden 1967) 3-20, esp. 12-15, lines 20-50.

[35]Bossert (*supra* n. 10) no. 728. Seal: *SBo* II no. 92; text: *KUB* 25, 32.

[36]Seal: *SBo* II no. 100; text: *ibid.* text 2, pp. 19 and 82.

[37]For easy reference see the plans in K. Bittel, *Hattusha, The Capital of the Hittites* (New York 1970) 75-83 and 56, respectively.

A few examples of bullae:

From the city mound at Gordion comes one example (fig. 10) found in 1965 in a rubble fill and published by Professor Young.[38] The knot of the string must have been too close to the sealed surface, so that the latter broke, destroying part of the inscription. From both the rather complex guilloche and the shape of the symbols LIFE and WELLBEING, the *crux ansata* and the triangle, this can be dated to the Old Hittite period.

A cone-shaped bulla from Tarsus has a string hole at the pointed end and a concave stamp impression on the base of the cone. In addition, a cylinder seal was rolled partially over the mantle of the cone.[39]

A bulla from Boğazköy (fig. 11) has oval impressions of a seal ring on its sides and narrow rollings over the top.[40] These could have been produced with the carved edge of a disc seal like one in the Louvre.[41]

Still another bulla from Boğazköy was attached to a wide strap or band, and its sides bear partial impressions (fig. 12) of the same royal seal that was impressed on its main surface: King Muwatalli protected by the Great Storm God (fig. 13). But this is not the only seal of this king: there is another seal which, while showing the same motif of the god protecting the ruler, differs in style (and in one of the king's names).[42] And a third seal contains only the name Muwatalli but has as the first hieroglyph the full image of the sacred animal of the Storm God.[43]

These three seals of Muwatalli raise the question of why there are so many seals bearing the name of one and the same king. Multiple seals of other kings can easily be found among the seals of Boğazköy and Ras Shamra.[44] Apparently there were officials authorized to use royal seals for government purposes. We do not know who they were, and there is no title corresponding to "Keeper of the Seal." One find confirms the fact that there were persons so authorized: this is the only seal of a Hittite great king of which we have the actual stamp, not just the impressions, and it was found at Ugarit![45] Certainly this stone, engraved on its convex side, must have been set in a ring or base, presumably of precious metal, and must have belonged to a person residing at Ugarit and authorized to use it.

In Ugarit a tablet was found with the text of an edict of "His Majesty" and the seal of Queen Pudukhepa alone.[46] Is the queen here writing and sealing for her husband? Or for her young son Tudhaliya? Or did the king use her seal?

Apart from this unusual case, there are many common seals of royal couples. They range from Arnuwanda and Ashmunikal (early fourteenth century) to Hattusili and Pudukhepa; in Ugarit, only Suppiluliuma I and Hattusili III appear on seals with their queens.[47]

However, the use of a seal by both a man and a woman was not restricted to the dynasty or royalty. Seal impressions from Korucutepe (fig. 14)[48] show the figure of a god and the name Ari-Sharruma, a local king as indicated by the KING sign. But his name is not alone: in smaller signs there is the name *Ki-lu-s-he-pa*, known from cuneiform texts as that of a lady, and next to it there are the signs GREAT and CHILD. Normally the latter sign has one straight and one angular line below the hand,[49] but here the

[38]*AJA* 70 (1966) 277 and pl. 74, fig. 25. For a similar inscription cf. *SBo* II no. 175; for dating, *WVDOG* 76, 59-61, "Gruppe XI," pls. 9 and II, esp. nos. 97 and 100.

[39]Cf. I. J. Gelb in *Tarsus* figs. 403, 407, no. 42.

[40]*SBo* II nos. 227-228, pl. VII.

[41]Delaporte, *Louvre* no. A.1015, pl. 100, 14; *PKG* 14, pl. 377b.

[42]*SBo* I nos. 38A and 39A, pl. II.

[43]*SBo* II no. 1, pl. I.

[44]*SBo* I *passim;* esp. *WVDOG* 76, pls. VI-XI; *Ug.* III pp. 2-21, figs. 2-26, and pp. 98-119.

[45]*Ug.* III 87-93, figs. 109-112, and Güterbock, *ibid.* 161-163; *PKG* 14, 448, fig. 142d.

[46]*Ug.* III pp. 13, 18, figs. 16, 23; p. 109; text: *PRU* IV, 118f.

[47]*SBo* I 60: Arnuwanda and Ashmunikal; 5-7: Suppiluliuma and Hinti; 8-11 and 36: Suppiluliuma and Tawananna, also *Ug.* III pp. 3-6, figs. 2-6, and pp. 98-103; *SBO* I 30-35: Mursili II and Tawananna; 37: Mursili II and Gasulawi; 42: Muwatalli and Tanukhepa; 43-44: Urkhi-Teshub (Mursili III) and Tanukhepa; 24-29: a Mursili (II or III?) and Tanukhepa; 49-51: Hattusili III and Pudukhepa, also *Ug.* III pp. 12-17, figs. 13-15, 17-22, and pp. 108-110. (*WVDOG* 76, pls. IX-XI, in different order and without *SBo* I 42).

[48]H. G. Güterbock, "Hittite Hieroglyphic Seal Impressions from Korucutepe," *JNES* 32 (1973) 135-147, no. 2. Fig. 14 is based on both impressions 2A and 2B.

[49]Signs L363 and L45, respectively, in Laroche's list (*supra* n. 13). In L45, the "crampon" above the hand is the word divider; only the lower one forms part of the logogram.

element below the hand lacks the angular line, and the only element present is a slender oval rather than a simple line. This then seems to be the sign for DAUGHTER as differentiated from SON. A clearer example can be seen on a bulla from Boğazköy (fig. 15),[50] where *Ga-su-la-wi* has the title KING'S DAUGHTER written with a clear oval which has a vertical groove in the middle. But this is not all!

It has long been observed that among the biconvex or lentoid seals there are some that have the same name on both sides but also some with two different names. When preparing such seals from Boğazköy (found in the so-called Südareal south of the Great Temple) for publication, I found again examples of both types: one such seal[51] shows a human figure on one side only but the same name, *La-hi,* on both. Lahi's title consists of the signs GOD + HOUSE (L249). Opposite it, but only on the side without picture, the sign L386, "line and angle," is found, surmounted by the triangle which we already know as GOOD, WELLBEING (L370). A seal in the Louvre[52] has on both sides the name of *Pa-la-tu-wa,* whose title is written with a pitcher (L354), again with the triangle and the line and angle (L370 + 386) on the right. There are many more such seals with identical inscriptions on both sides.

Another seal (fig. 16) from the same complex at Boğazköy[53] has two different inscriptions. One side has a name with the title CHARIOTEER (L289), but the other side reads *U-ma-ya* and has the triangle above a large, pointed, elongated oval. Now Umaya is known as a woman's name from cuneiform texts. Our sign lists register two oval signs: one (L79) with the meaning WOMAN, the other (L408) defined as a title because it appears beside names. It seems obvious now that the presumed "title" is the WOMAN sign, characterizing the name as that of a woman. Moreover, the combination "triangle over WOMAN" (L370-79) has a counterpart in L370 over L386, just like the pair "hand + L79" DAUGHTER and "hand + L386" SON. It would follow then that L386 means MAN or MALE.[54]

There are many seals with the names of a man and a woman, respectively, on their two sides, and it is an easy assumption that these seal owners are husband and wife. *Ku-tà-pi-ya* and *Ga-la-ya* are another such couple.[55] But there also is one seal with two men's names.[56]

On a tripod seal[57] the names of husband and wife are written on the only surface, in two columns side by side. The man's name, on the left in the impression, reads *Wa-la-zi-ya;* while the reading of the woman's name is uncertain, the WOMAN sign on the right is quite clear.[58]

---

[50]*SBo* I no. 104. For the combination KING + L45 see L46. Of the examples listed there under 2, "princesse," *SBo* I 37 and *Tarsus* no. 14 are damaged, while the late Malatya relief omits the element below the hand. But in *Tarsus* no. 17 the oval is well visible. It must be sign L79, WOMAN. (Did Shaushgamuwa have one seal, no. 3, together with his wife, a KING'S [DAUGHTER]? Cf. *Ug.* III p. 33, figs. 41-42, and p. 131.)

[51]*Boğ.* V no. 35 (cf. 36).

[52]Delaporte, *Louvre* pl. 102, 2, A.1044. For inscriptions on seals in Oxford and Paris see the articles by D. A. Kennedy in *RHA* 16, fasc. 63 (1958) 65-84 and 17, fasc. 65 (1959) 147-172 (hereafter *RHA* fasc. 63 and 65, respectively, with seal number). A.1044 is *RHA* fasc. 65, no. 5. Seals with identical names on both sides are too frequent to be listed.

[53]*Boğ.* V no. 37.

[54]Since there is another sign for MAN (L312 = 313), the relation of the two signs (L386 and L312/3) and of the word(s) (synonyms?) behind them remains to be investigated. The combinations L370-386 and L370-408, GOOD and MAN/WOMAN, respectively, are here taken as blessings like "well-being for the man/woman." Cf. now J. D. Hawkins, *Zeitschrift für vergleichende Sprachforschung* 92 (1978) 112; *idem, Florilegium Anatolicum Laroche* (Paris 1979) 153.

[55]*Boğ.* V no. 38. Of other two-faced seals with names of a man and a woman I noted: Alishar no. 78 (I. J. Gelb, *Inscriptions from Alishar and Vicinity*; OIP 27, Chicago 1935); Newell no. 387 (H. H. von der Osten, *Ancient Oriental Seals in the Collection of Mr. Edward T. Newell*; OIP 22, Chicago 1934); Oxford, *RHA* fasc. 63, nos. 15 and 20; Paris: *RHA* fasc. 65, nos. 8, 10, 14, 28; Yale, NBC 11014 and 11015 (B. Buchanan, *JCS* 21 [1967] 19-21, nos. 2 and 3).

[56]*Tarsus* no. 43: Halpa-ziti and Kukulana; the sign on side b is damaged L386, not L408!

[57]Giuseppe Furlani, "Un timbro hittito," *RendLinc, Classe di scienze morali* (etc.), ser. 8, vol. 5 (1950) 376-380. Also in Bossert, (*supra* n. 10) no. 688.

[58]For the sign L414 see Laroche's comments. On the Boğazköy seals it occurs in the secondary group (Nebengruppe); therefore he took it for a title. On the Furlani seal the two columns are facing each other, hence a title is not likely, and in addition there is WOMAN on the right.

Just like men, women could have a seal of their own, either inscribed on one side like a tripod in the Ashmolean Museum[59] or on both sides like the hemispheroid of Fig. 5 and a seal from Alishar where the name, *Arma-wi,* has long been recognized as a woman's name.[60]

This, then, explains the impressions on a tablet from Ugarit.[61] According to the cuneiform text the seals of Piha-ziti and Alalimi were impressed on the tablet, but the hieroglyphic name on the two stamp impressions reads *Ma-ni-na,* which fits neither these two names nor that of any of the other persons mentioned in the text. We now see that it is a woman's seal! And since the two impressions, while having identical inscriptions, differ in detail, it was one of the two-sided seals of women just mentioned. Apparently one of the two men who are said to have sealed used the seal of his wife! Since the other man used an uninscribed cylinder we cannot tell whether Manina was Mrs. Pihaziti or Mrs. Alalimi, but we can live without knowing that.

---

[59]*HS* no. 189 = *RHA* fasc. 63, no. 33; also a ring with circular bezel from Boğazköy, *RHA* fasc. 65, no. 1.

[60]Alishar no. 80; Newell no. 388 (*supra,* n. 55); one from Alalakh: L. Woolley, *Alalakh: An Account of the Excavations at Tell Atchana* (Oxford 1955) no. 156 on pp. 266f., pl. LXVII, bottom; R. D. Barnett in *AntJ* 19 (1939) 34 and pl. XIII.

[61]*Ug.* III pp. 57-59, figs. 80-83; p. 155; text: *PRU* IV 182-184.

Special abbreviations:

Boğ. V	K. Bittel *et al., Funde aus den Grabungen 1970* (Boğazköy V; Abhandlungen der deutschen Orient-Gesellschaft 18 [Berlin 1975]).
HS	D. G. Hogarth, *Hittite Seals, with Particular Reference to the Ashmolean Collection* (Oxford 1920).
Delaporte, *Louvre*	L. Delaporte, *Catalogue des cylindres orientaux, Musée du Louvre* II (Paris 1923).
KBo	*Keilschrifttexte aus Boghazköi.*
KUB	*Keilschrifturkunden aus Boghazköi.*
PKG 14	W. Orthmann, ed., *Der alte Orient* (Propyläen Kunstgeschichte 14; Berlin 1975).
PRU III	J. Nougayrol, *Le Palais royal d'Ugarit* III (Mission de Ras Shamra VI; Paris 1955).
PRU IV	J. Nougayrol, *Le Palais royal d'Ugarit* IV (Mission de Ras Shamra IX; Paris 1956).
SBo I	H. G. Güterbock, *Siegel aus Boğazköy, Erster Teil* (Archiv für Orientforschung, Beiheft 5; Berlin 1940).
SBo II	H. G. Güterbock, *Siegel aus Boğazköy, Zweiter Teil* (Archiv für Orientforschung, Beiheft 7; Berlin 1942).
Tarsus	H. Goldman, *Excavations at Gözlü Kule, Tarsus* II (Princeton 1956).
Ug. III	C. F.-A. Schaeffer *et al., Ugaritica* III (Mission de Ras Shamra 8; Paris 1956).
WVDOG 76	T. Beran, *Die hethitische Glyptik von Boğazköy,* I. Teil (Boğazköy-Ḫattuša V; Wissenschaftliche Veröffentlichungen der deutschen Orient-Gesellschaft 76 [Berlin 1967]).

Figure 1. Gordion "stud" seal, SS 70 (2:1)

Figure 2. Gordion "stalk" seal, B 464 (2:1)

Figure 3. Gordion stamp impression on jar handle, SS 117 (5:4)

Figure 4. Gordion seal impression on jar handle, SS 223 (2:1)

Figure 5. Hemispheroid seal, formerly in Collection Aciman, Ankara.
Photos in possession of author.

Figure 6. Old Hittite land deed with impression of royal seal, VAT
7463 (5:4). Courtesy of Vorderasiatisches Museum, Berlin.

Figure 7. Fragment of Old Hittite land deed, showing traces of strings coming out of hole in lower edge (5:4). Ankara Museum. Photo: Boğazköy expedition.

Figure 8. Fragmentary tablet with part of seal of Suppiluliuma I and his queen (5:4). Photo: Boğazköy expedition.

Figure 9. Fragmentary tablet with record of estate transfer and impression of seal probably belonging to responsible official (2:1). Photo: Boğazköy expedition.

Figure 10. Gordion bulla, SS 209 (2:1)

Figure 11. Bulla with impressions of seal ring on sides and narrow
rollings on top (2:1). Photo: Boğazköy expedition.

Figure 12. Side view of clay bulla, showing partial impressions of seal
of King Muwatalli (5:4). Photo: Boğazköy expedition.

Figure 13. Main surface of bulla of fig. 12 with full impression of seal: King Muwatalli under protection of the Great Storm God (5:4). Photo: Boğazköy expedition.

Figure 14. Seal of a king and a princess, from Korucutepe (5:4)

Figure 15. Impression on a clay bulla of seal of Princess Gasulawi (2:1). Photo: Boğazköy expedition.

Figure 16. Two sides of lentoid seal from Boğazköy; drawing by author from impressions (5:4): *left,* name of a man; *right,* name of a woman.

VI. CREMATIONS OF THE MIDDLE PHRYGIAN PERIOD AT GORDION

Ellen L. Kohler

In the Early Phrygian period at Gordion (the ninth and eighth centuries B.C.) the local culture showed strong affinities with the East (Urartu, Iran, Assyria, Phoenicia), and one would suppose, from its location well up on the Anatolian Plateau, that such affinities would continue during the Middle Phrygian period (seventh and sixth centuries B.C.). But instead the Lydian Empire rose and became powerful, and again in its turn surrendered to Cyrus of Persia in 546, so that the Central Anatolian area became first Lydianized and then Persianized. These new contacts with Lydia, and with a commercially expanding East Greece in the second half of the sixth century, are demonstrated by the first appearance of the burial custom of cremation at Gordion, where the Phrygians were beginning to receive a number of trade objects from those Western centers and were burying them both in the new cremations and in the wooden graves still being built according to Early Phrygian traditions.

In 1950 and 1951 the University Museum expedition opened four cremation-tumuli well scattered among the Phrygian mounds on the Northeast Cemetery Ridge (fig. 1). Tumulus A[1] is in the center of the modern village; F[2] is well in on the ridge, next to E, the largest of the group. Tumulus I[3] is the more westerly of the similar pair on the southwest edge of the ridge. M is higher up the slope, on a prominence commanding the west and south. There appears to be nothing clannish about their general grouping (fig. 2).

Tumulus F was dug in 1951. During the routine examination of the mound before its excavation, it was found to have a crater in the top left by stone- and clay-quarriers. The pit they had made extended all the way down to ancient ground level and had been almost refilled by erosion from wind and rain. This disturbance, fortunately, had not touched the burial, which was intact. The mound's greatest preserved height is 2 m., and its original diameter, measured after excavation, was found to be 28 m. (figs. 3 and 4).

Under the tumulus and sunken into a greenish-white clay floor was an earlier cist burial going back to the Chalcolithic period. Over this was a layer of gravel, fairly pure and water washed, into which Phrygians of the pre-tumulus period had built a house. Fragmentary walls and a pottery deposit of about the first half of the seventh century attest its presence.

During the excavation of the tumulus proper, an oval area approximately 2.40 m. east-west × 1.50 north-south, 5.90 m. from the calculated center of the mound and 0.36 m. below the sloping surface, was found to contain burned beam-ends and to have received the remnants of a cremation and a group of burial gifts. The deposit contained bronze, iron, and pottery finds in a scattered state over an oval area of mixed charcoal and earth (fig. 5), and since many objects looked unburned, it appears that the cremation

[1] R. S. Young, "Gordion—1950," *UMB* 16, 1 (1951) 17.

[2] R. S. Young, "Progress at Gordion, 1951-1952," *UMB* 17, 4 (1953) 31-32.

[3] *Ibid.*

took place somewhere else and that part of the ashes and of the offerings was subsequently transferred to this spot, where more gifts, unburned, were added.[4] Over this secondary cremation-deposit, then, the conical cap of clay was placed.

The pottery was burned and fragmentary, but at least eight gray-ware spherical jars (fig. 6) could be distinguished, as well as a gray-ware jug (fig. 7) and an imported Corinthian alabastron (fig. 8).[5] The latter was so badly burned that its decoration must be read from traces left by the missing paint. The vessel has a deep body-zone containing a pair of walking lions, head to head, with raised looped tails. The filling ornaments are circles of solid line with central dot, which according to the British method of dating place the alabastron between the years 640 and 625 B.C.[6] If a lag of a few years should be added, the date of the cremation could be pushed down to ca. 625/620 B.C.

Among the bronzes were a crushed and fused fragmentary bowl (fig. 9) with a bolster-shaped lifting device under the rim, akin to and in the later tradition of those from the Great Tumulus (MM, ca. 700 B.C.), and a spherical trefoil-mouthed jug now mended from many fragments (fig. 10).

Tiny pieces of ivory for inlay and appliqué, squares, lozenges, petals, triangles, etc., and a tiny knob, all shattered by the heat, could well be the decoration of a small wooden chest or pyxis which had been otherwise completely destroyed.

The gold jewelry, comparatively speaking, is simple and sparse: one earring of slim leech shape with the ends bound round in plain wire (fig. 11),[7] and fifty tiny die-cut sequins with rosette centers and carelessly punched-in sewing holes lay scattered about.[8]

A terracotta loom weight of the steep-sided pyramidal type lay among the finds.

The deposit of scattered bronze and iron fragments, showing clearly in fig. 5, furnishes several very interesting items. A long, forked iron bar was found associated with eight pairs of iron handle-rings, heavy, sturdy, and about the right size to be gripped by a human hand. Each had its two ends drawn out side by side, meeting, and entering a wooden pole, whose end was then wrapped by the cylindrical ferrule associated with each ring. Figs. 12 and 13 show one closed and one open revealing the nails for fastening. The only conceivable purpose for all these pieces, if fitted on the ends of poles, would be to form one very long bier or two shorter ones of fixed-floor type. If we add the pair of cylindrical bronze-sheet ferrules, possibly we have the decorative lead-ends of two poles which could have entered either four or eight pairs of ring-grips, making it convenient for four men as bearers. The forked rod, to judge from its position as found, may have been a support for the floor-frame.

Now where are the sequins to be placed? Since they are unburned, they could not have been on the clothing of the person buried here but must have been sewed to some scarf or drapery for a bier.

Only a few scraps of the cranium were recovered. The pyxis and the gold jewelry might be debatable as evidence for the sex of the deceased, but the loom weight tells us that we have to do with a female who will be asked to do weaving in the next world.

If we turn now to Tumulus M, we encounter a tumulus again ca. 28 m. in diameter. It is of the same composition as that of Tumulus F except that the underlying gravel layer is absent because it has sloped away to below the depth approached here. On the original ground level was a group of hearths, some with animal bones, but there were no other remains of pre-tumulus

---

[4]A proper cremation *in situ* requires a steep-walled pit ca. 1.30-1.50 m. deep with ventilation channels to sustain a sufficiently hot fire. Cf. R. S. Young, "Sepulturae intra urbem," *Hesperia* 20 (1951) 81ff.; D. Kurtz and J. Boardman, *Greek Burial Customs* (Ithaca 1971) 73ff.

[5]The listings of the objects as treated here are by no means complete inventories from these tumuli. Only a selection is provided of those pieces most important for the study of techniques of manufacture, the pattern of the combination of offerings, and for dating. It is planned that the complete inventories will be catalogued and discussed in the final publication.

[6]H. Payne, *Necrocorinthia* (Oxford 1931) pl. 12, 1 (for filling ornaments); pls. 12, 5 and 12, 6 (for similar alabastra of the Transitional period).

[7]Related to D. Curtis, *Jewelry and Goldwork* (Sardis XIII; Rome 1925) pl. 6, fig. 4.

[8]Young (*supra* no. 2) 33 and fig. 24.

habitation (fig. 14, section; fig. 15, plan). This bit of ground, commanding the whole plain to the south and southeast, would have made a fine location for soldiers or shepherds on watch.[9]

In 1951 Tumulus M offered the initial excavator only disappointments and false leads; in fact by early in the 1952 season it had worn out a second excavator, who decided he could spend his time better elsewhere, before a third, about at the end of her patience, one morning later in the 1952 season observed a small hole in a scarp through which a mouse had pushed a fragment of a miniature bronze jug. Pursuit of this clue was rewarded by the discovery of a cremation in the southern sector of the mound. It was, again, oval in shape, this time covered by stone slabs with a boulder on top. There were burnt logs *in situ* (fig. 16), which indicated that this was a pyre, not a secondary cremation-deposit.

Among the ashes were found several pots including a round-bodied lekythos (fig. 17) with one small vertical loop handle for a finger hold, a short narrow neck, and a round mouth with everted rim. It was painted in overlapping bands of black glaze from the top to near the bottom of the body. The clay is very micaceous and this combination of elements makes it clear that we are dealing with a Lydian import, dating to about 575 B.C. Add to this a local buff krater, a small gray plate, and a fragment of a ring-handled bronze bowl, crushed and fused (fig. 18), and resembling very closely that from Tumulus F. A bronze trefoil oinochoe fragment also parallels the one from F (cf. fig. 10).

The group from Tumulus M is smaller, poorer, for the most part of local ware, with only one import and that not particularly fine. There is nothing to indicate the sex of the deceased and there is no evidence for any conveyance.

The third member of the group is Tumulus I on the southwest edge of the ridge. (Tumulus H, its close neighbor, was a *proper* burial, as Dr. Young would say, because it contained *architecture*. He quite gleefully gave away to someone else for publication such wall-less, alphabetless

complexes as these cremations.) By comparison with Tumulus M, Tumulus I gave the excavator no trouble. On the fifth day of work, the cremation appeared, in Layer 3 (fig. 19). Layer 1 consisted of a loamy mantle; Layer 2 of covering fill (clayey type) which came down to the surface of the ancient ground. At only 90 cm. from the top surface in the southwest quadrant, the burned stratum appeared, containing a thorough cremation in an area 1.50 × .60 m. and .20 m. thick. The ashes of the skeleton lay upon three conifer logs about 1.20 cm. long.

The offerings appeared in a different combination this time, in that there was only one pot (a small black jar, coarse, faceted horizontally on the shoulder, with a plain collared mouth), a group of clay beads of several varieties, and two spindle whorls along with a collection of gold jewelry.

The jewelry lay scattered about: twenty sequins, some closely resembling those from F, spherical beads, a pair of earrings of the same leech type as those from Tumulus F but now decorated by flattish gold wires laid against the body in a sort of proto-filigree manner.[10] The circlets binding the ends of the leech are wire, which has been formed as a tube and made to resemble granulation.[11] There were also a pair of gold tubes, spirally ridged and ending in a dome with applied floret done in the elementary filigree method (fig. 20), and three spiral rings, usually called "hair-rings" for lack of another name (fig. 21). The basic spiral is of electrum and the added pyramids are this time of true granulation.

The dating of the group from Tumulus I must depend upon its resemblances to the burial gifts of the following group which are datable from imports.

The discovery and excavation of a fourth cremation, Tumulus A, was called by Rodney Young a "T.O.T.," a triumph of technique. This day's work will be described in a later paper, "Postscript," by Roger Edwards. Only a summary of the results is presented here.

---

[9]Another explanation might be that the family groups present at the funeral feast dined at these hearths which were subsequently covered by the tumulus. Such hearths were not observed near the other cremations, however.

[10]Such loops for suspension of pendants are seen on earrings from Sardis: Curtis (*supra* n. 7) pl. VI, fig. 7 and pl. VII, fig. 4.

[11]Young (*supra* n. 2) 33, fig. 25.

The mound itself happened to be low, already leveled partially by quarriers of clay for mud brick, and located inside the walls of a local landowner's barnyard. In ancient times it would have commanded a view to the north and east. Its circumference was still traceable in only a few places, but the curve could be extrapolated to yield a diameter of 31 m. Its height at the time of digging was about 1 m. above hardpan. At a depth of .80 m. below the modern truncated surface a burned layer was encountered (fig. 22). It was ca. 3 m. in diameter and located just south of the center of the mound. The ash layer, the greatest thickness of which was ca. 35 cm., tailed off round its edges to form a lens-shaped stratum resting at all points on a floor of soft white clayey material.

Finds from the top of the ashy lens consisted of a mixed fused mass of iron and diseased bronze clamps, sockets, plates, rods, etc. Upon the white floor lay lydions, an amphora, a stone alabastron, gold jewelry, a kore unguentarium, and much more (plan, fig. 23).

Through the white floor a shallow irregularly pentagonal pit, ca. .80 × .55, had been cut, which was also filled with charcoal, lumps of the white clay, chips of human bones, teeth, more gold, a silver mirror,[12] ivory[13] (some being inlays for a box of some type), and fragments of many objects, joining fragments from the floor at the level of the top of the pit. The materials from the pit and those above it were burned slightly and to the same extent, which means that both were filled and covered after the embers were dying. A mound of good clean earth was then spread above it all, to an unknown original height.

To give closer attention to only a few of the offerings—several pieces of gold jewelry, including a complete lion bracelet (Edwards, *infra,* fig. 2)[14] and fragments of perhaps two others, two pairs of gold earrings (Edwards, fig. 3), several types of pendants (fig. 24)—illustrate the technique of applying the preformed beaded wire

along edges, around ends, etc., to resemble granulation.[15] One group, acorn pendants (Edwards, fig. 4), illustrates also the mass-cutting of faceted surfaces into the metal to lend texture.[16] Several small lengths of chain held another type of pendant (fig. 25),[17] and a second, heavier, chain occurs, which is not of a continuously braided type but is made of many circular links bent double, each fitted into similar folded links above and below (fig. 26). The drawing (fig. 27) represents the wire as thinned lines so that the linking may be read. If we add to this profusion of jewelry a series of spindle whorls, we have ample evidence that the cremation is that of a young female.

One badly burnt object which aids with the dating is a terracotta unguentarium in the form of a young girl holding a bird (fig. 28). It belongs in a series found in several places in East Greece and in several combinations of front and back molds. One close to our back mold is from Camirus on Rhodes;[18] others, close to our front mold, are from Selinunte[19] and from Samos.[20] The latter was definitely buried in the period of the tyrant Polykrates, ca. 530 to 522. Our mold is worn, so, allowing a few years for wear, transportation to Gordion and placement in the grave, we may be approaching a date as late as 525 B.C.

A badly burned and fragmentary amphora of Lydian fabric (fig. 29), painted on the body in overlapping bands of red/black glaze, shows a

---

[12]Young (*supra* n. 1) 20 and pl. IX, fig. 1.

[13]*Ibid.* pl. IX, fig. 2.

[14]P. Amandry, "Orfèvrerie achéménide," *AntK* 1 (1958) 17.

[15]Young (*supra* n. 1) 18 and pl. VIII, figs. 1-4; R. S. Young, "Excavations at Yassihuyuk-Gordion," *Archaeology* 3 (1950) 199 and figs. 5 and 6.

[16]Young (*supra* n. 1) pl. VIII, fig. 3.

[17]Cf. similar blossoms on chains, said to come from the Maikop region: *From the Land of the Scythians,* exhibition catalogue of the Metropolitan Museum of Art (New York 1975) 157, no. 2.

[18]R. A. Higgins, *Catalogue of the Terracottas in the British Museum* (London 1954) 48, no. 57 (H. 0.260 m.), pl. 13, probably from the Kechraki Cemetery; Higgins's date "530-500, nearer 530."

[19]E. Gabrici, "Il Sanctuario della Malophoros à Selinunte," *MonAnt* 32 (1927) pl. 38, 1, 1a. It was excavated by him and dated to the "last half of the sixth century, in the early period of the Megarian colonization." H. 0.263 m.

[20]E. Buschor, *Altsamische Standbilder* II (Berlin 1934) figs. 134, 135 and p. 35. Buschor places these in the period of Polykrates, 532 (Eusebius) to 522, and he believes them to be Samian in origin.

zone of hooks on the shoulder, done with a multiple brush. Such an amphora is usually dated about 550 B.C. A further group of pottery consists of lydions (Edwards, fig. 1), some actually from Lydia, others local copies, and of course the ever-present Phrygian jug in coarser local ware. One gray-ware open bowl with rim pulled out in three places, may be construed as an early lamp (fig. 30).

From that scattered mass of bars, clamps, etc., mentioned earlier, we are able to gather the parts of a wagon (fig. 31): iron tires, sprung in the heat (A-E), bands to secure the inner and outer surfaces of the wheel-naves (M and N), and the axle-caps which have holes for linch-pins (not illustrated). In addition there is a series of double clamps, four keystone-shaped (I), eight long rectangular (F-H), four shorter rectangular (J), and pin-bolts, etc., (K) as fasteners for the harness.[21] For the horses themselves we have part of one frontlet (not illustrated) and one and one-half snaffle bits (L).

Thus we know that the means of conveyance for the remains of the already burned body with its initial group of offerings was a sturdy wagon drawn by a pair of horses with decorative harnessing. There are several choices for the type of wheel, exact evidence for which is lacking. One might look in the direction of those romantic squeaky solid-wheeled wagons that are still used up on the central plateau, at Alaca and Boğazköy, for example, with axles barely rounded at the center and held in place by spikes,[22] but we have no such spikes in our Tumulus A group. However, right at Gordion an example of a technically more advanced wheel emerged from the excavation of the mud-brick building on Küçük Hüyük, the smaller mound of the Lydian period, ca. 580-546 (fig. 32). This type, lighter from having had much of its bulk eliminated, would still be strong if bound with a tire such as those from Tumulus A. The form of the body of the wagon is difficult to determine precisely, as the undercarriage and box could have employed the preserved pairs of clamps in any of several ways.

These four cremation mounds, dating from the late seventh through the sixth centuries, yield evidence for the introduction of several changes into the Phrygian way of life and show a sort of progression (not progress, necessarily) among themselves. The types of gold earring, for instance, moves from the plain leech to that decorated with filigree and then with granulation. In regard to the jewelry in general Tumulus F shows false granulation and A shows a combination of mass cutting, false granulation, and true granulation. The imported types of Lydian pottery change with Lydian taste in form and decoration. One constant element, however, throughout the period is the formula employed by the Greeks, and here at least approached by the Phrygians, for the combination of offerings to be put in a grave.

Rodney Young himself excavated an archaic cemetery in the Agora[23] not far from the Poros Building which Eugene Vanderpool has taken to be the State Prison of Athens (supra). In that cemetery, out of forty-eight burials of the Geometric and Archaic periods twenty-two were interments and twenty-one were pyres, none, however, demonstrably under tumuli, as much of the top soil had been removed by later builders. There was no strict pattern of offerings, but there was usually some combination of ointment jars such as alabastra or unguentaria, plates with two handles at the rim, lamps, small boxes or pyxides, cups, saucers, miniature pieces, and the ever-present jug for filling the cups. This grouping of gifts was about standard in the Greek world at this period.

The Greeks on the Mainland built many mounds, but only a very few over cremations.[24] To find a preference for tumuli over all kinds of

---

[21] For similar circular bands and rectangular clamps, cf. H. Müller-Karpe, "Metallbeigaben der Kerameikos früheisenzeitlichen Gräber," *JdI* 77 (1962) 102 (Grave 13, fig. 21) and 103 (Grave 58, fig. 20).

[22] H. Z. Koşay, *Alaca-Höyük, Das Dorf* . . . (Turk Tarih Kurumu Yayınlarından, ser. VII, no. 21; Ankara 1951) pls. 15 and 16.

[23] R. S. Young, "Sepulturae intra urbem," *Hesperia* 20 (1951) 67-134. Cf. especially burials of the sixth century, pp. 87-102 and pl. 33.

[24] The most famous example is the large tumulus (VIII) of the archaic period (after 540 B.C.) in the east portion of Eridanos Cemetery (South) in the Kerameikos (Grave 33, h.S. 128). See B. Schlörb-Vierneisel, "Eridanos—Nekropole," *AthMitt* 81 (1966) 19 and pl. I (section).

graves one must look to East Greece, Lydia, and Anatolia. A few tumuli over cremations occur at Nisyros,[25] Samos,[26] and in Lycia at Karataş (Elmalı), where the third[27] and fourth[28] mounds

---

[25]*Clara Rhodos* VI-VII (Rhodes 1932-33) 471ff.

[26]K. Tsakos, "Samos—Dutike Nekropolis," *AAA* 2 (1969) 202-205. Note also the "hair-rings" from pyre 6, p. 203, fig. 3.

[27]M. J. Mellink, "Excavations at Karataş-Semayük and Elmalı, Lycia, 1971," *AJA* 76 (1972) pl. 57, fig. 11.

[28]*Ibid.* pl. 56, figs. 6-10.

on the Karaburun ridge covered the remains of two cremations of the sixth century. The greatest mound-builders of the seventh and sixth centuries were, however, the Lydians and the Phrygians themselves, as the earlier papers have shown. It is thus evident that the period from the late seventh to the late sixth centuries B.C. is one in which the ties of Lydia and East Greece with inner Anatolia are strengthened, and alongside the normal survivals a new kind of Phrygian culture pattern emerges, long before the coming of Alexander.

Figure 1. Aerial view of Gordion from south. The northeast cemetery-ridge is in the center, with the village of Yassihüyük on its northwest corner.

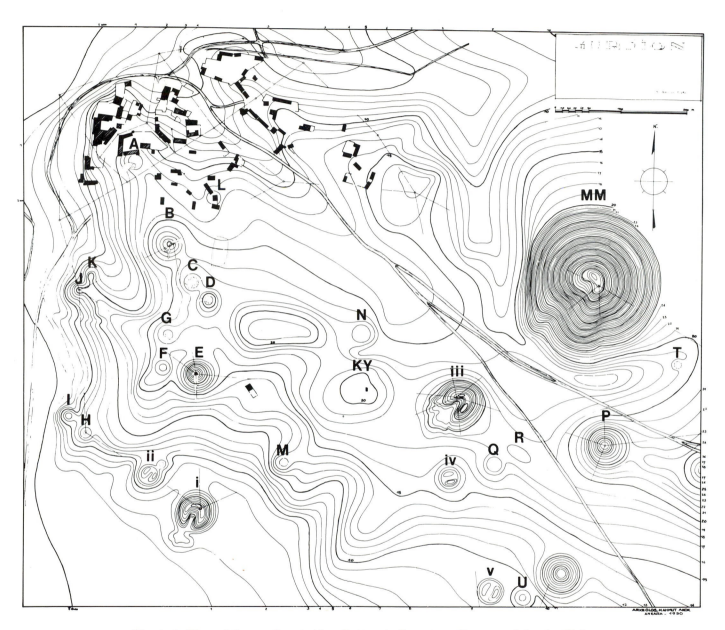

Figure 2. Plan of the northeast ridge. Letters indicate tumuli surveyed by the University Museum expedition in 1950-1973; small Roman numerals indicate those dug by Gustav and Alfred Körte in 1900. Cf. *Gordion, JdI*, 5th Ergänzungsheft (Berlin 1904). Drawn by Mahmut Akok.

Figure 3. Tumulus F: section A-A′ (see fig. 4). The cremation disturbed remains of Phrygian and possibly earlier house walls. *I*, surface loam; *II*, clay of tumulus cover; *III*, gravel and earth mix; *IV*, layer of natural gravel; *V*, brown hardpan. Drawn by Dorothy H. Cox.

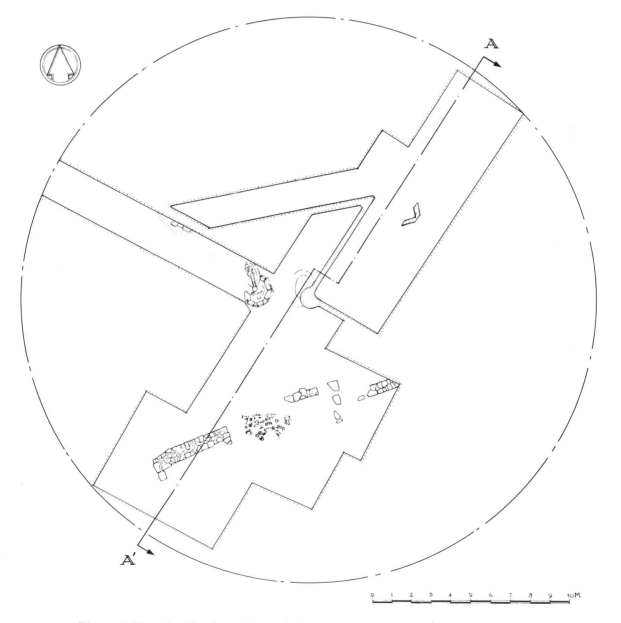

Figure 4. Tumulus F: plan of the main features. The cremation is in the southwest quadrant. Drawn by Dorothy H. Cox.

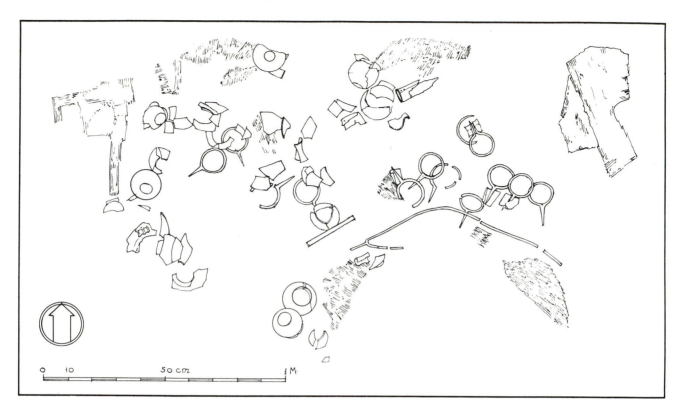

Figure 5. Tumulus F: plan of cremation offerings as found, drawn by
Dorothy H. Cox

Figure 6. Gray-ware jar, P 334, Tumulus F.
H. 0.12 m.

Figure 7. Gray-ware jug, P 252, Tumulus F.
H. 0.19 m.

Figure 8. Corinthian alabastron of the Transitional period, P 291,
Tumulus F. Max. dim. 0.096 m.

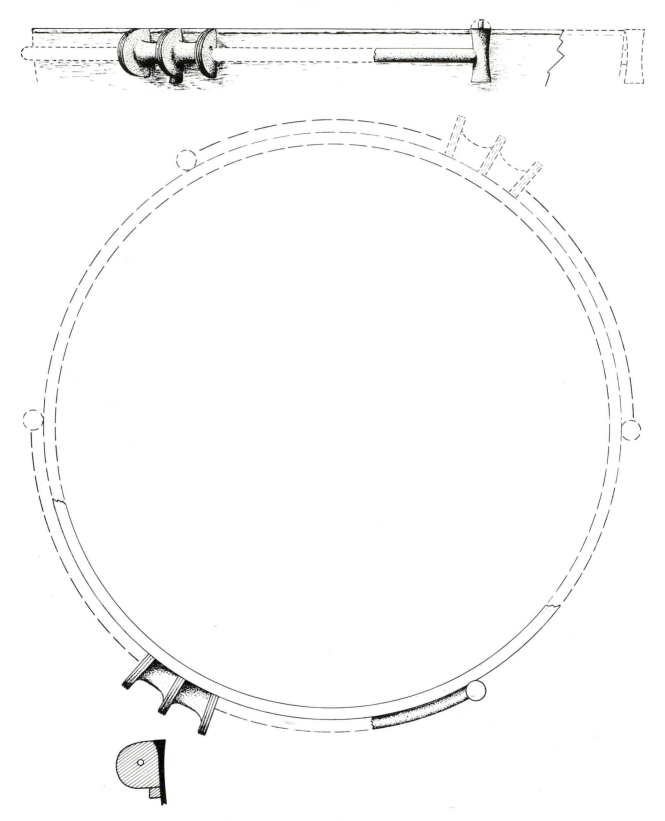

Figure 9. Fragments of a two-handled bronze bowl, B 468, Tumulus F, drawn by
M. Kutkam. Est. D. rim 0.35 m.

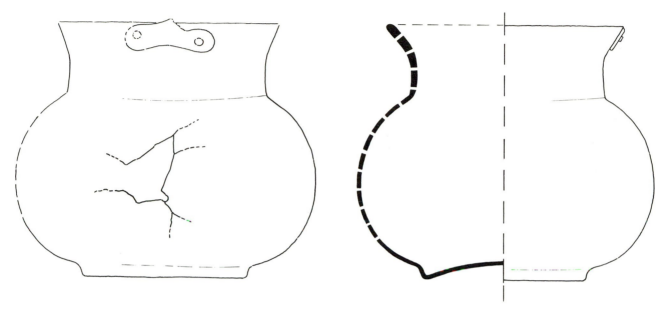

Figure 10. Fragmentary trefoil jug, B 469, Tumulus F, drawn by M. Kutkam.
Est. max. H. 0.136 m.

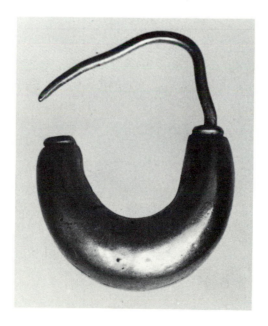

Figure 11. Hollow gold leech-earring, J 36,
Tumulus F. Max. W. 0.013 m.

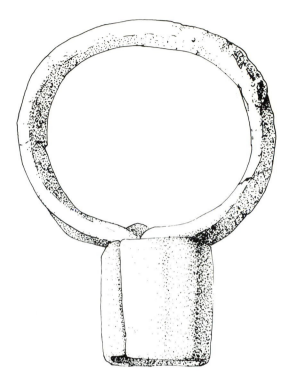

Figure 12. Iron handle with closed ferrule, ILS 471, Tumulus F, drawn by Maria Shaw. D. ring 0.097.

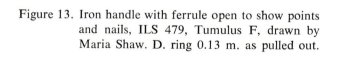

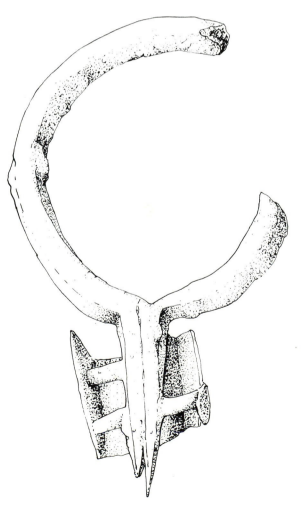

Figure 13. Iron handle with ferrule open to show points and nails, ILS 479, Tumulus F, drawn by Maria Shaw. D. ring 0.13 m. as pulled out.

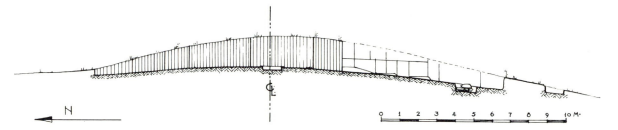

Figure 14. Tumulus M: section A-A′ (see fig. 15), drawn by Dorothy H. Cox

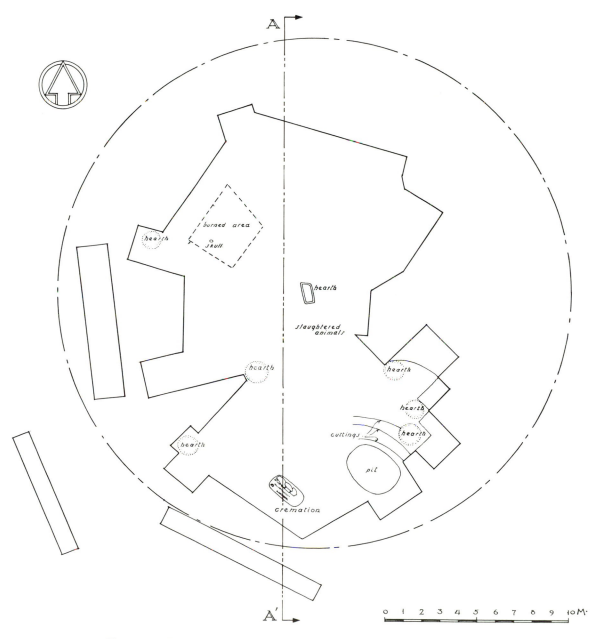

Figure 15. Tumulus M: plan of features encountered in digging. Cremation
appears near the south edge. Drawn by Dorothy H. Cox.

Figure 16. Tumulus M: cremation group *in situ*

Figure 17. Lydian round-bodied lekythos, P 762, Tumulus M. H. 0.229m.

Figure 18. Crushed two-handled bronze bowl, B 466, Tumulus M. Est. D.
rim 0.32 m. Similar to that in Tumulus F; see fig. 9a, b.

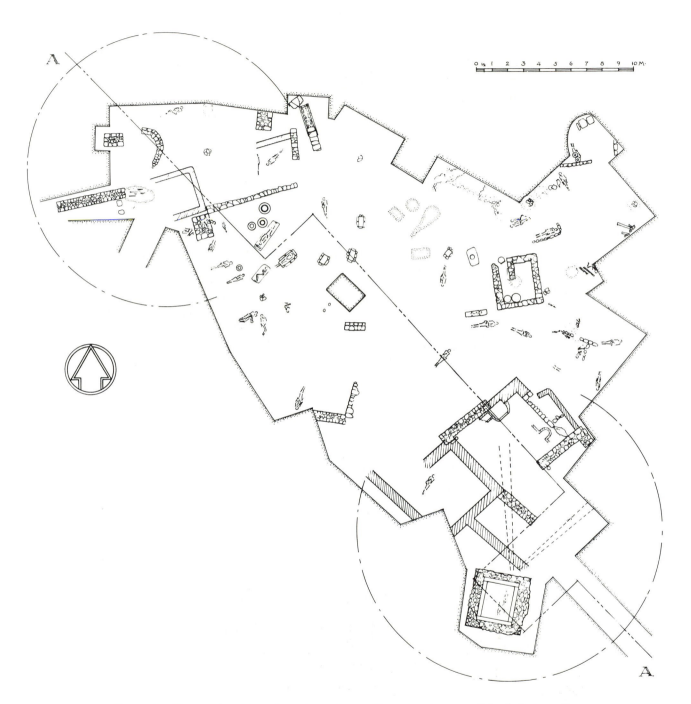

Figure 19. Tumuli I and H: plan. Cremation in Tumulus I (*upper left*) is just southwest of center. Other features included are the main burial in Tumulus H
(*lower right*), and the pre-tumulus evidence for habitation walls and the
cemetery encountered when the excavations of H and I were taken down
to hardpan. Drawn by Dorothy H. Cox.

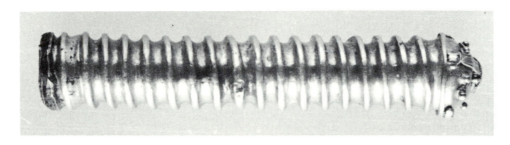

Figure 20. Gold tube, J 38, Tumulus I: side view, detail of end. L. 0.073 m.

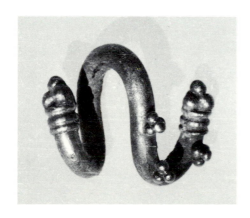

Figure 21. Electrum "hair-ring," J 49, Tumulus I. Max. dim. 0.022 m.

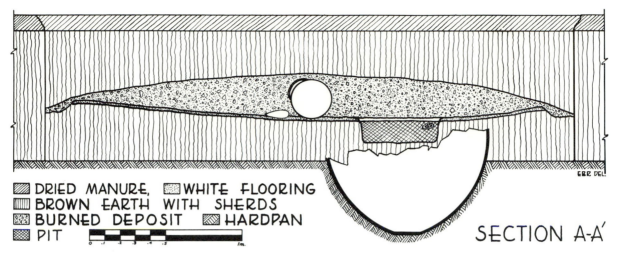

DRIED MANURE, WHITE FLOORING
BROWN EARTH WITH SHERDS
BURNED DEPOSIT HARDPAN
PIT

SECTION A-A´

Figure 22. Tumulus A: section through lens of cremation ash, showing the pit and a destroyed pre-tumulus storage jar, drawn by E. B. Reed

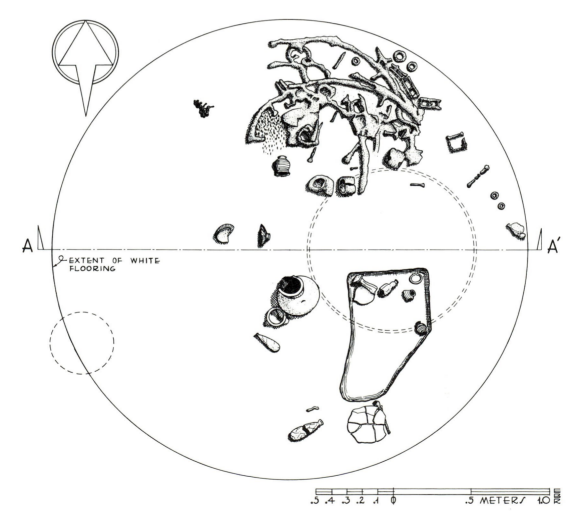

A ─────── EXTENT OF WHITE FLOORING ─────── A´

.5 .4 .3 .2 .1 0 .5 METERS 1.0

Figure 23. Tumulus A: plan of the cremation area with offerings, drawn by E. B. Reed

Figure 24. Gold and electrum pendants illustrating the use of preformed beaded wire, Tumulus A: *left,* J 16, H. 0.014; *right,* J 15, max. L. 0.015 m.

Figure 25. Gold chain with small blossompendants, J 19, Tumulus A. H. blossom 0.012 m.

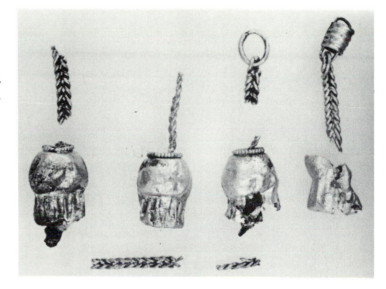

Figure 26. Heavier gold chain, J 20, Tumulus A. Th. 0.004 m.

Figure 27. Schematic detail of chain in fig. 26, drawn by M. Kutkam

Figure 28. Molded unguentarium: kore holding a bird, T 1, Tumulus A.
H. 0.268 m.

Figure 29. Burned Lydian neck-amphora with multiple hooks on shoulder,
P 1, Tumulus A.   H. 0.293 m.

Figure 30. Coarse open-bowl lamp in gray ware, P 10, Tumulus A.   D. 0.255 m.

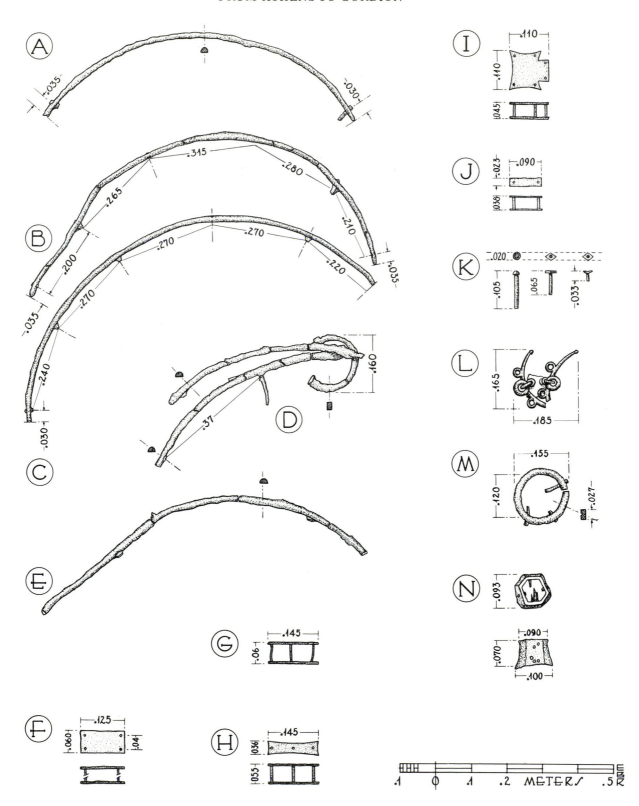

Figure 31. Burned iron wagon parts, Tumulus A, drawn by E. B. Reed

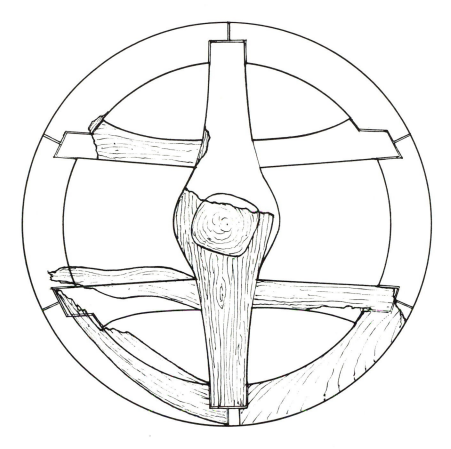

Figure 32. Wheel from Küçük Hüyük at Gordion, dated to the Lydian period (ca. 580-546 B.C.), drawn by Dorothy H. Cox. Restored D. 1.15 m.

VII. ARCHAIC WALL PAINTINGS FROM GORDION

Machteld J. Mellink

In the excavation seasons of 1953 and 1955 evidence for wall paintings of East Greek style came to light at Gordion in a small building of the archaic level, the so-called Painted House, initially excavated by Jeanny Vorys (Canby), later by Mabel Lang.[1] The Painted House stood between Megara C and G, large buildings which belonged to the post-Kimmerian reconstruction program (fig. 1). The megara faced north ("notebook north" equals true northeast) in the first court behind the archaic East Gate, similar in layout to their predecessors Megara 1 and 2 in the pre-Kimmerian East Court. Megaron C had gone through a period of use and a complete reconstruction before the Painted House was built. The latter was fitted in tightly. Its east wall was built against the reconstructed west wall of C, and its west wall touched the east wall of G, or at least what was left of its foundations. Even on its north side the Painted House apparently had a neighbor built right up against it.

This blocked-in situation of the Painted House was part of a deliberate design. The main unit was a room of 4.50 × 3.75 m. with its floor level sunk about 1 m. below the level of the courtyard and the floors of the neighboring megara. The door was in the center of the south side, but it was reached from the alley at the rear of Megara C and G in an indirect manner (fig. 2). Four steps at the corner of Megaron C descended to a landing outside of the southeast corner of the Painted House; here a left turn and

one more step down led into the vestibule, and from there a right turn was needed to reach the door of the painted room. This makes a devious and dark piece of architecture, resembling a tomb or a heroon rather than a functional habitation unit. We do not know the nature of Megaron C, which was large enough to be a temple. The Painted House is not exactly an annex of Megaron C, as it was first labeled, but it may have had a special connection with the purpose of its impressive neighbor.

The special nature of the Painted House is in its architecture therefore as much as in its decoration, but its interpretation will depend more on the latter. The vestibule had walls decorated with a mosaic of terracotta pegs, nearly one thousand of which were found in its debris. The room unit proper had wall paintings, fragments of which were found in thick piles of debris on a well-preserved floor. The floor itself was a gray blue stucco. Stone robbers had pulled the walls of the archaic level apart, and the Painted House had not escaped their attention. The lower walls of the semi-subterranean room had been built of trimmed rectangular blocks, left only partly *in situ*. Over the stone socle ca. 0.40 m. high had been a beam course as the support for a mud-brick superstructure. Of this, only fallen, unburned debris remained. The walls had been covered with white plaster as a background for painting. Some of the plaster was found still adhering to the stone socle, but most of it had tumbled down in the collapse of the ruined structure or had crumbled off the stones as they were pillaged.

---

[1] *AJA* 59 (1955) 8-10; *AJA* 60 (1956) 255-256.

The salvage of the thousands of pieces of broken and fused plaster is due to patient excavation by Jeanny Vorys and Mabel Lang. The preliminary sorting, recording, and cleaning of the fragments was a joint effort by the excavators and several other staff members, principally Grace Muscarella and Piet de Jong. Much time was spent on the reconstruction of the designs that emerged from the jigsaw puzzle. Piet de Jong made a series of water colors, some of which have been on display in the University Museum. The actual fragments are now preserved in the study rooms of the Museum of Anatolian Civilizations in Ankara. They have been analyzed and catalogued in a provisional fashion.[2]

The preliminary stage of study has led to the following results. The technique of the paintings is tempera on a fine white plaster. Preliminary contours are in red, final outlines in black. Colors are applied in solid washes. Red is the most prominent and appears in several shades; blue and green are also common. Brown is used less often, as are yellow and light buff.

The composition of the designs is in friezes. The main frieze was probably set over the (blank?) dado which covered the stone socle. Human figures moving to the right and left are part of this frieze, which is about two feet in height. The bare feet of the figures stand on the red base line, which is set, architecturally, over a horizontal wooden beam in the wall face. The heads are just about an inch away from a similar slightly profiled edge of the plaster. The figures moving to the right are thought to have formed a continuous frieze starting to the north of the doorway and continuing along the north wall to the center of the east (rear) wall. Other figures move to the left on the opposite walls and meet their counterparts on the east wall.

The figures are best preserved in large fragments of drapery patterns. They show considerable overlapping of individuals. Those coming from the left are mostly recognizable as women. The costumes, underneath which the anatomy of ankles, knees and legs is shown in black contours, are of two main variants: we see crinkly chitons covered by himatia with broad linear (no

zigzag or stacked) folds; we also have smoother, simpler chitons. The costumes belong to East Greek fashion. Less familiar and more Anatolian are the various turbans and veils worn as headgear and shawls. The colors dominating in the drapery, as seen especially on the himatia, are red, blue, and green. Some of the himatia have embroidered patterns on the fabric or woven meander borders, while the crinkly chitons have thick black borders near the hem and the smoother chitons have broad colored borders at the neck, shoulders, and sleeves. The drapery often is somewhat cursorily delineated, but it is clear that experienced hands were at work in the drawing.

The heads are the most carefully done. The facial profiles have fleshy double contours and bright red lips. The women are wearing their best jewelry. Prominent are necklaces, bracelets, and earrings, the last-named being an elaborate kind with a fluted crescent-shaped ornament over the top of the ear and various pendants and discs attached to the lobe. The hair styles vary. Neatly drawn little curls lie on the forehead, and long brown tresses hang down shoulders and back.

It has not yet been possible to join a complete figure from head to foot, but the general proportions and types of figures moving to the right can be reconstructed. Of the gestures, one is recognizable. A young woman in the procession wearing a straight chiton and well-provided with jewelry raises her right hand in front of her mouth, not touching her lips (fig. 3). This gesture is known in Achaemenian art as that of respectful silence or silence before speech of a person approaching a king or a dignitary. Another figure raises both hands and firmly grasps what looks like a reed.

Among the figures coming from the right are two overlapping standing figures with a kneeling figure behind. The bent foot of the kneeling figure is well preserved, and a large group of adjoining fragments shows that the kneeling figure stretched out a hand to the left, holding a reed or tube. A fragmentary contour of a spouted pitcher standing in front of the kneeling figure makes it probable that a beverage is being offered to be sipped through a drinking tube, a custom familiar enough from the Near East but especially known through Xenophon's reference to beer drinking in Eastern Anatolia (*Anabasis* IV, 5, 26). It is

[2]*Year Book of the American Philosophical Society* 1960, 563-565.

probable that the reeds seen in other fragments of the procession belong to the same context and are carried in anticipation of a festive refreshment. Some of the figures did not have to wait. Fragments which originally were thought to show trumpeters, with the addition of new pieces became revelers drinking from small beaked pitchers in an unexpected and to us unceremonial manner (fig. 4).

One of the most expressive moments of the celebration is preserved in a group of two figures facing each other, the ones popularly nicknamed Orpheus and Eurydice (fig. 5). It looks as if the mood has become more intimate and sentimental with the enjoyment of the good beverage. The two best preserved faces belong to this scene: deep-gazing eyes show the effective use of red for the pupils and corners; the radiating eyelashes are at their most emphatic; the lips are painted in red brush strokes; the facial contours sag slightly to show the full features of the Anatolian-East Greek type. These two figures, perhaps both female, perhaps man and woman, wear elaborate turbans and veils in contrasting colors, the turbans embroidered with tiny black crosses. The figure to the right holds a small black pitcher with beak spout. Piet de Jong made three figures out of this complex, not convincingly. The two figures are joined by the gesture of an arm around a shoulder; one may wonder if they were reclining on a couch rather than walking in a procession. There are fragments of furniture among the debris of the friezes. A "banquet scene" would make good sense as the centerpiece of the main frieze.

There is no red or light red skin tone to differentiate male figures in these paintings. Some of the figures coming from the right are bearded (one with blue hair) but have white skin. Other participants wear griffin crowns (fig. 6). It took a while to understand the meaning of the miniature griffin heads, which were among the fallen bits from the procession. A series of them joined a human head with the customary locks of hair and earrings. As many as six griffin protomes are fastened to a diadem. As we were wondering about this exotic headgear in the Gordion procession, the British excavators of the archaic temple at Emporio on Chios found nine little griffin protomes of lead, attributed to the wooden statue of a goddess in the temple where they survived.[3] The Gordion figures wearing griffin crowns, whether male or female, must have ceremonial importance. Such crowns are not everyday attire. There are other diadems (floral, laurel branches, beads) worn in the procession, but the griffin crowns are of special rank and importance.

The main frieze hypothetically would have formed a zone from about 0.40 to 1.00 m. above floor level. Other decorations were painted on a smaller scale. They may have belonged to panels and friezes at higher levels. Fragments showing athletes, musicians, architectural elements, painted columns and mouldings, birds, trees, and a girl picking fruit from a tree belong to the "miniature" series. Enough variety was found for us to assume that the colorful decoration of the room went to ceiling level. The roof was tentatively thought to be gabled because animal decoration (spotted felines, snakes) would form appropriate pedimental fillers. Red geometric designs and stripes on coarse plaster with reed impressions could have come from the ceiling proper.

The East Greek affinities of the figures on the walls of the Painted House at Gordion were never doubted. The ample forms, the luxurious attire of the figures in the procession, and the full facial contours were recognized as characteristic also of East Greek sculpture and vase painting. Sculptures from Ephesus, terracottas from Sardis, lead griffins from Chios, painted vase fragments from Phocaea, jewelry from Bayraklı (on the terracotta statue) and Ephesus (on the ivory votary with Phrygian bowl and pitcher), details of figures on Clazomenian sarcophagi all helped to determine the milieu of the wall painters who worked at Gordion and their approximate date of ca. 525 B.C. But the main and surprising revelation was the actual preservation of East Greek wall painting in samples from very near its homeland, the first demonstration of what kind of East Greek wall painting stood behind the Etruscan tradition and what prototypes Etruscan artists could have drawn upon. Etruscan wall painting is admittedly a reflection of East Greek monumental painting. The direct study of its models

[3] *JHS* 74 (1954) 164; more recently, J. Boardman, *Excavations in Chios 1952-55, Greek Emporio (BSA* supplementary volume 6, 1967) 26-28, 203-205, pls. 84-85.

became conceivable through the discoveries at Gordion.

In 1960, when trying to reconstruct the decoration of the semisubterranean room at Gordion, we interpreted the Painted House as a symbolic tomb or heroon and used Etruscan tomb chambers as indirect evidence for a tentative restoration of a series of painted friezes and a decorated, painted ceiling.

As slow progress was made in the study of the fragments in the Ankara Museum, new discoveries came to the rescue. The painted tomb chamber found in 1969 at Kızılbel near Elmalı in Northern Lycia proved that East Greek painted friezes indeed decorated gabled chambers, that friezes of various scales were combined, and that decorations covered all available wall, floor, and ceiling surfaces. The style and technique of the Kızılbel paintings were close to the Gordion pieces. Processions of draped figures and details of costume could be compared, but Kızılbel offered much more variety in subject matter and, above all, in spite of much damage, what survived was found *in situ* on the walls.[4]

The discovery of a second painted tomb in the Elmalı area, the Graeco-Persian tomb at Karaburun, has added to the conviction that there was a long-standing tradition of wall painting in Anatolia and East Greece. The Etruscan tradition can now be measured against a more substantial Anatolian representation.

The Painted House of Gordion with its pseudo-funerary decorated chamber, in proportions comparable to those of the Kızılbel chamber (wide rather than long), will be restudied in the new context. Rodney Young was much pleased that good luck had brought new information and new discoveries together in one study project. He discussed with me the promising results of the first technical tests made by Franca Callori di Vignale, the restorer of Kızılbel, on the fragments of the Gordion paintings. A new conservation project will be planned. The Gordion fragments will be cleaned and consolidated according to the newly gained experience and by restorers who have had years of practice with Etruscan and now Anatolian wall painting. The Painted House will in the outcome be much better understood and appreciated. The restoration of the friezes can then be undertaken in the laboratory, and large sections of the original paintings can be prepared for display in the Ankara Museum.

ADDENDUM

Franca Callori di Vignale began the new conservation project in the summers of 1978 and 1979. All fragments of the Gordion wall paintings and their unpainted background have been brought to the workrooms of the Archaeological Museum in Ankara for treatment and study. The cleaning of the pieces and the consolidating of the colors have commenced. The entire complex will be restudied for joins and original composition.

---

[4] *AJA* 74 (1970) 251-252; *AJA* 75 (1971) 246-249.

Figure 1. Plan of archaic level, Gordion. *PH* designates the Painted House.

Figure 2. View of Painted House at end of excavation

Figure 3. Woman with hand by mouth (2:3)

Figure 4. Reveler drinking from pitcher (2:3)

Figure 5. "Orpheus and Eurydice" (2:3)

Figure 6. Head with griffin crown (2:3): restored drawing by Piet de Jong

VIII. ON LYDIAN SARDIS

George M. A. Hanfmann

To honor the memory of Rodney S. Young, it was my original intention to make a comparison of urban organization of Lydian Sardis with Phrygian Gordion and to integrate into this discussion examples of Lydian sculpture which have a bearing on the architectural aspects of the city. This proved too large a subject for a short paper. In this essay, then, I shall limit myself to presenting some observations on the fragmentary archaeological evidence for various aspects of urbanism at Sardis: first, on the royal cemetery and royal burials, a component of a royal capital and, as city of the dead, a counterpart of the city of the living; then on the extent of the urban area, on the defenses of the acropolis, and on the problem of the royal palace; and assess what data we have for religious architecture of Lydian Sardis. I shall conclude with a sketchy view of the important material on the industrial, commercial, and domestic aspects of Sardis under the Mermnad dynasty and the Persians (ca. 680-334 B.C.). From time to time we shall turn our eyes eastward, toward Gordion, and seek to discern something of the similarities and differences of the two capitals, without pretending to a systematic comparison.[1]

Lydian Sardis owes much to Phrygian Gordion —and the Sardis Expedition owes much to Rodney S. Young. Rodney had been digging for several years at Gordion before we began at Sardis. To learn the management of a dig in Turkey from Rodney and the workings of the Gordion recording system from Ellen Kohler, Mrs. Hanfmann and I made a special pilgrimage to Gordion in 1957. Thereafter Rodney became a stalwart friend. With Greenie, Professor C. H. Greenewalt, Jr., as a staff member of both expeditions and a living link, this friendly cooperation continued. It culminated in 1963. Seven years earlier (1956), Rodney had made archaeological history by his successful use of an oil rig to discover the chamber in the Great Tumulus of Gordion (fig.

[1]M. Hammond, with L. J. Barston, *The City in the Ancient World* (Cambridge, Mass., 1972) chap. 11, section 3, "Phrygian Gordion and Lydian Sardis," 144-146, with literature 466-468, is a brief suggestive attempt to evaluate the historic position of the two capitals in the development toward the Greek city state. Archaeological summaries and literature in E. Akurgal, *Ancient Civilizations and Ruins of Turkey*, 3rd ed. (Istanbul 1973)

124-131, 279-283, 362, 365. For Sardis, J. G. Pedley offers a fine sketch which includes historical evidence in his *Sardis in the Age of Croesus* (Norman, Okla., 1968), and he presents the ancient documentary evidence in his *Ancient Literary Sources* (Archaeological Exploration of Sardis, Monograph 2; Cambridge, Mass., 1972). The epichoric inscriptions are treated by R. Gusmani, *Neue epichorische Schriftzeugnisse aus Sardis, 1958-1971* (Archaeological Exploration of Sardis, Monograph 3; Cambridge, Mass., 1975). An up-to-date survey and summation of data on urban development of Sardis appears in G. M. A. Hanfmann and J. C. Waldbaum, *A Survey of Sardis and the Major Monuments Outside the City Walls* (Archaeological Exploration of Sardis, Report 1; Cambridge, Mass., 1975) chaps. 1-2. For its numerous illustrations, cf. also G. M. A. Hanfmann, *Letters from Sardis* (Cambridge, Mass., 1972). An attempt to integrate Sardis into a panorama of Western Anatolian cultural development is made in G. M. A. Hanfmann, *From Croesus to Constantine* (Ann Arbor 1975). See also Addendum, *infra*.

1).[2] We wanted to emulate Rodney, and he very willingly lent us the oil drill rig complete with his wonderful foreman Abdullah. We put the rig into operation on the central of the three giant mounds in the royal cemetery of Bin Tepe, ca. seven miles north of Sardis (fig. 2).

It would have been a glorious "one-two punch" for American expeditions, if the discovery of the burial of King Gordios of Phrygia—in the Gordion mound (fig. 3)—had been followed by the discovery of the burial of King Gyges of Lydia—at Sardis—in the similar giant mound (the Gordion mound, 250 m. diam., ca. 50 m. height; the Sardis one, 220 m. diam., ca. 40-45 m. height; figs. 4-6).

This was not to be. In all of our twenty-six drillings (fig. 2), the drill was stopped by large pieces of limestone without reaching depths greater than 14 m.[3]

In three seasons of valiant underground search (1964-1966) Greenewalt did not find the chamber. We did find an astonishing Lydian monumental limestone wall, which we followed for more than a third around the circle (ca. 105 m.; figs. 5-6).[4]

About 85 m. in diameter and partly unfinished, this crepis wall includes masonry blocks of well over 6 feet (1.90 m.) long. I continue to believe that it originally circumscribed a smaller mound. As to the strange sign (in the drawing fig. 6*b*),

Roberto Gusmani in his monograph on epichoric inscriptions would read it as a combination of the Lydian *v* and *e*. I read it as a gamma of Greek form plus Lydian upsilon and as a monogram for GuGu or King Gyges.[5] The identification as the mound of Gyges is, in any case, made probable by a poem of the archaic Ephesian poet Hipponax.[6] The wall and the monogram would then date around 645 B.C., the year King Gyges fell battling the Kimmerian invaders in front of Sardis. The wall gives an impressive notion of stone-working skill available in Sardis at this early date.

If we failed to find the burial chamber of King Gyges, we do know the burial chamber of King Alyattes, the father of Croesus. He died around 560 B.C. Lying some 30 m. off center in the largest mound of all (355 m. in diameter), the marble chamber was discovered by H. Spiegelthal in 1853 and remeasured by us in 1962. It measures only 11 by 8 feet (3.33 by 2.37 m.) compared to 21 by 17 feet for the big wooden chamber of the Gordion mound (6.20 by 5.15 m.). The heavy marble blocks are fitted with hairbreadth precision. The ceiling block over the entrance weighs nearly 16 tons (1.93 by 3.75 by 0.93 m., at 2.75 tons per cu. m.). Made in 1962, our architectural drawings of the chamber of the Alyattes mound show it half filled with rubble collapsed into it from the antechamber (fig. 7).[7] The chamber of Alyattes had been plundered. Only a few Lydian and Greek pot fragments were

---

[2]The drilling is discussed and illustrated in R. S. Young, "The Campaign of 1955 at Gordion: Preliminary Report," *AJA* 60 (1956) 250, 264-265, pl. 95, fig. 53. It began in 1955, but the definitive location of the chamber was made in 1956. See R. S. Young, "Gordion 1956: Preliminary Report," *AJA* 61 (1957) 319, n. 1, and for the excavation and tunneling, R. S. Young, "The Gordion Campaign of 1957," *AJA* 62 (1958) 147-154.

The aerial photograph with the mound, here fig. 9, appeared in Young's first report, "The Excavations at Yassihuyuk-Gordion," *Archaeology* 3 (1950) 196, fig. 1.

[3]G. M. A. Hanfmann, "The Sixth Campaign at Sardis (1963)," *BASOR* 174 (1964) 55. For the location of Bin Tepe, see Hanfmann and Waldbaum (*supra* n. 1) 11-12, fig. 2.

[4]C. H. Greenewalt, Jr., in *BASOR* 182 (1966) 27-30; in *BASOR* 187 (1967) 43-47, fig. 25; and in G. M. A. Hanfmann, *Letters from Sardis* (Cambridge, Mass., 1972) 146-148, 153-159, 164-166, 171, 183, 193-194, figs. 106, 108-112. Greenewalt cites the lengths of ashlar blocks as 0.85-1.77 m. and of pieces of the rounded bolster top course as 0.875-1.90 m.

[5]Gusmani (*supra* n. 1) 68, figs. 38-39. G. M. A. Hanfmann, "The Seventh Campaign at Sardis (1964)," *BASOR* 177 (1965) 34. Hanfmann (*supra* n. 4) 154, fig. 107.

[6]O. Masson, *Les fragments du poète Hipponax* (Paris 1962) 65, 129-134. J. G. Pedley, *Ancient Literary Sources* (Archaeological Exploration of Sardis, Monograph 2; Cambridge, Mass., 1972) 77, no. 280, with up-to-date commentary. Hanfmann (*supra* n. 5), 34, presented the interpretation of the fragment as enumerating the three great mounds of Bin Tepe from east to west.

[7]For the location cf. our fig. 12, legend "Tumulus of Alyattes." H. Spiegelthal and J. F. M. von Olfers, "Über die lydischen Königsgräber bei Sardès," Kgl. Preussische Akademie der Wissenschaften, Berlin, *Abhandlungen* (1858) 539-556, pls. 1-5. G. M. A. Hanfmann, "The Fifth Campaign at Sardis (1962)," *BASOR* 170 (1963) 52-57, figs. 39-41. J. J. Coulton, "Lifting in Early Greek Architecture," *JHS* 94 (1974) 3, n. 15, gives 2.75 tons for 1 cu. m. of marble. See also Addendum, *infra*.

found,[8] but objects from nonregal Lydian burials, such as golden lions of the time of Alyattes, hint at the splendors Lydian royal burials may have held. Four such lions, each about one inch long, were attached perhaps to a lid of a chest. They came from a grave (no. 75) discovered in 1910 or 1911 by our predecessors, the Princeton Expedition to Sardis.[9]

Three large royal mounds and about one hundred other mounds constituted the cemetery for kings and princes at Bin Tepe (figs. 2, 8, 12).[10] In their paper, C. H. Greenewalt and L. J. Majewski discuss one of the smaller burials.[11] In addition, one thousand chamber tombs were cut into the rock cliffs above the city to house several thousand middle- and perhaps lower-class Lydian dead.[12]

The weight given to the mound cemetery and the symbolization of royal power and aristocratic privilege through especially large mounds are the same in Gordion and Sardis, though at Gordion (fig. 9, air view of Gordion) the mound

cemeteries lie closer to the city. Indeed, several of the later mounds (F, H, I, E) (fig. 11) on the so-called "Eastern Ridge" are built over earlier habitations.[13] This may indicate a contraction of population after the Kimmerian catastrophe, if outlying areas were abandoned; they may equally have been abandoned because of a tightening of settlement into a more densely built up, more urban pattern. The great wealth of the mounds, built over earlier dwellings during the period of Lydian domination, indicates no rapid decline for archaic Gordion.[14] In any event, it is clear that the pattern of city plus mound-cemetery was continued even after the end of the Phrygian kingdom.

We turn now from the cities of the dead to the cities of the living and perceive here some resemblances but also some important differences. Both Sardis (fig. 10, view from acropolis; fig. 12, plan of Sardis area with Bin Tepe) and Gordion (fig. 11, Gordion plan) are cities at east-west crossings of river fords—the Sangarius at Gordion, the Pactolus at Sardis; Sardis, in fact, may have controlled a second, larger north-south crossing—that of the river Hermus. This may have been done by means of an advanced post and a separate suburb, for we have no indication that the Lydian city reached the two miles or so northward, which separate the known Lydian city area remains from the present course of the Hermus (Gediz Çay, fig. 12).[15]

Both cities lay in fact on the great east-west road from the Aegean coast across Anatolia, the

[8]Spiegelthal and von Olfers (*supra* n. 7) pl. 5. Hanfmann (*supra* n. 7) 56-57.

[9]C. D. Curtis, *Jewelry and Gold Work* (Sardis XIII, 1; Rome 1925) 34, pl. 8, figs. 7a-c, no. 86. L. 0.0205 m.; weight 2.7-2.8 grams. Twelve holes are along the edges of the base. Three lions are in Istanbul, and one is in the Ashmolean Museum, Oxford, 1928.323.

[10]Fig. 2 is taken from the great central mound, BT 63.1, the tumulus of Gyges. Fig. 8 shows the great western mound; it is not marked on the plan, fig. 12. For its location cf. Hanfmann (*supra* n. 3) 54, fig. 34, Kir Mutat Tepe. Cf. also Hanfmann and Waldbaum (*supra* n. 1) 5, fig. 2, Regional Map of Sardis.

[11]"Lydian Textiles," *infra* 133-147; Hanfmann (*supra* n. 3) 55, 57, figs. 35, BT 63.2. Other small mounds opened by the expedition: Hanfmann (*supra* n. 7) 57-59, figs. 42-44 and G. M. A. Hanfmann, "The Ninth Campaign at Sardis (1966)," *BASOR* 187 (1967) 38-43, 47-52, figs. 27-36, BT 63.3, 66.1-6.

[12]They are summarily described by H. C. Butler, *The Excavations* (Sardis I, 1; Leiden 1922). In his unpublished file of tombs made in 1914, G. H. Chase cited 1107 as the last tomb number. A few additional graves were opened by the Harvard-Cornell expedition. G. M. A. Hanfmann, "Excavations at Sardis, 1959," *BASOR* 157 (1960) 10-12, fig. 1; G. M. A. Hanfmann, "The Fourth Campaign at Sardis (1961)," *BASOR* 166 (1962) 24-30, figs. 1, 19-23; G. M. A. Hanfmann, "The Ninth Campaign at Sardis (1966)," *BASOR* 187 (1967) 37-38, figs. 1, 16, 17; A. Ramage, "The Fourteenth Campaign at Sardis (1971)," *BASOR* 206 (1972) 11-15, figs. 1-4.

[13]R. S. Young, *Gordion, A Guide to the Excavations and Museum,* 2nd ed. (Ankara 1975) 18, speaks of thirty excavated tumuli and of houses covered by them. Cf. R. S. Young, "Gordion 1956: Preliminary Report," *AJA* 61 (1957) 324-331, and R. S. Young, "The Gordion Campaign of 1957," *AJA* 62 (1958) 147-154, pls. 23-27. For the walls under the mounds F, H, I and "a fairly well-preserved house complex below tumulus E," cf. R. S. Young, "Progress at Gordion, 1951-1952," *UMB* 17, 1 (1953) 30, figs. 22-23. Cf. n. 16, infra.

[14]R. S. Young, "Gordion, Preliminary Report, 1953," *AJA* 59 (1955) 16, pls. 90-96. Cf. also E. L. Kohler, "Cremations of the Middle Phrygian Period at Gordion," *supra* 65-89.

[15]Gordion: R. S. Young, *Gordion, A Guide to the Excavations and Museum,* 2nd ed. (Ankara 1975) 1, 17. Sardis: Hanfmann (*supra* n. 4) map 2; Hanfmann and Waldbaum *supra* n. 1) 18, fig. 2.

later Royal Road.[16] In Gordion (fig. 11) after crossing the river north of the palace mound, the road bore past the traces of inhabited areas and the big mound of King Gordios or Midas (MM; fig. 9).[17] In Sardis, it may be surmised with fair certainty to have passed just north of the Lydian Market area (HoB) and then across the Pactolus, following in general a course not too different from the later Roman Main Avenue. It is possible, however, that this was only a detour from the major east-west road, in order to reach Sardis, for the passage from Hipponax which speaks of a wanderer from the interior passing the three large royal mounds of Bin Tepe is plausible only if the major east-west road ran sufficiently close for the three great mounds to be clearly seen. This would be the case if the road followed the Hermus. But, as at Gordion, it may have gone straight by the great royal monuments somewhat in the way of the modern highway from Salıhlı to Akhisar (broken line in fig. 12).[18]

Standing on the Sangarius river, the city mound of Gordion is a typical Near Eastern, flat-topped habitation mound composed of eighteen layers (figs. 9, 11, 13). The main hill measures 500 by 350 m. and rises nearly 15 m. above the plain. Thus the city mound area proper is only around

4½ acres. Rodney S. Young himself remarked in his admirable Gordion guide that "the town should probably be regarded as the seat of the king, and of his bureaucracy and garrison . . . and of such population as was needed to provide for the needs of the court," and he continued, "The common people for the most part must have lived in the countryside perhaps going to town to market and sheltering behind its walls in time of danger. . . ."[19] We note in the aerial view that the royal cemetery with the mounds is fairly nearby, whereas at Sardis it is several miles away (figs. 2, 8).

Lydian Sardis, too, had a fortified center, but its citadel was a typical acropolis rising over precipitous cliffs to a height of well over 300 m. (1,000 feet) above the plain of the Hermus river —7 miles away from the royal cemetery of Bin Tepe (figs. 10, 12, 18).

At Gordion, apparently only scattered dwellings are known in the plain. "A number of houses of various periods have been found on higher ground at the east, above the present village . . . some covered by tumuli . . . others burned . . . at the time of the Kimmerian raid. . . ."[20] The density of structures in the built-up areas is attested by walls under the mounds F, H, and I and "a fairly-well preserved house complex below Tumulus E."[21]

For the moment, the distance of over half a mile from the palace mound suggests that we have perhaps here the survival of the Bronze Age type of settlement in several villagelike agglomerations in the countryside around a fortified refuge castle, *kata komas* as Thucydides (I, 5) had said of early Greek towns (cf. also II, 15-16, on Athens). For Sardis, literary sources and our excavations prove the existence of a densely built-up lower town. Herodotus (V, 101) speaks of the burning of Sardis in 499 B.C. in terms which suggest a densely built-up area around the agora at the crossing of the torrent Pactolus.

We have exposed one sizable, built-up area of industrial installations—the so-called gold re-

---

[16]Royal Road: for its general course, Hanfmann and Waldbaum (*supra* n. 1) 18-19, fig. 8. No identifiable remnant of the Lydian or Persian Royal Road was found at Sardis. Cf. G. M. A. Hanfmann, "The Fourth Campaign at Sardis (1961)," *BASOR* 166 (1962) 45; Hanfmann and Waldbaum (*supra* n. 1) 29, fig. 10. I am informed by K. DeVries that the paved road at Gordion initially identified as part of the Royal Road is now considered to be Roman in its present state. Cf. R. S. Young, "Gordion 1956: Preliminary Report," *AJA* 61 (1957) 319, pl. 87, and R. S. Young, "The Gordion Campaign of 1957," *AJA* 62 (1958) 140-141. DeVries remarks (in a letter of February 21, 1976): "An early road is almost certainly indicated by two more or less parallel lines of tumuli to the east of the MM Tumulus and to the south of the apparently Roman road. . . . A road fringed by tumuli does, I suppose, make for an even closer parallel to what you are suggesting for Sardis."

[17]R. S. Young discussed the course of the road from Gordion up the valley of the Tembris to Dorylaion in "Gordion 1956: Preliminary Report," *AJA* 61 (1957) 319, and "The Gordion Campaign of 1957," *AJA* 62 (1958) 139, n. 3.

[18]Clive Foss in Hanfmann and Waldbaum (*supra* n. 1) 19, fig. 2, suggests that this road from the north "provided the main east-west thoroughfare when it reached Sardis."

---

[19]Young (*supra* n. 15) 17.

[20]Young (*supra* n. 15) 11.

[21]R. S. Young, "Progress at Gordion, 1951-1952," *UMB* 17, 4 (1953) 30, figs. 22-23. Cf. E. L. Kohler, *supra* 65.

fineries[22]—as well as dwellings at Pactolus North (fig. 27), marked PN on the plan (fig. 14), and we have smaller exposures of continuous urban structures—probably houses—in two other areas of the Pactolus Valley: Pactolus Cliff[23] (PC on the plan) and Northeast Wadi,[24] northeast of the Artemis temple. We have found commercial structures and possibly some dwellings in the Lydian Market area,[25] HoB Market on the plan (fig. 14).

Yet much remains uncertain. Andrew Ramage, who has written a careful study of all remains of domestic Lydian architecture we have found, comes up with a plan for Lydian Sardis which is essentially a north-south ribbon development. My reconstruction is based on a north-south–east-west cross (fig. 14).[26] We agree in having a road along the Pactolus and another diagonally from Pactolus North toward the Lydian Market. We agree in allowing a considerable built-up area on the order of between 200 and 350 acres, much

larger than the "city mound" of Gordion.[27] Yet we have exposed a total of only about 10,000 sq. m. (about 4 acres) in eight different Lydian locations; even the exact position of the agora is uncertain; and no excavations have been made in the central, eastern, and northern areas.[28] There is still work to be done to ascertain the major features of the city plan and to discover whether the lower town of Sardis had any defensive wall before the Hellenistic Age.[29]

Let us now turn to the acropolis, its defenses and the problem of the royal palace.[30] Literary sources (Herodotus I, 84) say that King Meles fortified the citadel, presumably around 700 B.C., and that Alexander the Great in 334 B.C. admired the fortress with its triple wall (*triplo teichei pephragmenon,* Arrian I, 17, 3). Yet so much of the acropolis has sheared off by erosion that it came as a surprise when C. H. Greenewalt, Jr., in 1972-1973 discovered three fragments of the defensive wall. They were found on the south slope, just below a Byzantine redoubt (figs. 15, 17).[31]

Preserved up to eight courses and having a thickness of ca. 12 feet (3.5 m.) the wall consists of two faces of roughly squared masonry, its joints chinked with slivers of stone, and a core of river stones cemented with mud. Compared to Gordion's mighty gate[32] (fig. 16), this does not

[22]G. M. A. Hanfmann and J. C. Waldbaum in J. A. Saunders, ed., *Near Eastern Archaeology in the Twentieth Century* (Garden City, N.Y., 1970) 310-313, fig. 1, pl. 34. Hanfmann (*supra* n. 4) 230-234, 248-249, figs. 172-179. G. M. A. Hanfmann, *From Croesus to Constantine* (Ann Arbor 1975) 5-6, figs. 10-11, 13. A. Ramage in *BASOR* 199 (1970) 16-26. S. M. Goldstein, *ibid.,* 26-28, figs. 7-14, with plans. G. M. A. Hanfmann, "The Sixteenth Campaign at Sardis (1973)," *BASOR* 215 (1974) 33, fig. 3 (axonometric drawing).

[23]G. M. A. Hanfmann, "Excavations at Sardis, 1959," *BASOR* 157 (1960) 12-19, and "The Third Campaign at Sardis (1960)," *BASOR* 162 (1961) 17-24, plan, fig. 7.

[24]C. H. Greenewalt, Jr., in Hanfmann and Waldbaum (*supra* n. 1) 118-125, figs. 283-285, 292-319.

[25]G. F. Swift, Jr., in *BASOR* 187 (1967) 31-37 and *BASOR* 199 (1970) 28. The Lydian levels and their stratigraphy are discussed by Swift in *BASOR* 174 (1964) 8-14, figs. 2-7 and *BASOR* 182 (1966) 8-15, figs. 4-11. For complete listings of reports, cf. Hanfmann and Waldbaum (*supra* n. 1) 13, Sector Index, #4-5.

[26]Cf. A. Ramage, "Studies in Lydian Domestic and Commercial Architecture at Sardis" (Dissertation, Harvard University 1969, unpublished); summary in *HSCP* 75 (1971) 214-215. Some of the results appear in A. Ramage, *Lydian Houses and Architectural Terracottas* (Archaeological Exploration of Sardis, Monograph 5; Cambridge, Mass., 1978). Cf. also G. M. A. Hanfmann, *From Croesus to Constantine* (Ann Arbor 1975) 5-7, fig. 9, and Hanfmann and Waldbaum (*supra* n. 1) 28-29, fig. 7. See Addendum, *infra.*

[27]Young (*supra* n. 15) 19 gives ca. 500 by 350 m. as maximum dimensions; hence the area of the city mound is around 40 acres.

[28]Cf. Hanfmann and Waldbaum (*supra* n. 1) 3-5, fig. 1, for overall plan.

[29]R. S. Thomas in Hanfmann and Waldbaum (*supra* n. 1) 35. We were in error, however, p. 28, in placing the Persian camp west rather than east of the Pactolus river during the battle of 395 B.C. Cf. the excellent discussion by J. K. Anderson, "The Battle of Sardis in 395 B.C.," *California Studies in Classical Antiquity* 7 (1974) 27-53, especially 41-42, 52: "The Greeks drove the Persians into the Pactolus and then crossed to capture the Persian camp."

[30]C. H. Greenewalt, Jr., in *BASOR* 206 (1972) 15-20. Hanfmann and Waldbaum (*supra* n. 1) 4, 14, Sector Index, #20-22, with references, fig. 4, plan.

[31]C. H. Greenewalt, Jr., "The Fifteenth Campaign at Sardis (1972)," *BASOR* 211 (1973) 31. G. M. A. Hanfmann, "The Sixteenth Campaign at Sardis (1973)," *BASOR* 215 (1974) 31-33, figs. 1-2.

[32]R. S. Young, "The Campaign of 1955 at Gordion: Preliminary Report," *AJA* 60 (1956) 257-260, pl. 87, fig. 25 and pl. 91, fig. 36; R. S. Young, "The Gordion

look like much, but it is the same type of wall (fig. 17). In Gordion, too, the wall, 13-14 feet (4 m.) thick, consists of two chinked masonry faces with a rubble core (fig. 16). What is preserved at Sardis (fig. 17) corresponds to the lower part of the Gordion wall, but instead of the twenty courses of masonry rising above the lower (eight-course?) part, one might assume in Sardis an equivalent height of mud brick.

The preserved fragment runs downhill for about 10 m.; a triangular construction below and a platform above do not add up to anything immediately intelligible (fig. 15). Sherds found in the core are pre-Hellenistic but not closely datable. To stimulate thoughts about the possible function of this remnant of Sardian defense, one may look back to Gordion's great gate and the plan of the palace area with its majestic megarons (fig. 13).

Even the location of the palace is controversial at Sardis.[33] A Hellenistic source used by Vitruvius (II, 8, 9-10: Pedley, no. 291, with comments) says that the Palace of Croesus became the seat of the city senate, the *gerousia,* after Alexander captured Sardis. On the theory that senior citizens would not have climbed to the top of the acropolis every time the city senate met, we used to favor a hillock now crowned by a Byzantine fort with a tree as a candidate for the palace site,[34] especially as tunnels—unfortunately undatable—seem to descend in this direction from the top of the acropolis.[35] In so doing, we over-

looked a much earlier and better literary tradition. Speaking of the Ionian attack on Sardis in 499 B.C., the historian Charon of Lampsakos, who wrote around 400 B.C., stated clearly that the Greeks failed to take "the (fortress) wall of the royal palace," *teichos tou basileiou*; and from other sources we know that what the Greeks failed to take was the acropolis. The fortified palace was therefore on the acropolis.[36]

The discovery by Greenewalt of monumental, beautifully worked—though partly unfinished—Lydian limestone and sandstone terracing walls with Lydian mason marks just below the top of the north side of the acropolis has now vindicated Charon of Lampsakos. There was a palatial structure on the acropolis. The technique of limestone masonry is the same as in the Gyges mound, and one of the walls shows traces of an external (outside) staircase (fig. 19).[37]

Nothing can be made of the plan except that the buildings rose one above the other. I believe they had staircases, platforms, and possibly door frames of stone with walls of mud brick, like the later Achaemenian palaces of Persia.

Vitruvius' source said that the upgoing walls of the Palace of Croesus were of mud brick. The buildings may have had pitched roofs and were possibly decorated with painted terracotta tiles. The fragment of a horse (T 74:1) was found near the terracing walls, and a winged horse in another part of the acropolis.[38] The general effect may have resembled the fortified mountain pal-

---

Campaign of 1959: Preliminary Report," *AJA* 64 (1960) 233-234; Young (*supra* n. 15) 23-24 and illustrations. E. Akurgal, *Die Kunst Anatoliens* (Berlin 1961) 105, color pl. II.

[33]Hanfmann (*supra* n. 26) 8-9, fig. 17, with references, discusses the possibility of two palaces, one on the citadel, one below. A detailed consideration of the various problems and solutions appears in U. Höckmann and A. Krug, eds., *Festschrift für Frank Brommer* (Mainz 1977) 145-154.

[34]Hanfmann and Waldbaum (*supra* n. 1) 14, fig. 1, no. 23, and fig. 15. C. Foss, *Byzantine and Turkish Sardis* (Archaeological Exploration of Sardis, Monograph 4; Cambridge, Mass., 1976) 60, 75, plans I-IV. The plan and photographs of the Byzantine fort will be published by R. L. Vann in his study of "unexcavated buildings" of Sardis.

[35]Tunnels: G. M. A. Hanfmann, "The Fifth Campaign at Sardis (1962)," *BASOR* 170 (1963) 35-37, fig. 24; "The Seventh Campaign at Sardis (1964)," *BASOR* 177 (1965) 8-10; and Hanfmann (*supra* n. 4) 105-106,

figs. 69-70. Location: Hanfmann and Waldbaum (*supra* n. 1) fig. 1, no. 21, and fig. 4.

[36]The same wording is preserved by Aristotle, *Analytica posteriora* 94 a-b, cf. Pedley (*supra* n. 6) no. 148, hence before Alexander the Great captured Sardis, and by Plutarch, *De Herod. malign.* 24 (861 B), who specifically attributes the passage to Charon of Lampsakos; cf. Pedley, *ibid.,* no. 155.

[37]G. M. A. Hanfmann, "The Third Campaign at Sardis (1960)," *BASOR* 162 (1961) 37-39, figs. 21-22. Greenewalt (*supra* n. 30) 15-20, figs. 5-7, with revised dating. Hanfmann (*supra* n. 4) 306-307, figs. 229-230. G. M. A. Hanfmann, "Excavations and Researches at Sardis, 1974," *TürkArkDerg* (1976) 57-58.

[38]G. M. A. Hanfmann, "The Fifth Campaign at Sardis (1962)," *BASOR* 170 (1963) 32, fig. 22; Hanfmann (*supra* n. 26) 9, figs. 14-15; G. M. A. Hanfmann, "Excavations and Researches at Sardis, 1974," *TürkArk-Derg* (1976) 58, fig. 10, T 74.1. Cf. in general A. Ramage in *BASOR* 215 (1974) 54-58, figs. 23-26, with references; Ramage (*supra* n. 26; 1978) 20, no. 19, color.

ace shown in the reliefs of Trysa.[39] And this is all that can presently be said about the palace of the Lydian kings and royal architecture on the acropolis.

We now turn to Lydian religious architecture. It is represented so far by two altars, one in the center of the gold purification plant at Pactolus North (fig. 20; plan, fig. 27),[40] the other in the Artemis precinct (fig. 21).[41] They are remarkably different. The Artemis altar is built of carefully fitted, partly clamped limestone masonry. The hole in its center is due to recent robbing. The altar in the refinery is known from a graffito to be sacred to the native goddess Kuvava, or Cybele;[42] it is made of river stones and originally had four eastward-roaring sandstone lions set on its corners.

At its west side it had a step for the sacrificer to stand on; he was thus facing east. The Artemis altar (fig. 21), contrariwise, possibly had steps on the east (fig. 22, tentative reconstruction), and the sacrificer faced west, toward the graves of the Cemetery Hill, which according to Lydian inscriptions were under the protection of Artemis. Thus Artemis protected the dead aristocrats, Cybele the living workmen. Her altar, dating around 560 B.C. stood free in the center of the gold-working precinct (fig. 20). It had no obvious relation to any templelike structure. As to the Artemis altar, our colleague K. J. Frazer would like to put an archaic temple west of the altar (fig. 22), but the evidence is, in my view, insufficient to prove the existence of such a temple. A fine limestone Ionic profile may belong to the Artemis altar,[43] and there are preserved two and a half sandstone lions from the altar of Kuvava.[44]

We have evidence of a different kind for archaic Lydian shrines and temples. The plan of a shrine of Cybele (figs. 23-25) is derived from what seems to be a faithful model of a real shrine of the time of Alyattes or Croesus—a marble model two feet high, given originally, I believe, by the donor of the actual building to the goddess. Although damaged at the top, this is an important witness for the experimental phase of archaic Ionic order. The odd number of columns at the back (on axis), the use of half columns with square pedestals, simple torus bases, and slender fluted shafts (with eighteen fillets), and a nearly Doric abacus surmounted by Ionic volutes seem to reflect a remarkable structure.[45]

The image of the goddess is flanked by snakes, but the heraldic lions shown in panels of the reliefs (fig. 24), which rise in three zones on the side walls, speak for Cybele whose archaic shrine was burned down by the Ionians in 499 B.C. The Sardis model resembles a flat-roofed shrine shown on an Attic black-figure amphora of ca. 530 B.C. in the British Museum which Beazley, because of the lion on the roof, described as that of Cybele (with question mark). Perhaps this reflects a remembrance of Sardis(?) or a shrine in Attica(?).[46]

On the Sardis shrine, priestesses are shown proceeding to the front to worship the goddess. We seem to have found two small (H. 0.40 m. = 14 inches) marble figurines of priestesses wear-

[39]F. Eichler, *Die Reliefs des Heroon von Gjölbaschi-Trysa* (Vienna 1950) 61-62, 223-226, pl. 18, fig. 8. Cf. also Hanfmann (*supra* n. 26) 8ff., 18, fig. 39, on Larisa, with literature.

[40]Hanfmann (*supra* n. 26) 14, figs. 10, 13, 31-32, with references.

[41]Detailed publication by K. J. Frazer in Hanfmann and Waldbaum (*supra* n. 1) 88-95, 103, figs. 103, 132, 181-207. Tentative reconstruction: Hanfmann (*supra* n. 26) 7, fig. 16.

[42]Gusmani (*supra* n. 1) 28-30, A II 5, figs. 12-13, dated 600-575 B.C.

[43]Hanfmann and Waldbaum (*supra* n. 1) 94, fig. 210.

[44]A. Ramage in *BASOR* 191 (1968) 11-12, figs. 9-11. Hanfmann (*supra* n. 26) 14, fig. 31; Hanfmann (*supra*

n. 31) 44, fig. 17, reconstruction with modern casts of lions; Hanfmann (*supra* n. 4) 221-222, figs. 169-170. G. M. A. Hanfmann and N. Ramage, *Sculpture from Sardis, The Finds through 1975* (Archaeological Exploration of Sardis, Report 2; Cambridge, Mass., and London 1978) 66-67, nos. 27-29, figs. 105-117.

[45]Hanfmann and Ramage (*supra* n. 44) 43-51, with literature, and figs. 20-50. B. Wesenberg, *Kapitelle und Basen, Beobachtungen zur Entstehung des Griechischen Säulenform* (Düsseldorf 1971) 111-112, no. 3, fig. 232.

[46]British Museum no. B 49. J. D. Beazley, *Attic Black-Figure Vase-Painters* (Oxford 1956) 326, 715 ("Cybele?"). *CVA*, British Museum III (London 1927) pl. 35, 2a. Wesenberg (*supra* n. 45) 84, fig. 175. M. P. Nilsson, *Greek Popular Religion* (New York 1940) 91 ff., fig. 35 (Magna Mater).
I. Papachristodoulou, Ἄγαλμα καὶ ναὸς Κυβέλης ἐν Μοσχάτῳ Ἀττικῆς, *ArchEph* (1973) 189-217, has published a definitive account of the newly discovered statue of Cybele together with a general account of the cult of Cybele in Attica. Cf. H. W. Catling, *Archaeological Reports for 1974-1975* (Society for the Promotion of Hellenic Studies 21; London 1975) 3.

ing a peculiar belt with wide ends hanging down —possibly from Cybele's precinct.[47]

A problem connected with religious architecture is presented by the numerous lions—twenty-two out of a total of sixty Lydian- and Persian-period sculptures. Curiously, none of the lions has been found near a tomb or a grave. Four originally guarded Kuvava's altar (fig. 20); two pairs probably flanked a divine image.[48] One wonders whether some of the other lions might not have guarded the façades and gates to palaces or sacred precincts as at Gordion.[49] A five-foot-long Lydian marble lion (fig. 26) was re-used as heraldic symbol in the main avenue of Roman Sardis. We have also found a fragment of its counterpart. The lion may date before 550 B.C.[50]

And might not other lions have flanked a sacred road to the Artemis precinct, as did the lions along the road to Apollo's sanctuary at Didyma? Or a terrace, like the famous lions at the Sacred Lake of Delos?[51]

If we look back, we see that at Sardis the evidence for defensive, palatial, and religious architecture is so far very fragmentary, amounting to hints about possibilities rather than firm data for reconstructible probabilities. Evidence for commercial and industrial aspects is more extensive and tangible. It was partly worked up by the late Gustavus F. Swift, Jr., for the commercial Lydian market (figs. 28-29, plans) and by Andrew Ramage and Sidney Goldstein for the gold-working industries and other shops on the Pactolus (fig. 27, plan). Their preliminary findings were reported to the Tenth Congress of Classical Archaeology.[52] I shall make here only one general observation. In the commercial market area (figs. 28-29) of which nearly 6,000 sq. m. were exposed, emphasis seems to lie on utilitarian, nonluxury trades, casting and finishing of bronzes, and making and repair of lamps and pottery; thus ten unused lamps were found together (fig. 30).[53] By contrast, the region of the gold-purifying plant at Pactolus North (figs. 27, 20; and n. 22, *supra*) has yielded evidence of jewelry in gold (fig. 31, golden lamb earring) and in rock crystal[54] and was probably a quarter of gold-workers and jewelers.

Phrygian Gordion and Lydian Sardis have been linked by Mason Hammond in a recent book, *The City in the Ancient World,* as examples of the way in which the Indo-European tribes invading Asia Minor were introduced to urban living.[55] As we have seen, both cities were dominated by their kings; both had fortified refuge-palace areas; both had mighty royal mounds; both were centers of agricultural wealth and industrial production.

But Sardis, famed as world capital and pioneer of monetary economy, seems to show incipient

---

[47]G. M. A. Hanfmann, "The Sixteenth Campaign at Sardis (1973)," *BASOR* 215 (1974) 41, fig. 11. Hanfmann and Ramage (*supra* n. 44) 41-42, nos. 4-5, figs. 11-15.

[48]Kuvava's altar: *supra* n. 44. Flanking: D. G. Mitten in Hanfmann (*supra* n. 3) 38, fig. 23; Hanfmann (*supra* n. 4) 138, fig. 98; Hanfmann and Ramage (*supra* n. 44) 63-65, no. 25, figs. 92-101.

[49]R. S. Young, "The Campaign of 1955 at Gordion: Preliminary Report," *AJA* 60 (1956) 262, pl. 92, figs. 42-43. Young (*supra* n. 15) 34 "re-used in foundations of buildings of the Persian level were the two lions' heads of poros . . . assigned with great probability to M[egaron] 2 . . . adorning its façade at either side."

[50]Hanfmann (*supra* n. 47) 52, fig. 22. G. M. A. Hanfmann, "Excavations at Sardis, 1973," *Archaeology* 27 (1974) 138, ill. Hanfmann and Ramage (*supra* n. 44) 68, no. 31, figs. 119-122. The fragment of a possible counterpart, S 70:10; 8112, is published in Hanfmann and Ramage, 68-69, no. 32, fig. 123.

[51]K. Tuchelt, *Die archaischen Skulpturen von Didyma* (Istanbuler Forschungen 27; Berlin 1970) 212-213, denies the suggestion first advanced in 1850 by Ludwig Ross that the lions flanked the Sacred Road in the manner of an Egyptian processional avenue. Tuchelt argues that the lions and seated statues were first placed alongside the Sacred Road to Didyma in the fifth or fourth century B.C. For Delos cf. H. Gallet de Santerre, *La Terrasse des lions, le Létoon, le Monument de granit à Délos* (Exploration archéologique de Délos 24; Paris 1959) 28ff., pls. 41-49.

[52]G. F. Swift, Jr., "The Chronology of Lydian Culture," unpublished paper delivered at Tenth International Congress of Classical Archaeology, Ankara and Izmir, September 1973. A. Ramage, "Gold Refining at the Time of the Lydian Kings of Sardis," *The Proceedings of the Xth International Congress of Classical Archaeology, Ankara-Izmir . . . 1973* II (Ankara 1978) 729-735.

[53]Bronze working: G. F. Swift, Jr., in Hanfmann (*supra* n. 16) 7. Pottery repair: G. M. A. Hanfmann, "Excavations at Sardis, 1958," *BASOR* 154 (1959) 27-29, fig. 13. Lamps: G. M. A. Hanfmann, "The Third Campaign at Sardis (1960)," *BASOR* 162 (1961) 12; also, *in situ*, Hanfmann (*supra* n. 4) 80, fig. 51.

[54]G. M. A. Hanfmann, "The Seventh Campaign at Sardis (1964)," *BASOR* 177 (1965) 7, fig. 7, rock crystal. Ramage (*supra* n. 44) 13, fig. 13. Hanfmann (*supra* n. 4) pl. IV, opposite p. 226, color reproduction of jewel with lamb.

[55]Hammond and Bartson (*supra* n. 1) 144-146.

specialization of markets and possibly industrial quarters allotted to special trades and is thus closer to commercial cities of the Levant and Greece. By contrast, Gordion has an air of rugged, feudal power and, as K. DeVries shows (*supra*), of patriarchal Homeric living. Its social and economic organization with its 300 spinning and baking women may have been closer to the palace-oriented economies current in the Bronze Age, or—in more sophisticated form—in Late Hittite principalities, than to the Phoenician or Greek cities of the Iron Age.[56]

What I have presented here are only sketchy remarks reflecting evidence which is still very fragmentary. Yet through the work of scholars like Rodney S. Young it is growing ever more

tangible and solid. Not so long ago, Gordion with its Gordian knot was little more than a myth, an evocative verbal image; Rodney Young gave half of his scholarly life to make it a concrete human reality. We hope that his successors will continue and complete his work.

ADDENDUM

The preceding paper was written in 1975. Since that time, huge Lydian (city?) walls have been found in the lower city; the mound of Alyattes has yielded more pottery; and new data on the extent and settlement density of the urban area of Sardis have been gained.[57]

---

[56]The concentration of economic and industrial productivity in the palaces can be reconstructed from written documents for such north Mesopotamian and Levantine (Canaanite) cities as Mari, Alalakh, and Ugarit; and the same general type of "palace-oriented" economies emerge from the archives of Knossos and Pylos. "Late Hittite" cities like Kargamiş, Sencirli, and Malatya seem to have preserved the dominance of the palace. Virtually all major examples of urban sites with palaces from the prehistoric to Iron Ages are discussed—but from the historical rather than the architectural-urbanistic point of view—by Hammond and Bartson (*supra* n. 1) chapters 3-13, with an excellent selection of bibliography.

Anatolian and Syrian palaces are surveyed architecturally by R. Naumann, *Architektur Kleinasiens von ihren Anfängen bis zum Ende der Hethischen Zeit*

(Tübingen 1955) 347-378. For the architectural-urbanistic surveys, cf. P. Lampl, *Cities and Planning in the Ancient Near East* (New York 1968) for the Near East; also H. Frankfort, "Town Planning in Ancient Mesopotamia," *The Town Planning Review* 21, 2 (1958) 98-115. For the role of the palace in Anatolia, cf. the brief discussion in Hanfmann (*supra* n. 26) 4-11, figs. 7-9, 17-19, where the industrial and commercial aspect of Sardis is perhaps underemphasized. For some interesting remarks on the transition from the Aegean palace to the Greek polis, cf. J. B. Ward-Perkins, *Cities of Ancient Greece and Italy* (New York 1974) 8-13, figs. 1-5.

[57]C. H. Greenewalt, Jr., "Sardis Campaign of 1976," *BASOR* 229 (1978) 56-73, fig. 19 (Alyattes); *idem*, "The Sardis Campaign of 1977," *BASOR* 233 (1979) 1-26.

Figure 1. Drilling rig on the Great Tumulus (MM), Gordion

Figure 2. Mound of Gyges (BT 63.1) and the Bin Tepe cemetery at Sardis. Drilling rig from Gordion in use. View looking south toward acropolis.

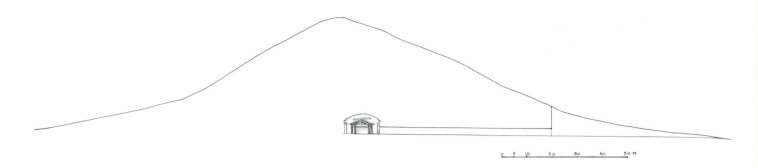

Figure 3. Gordion: the Great Tumulus (MM). Section showing tunnel and chamber.

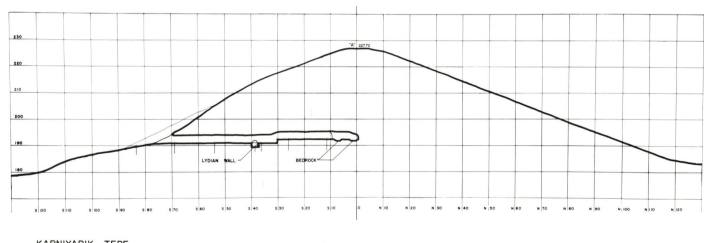

KARNIYARIK TEPE
SOUTH-NORTH SECTION

BT·19

Figure 4. Sardis: mound of Gyges (BT 63.1). Section showing tunnels and Lydian
wall around inner mound.

110

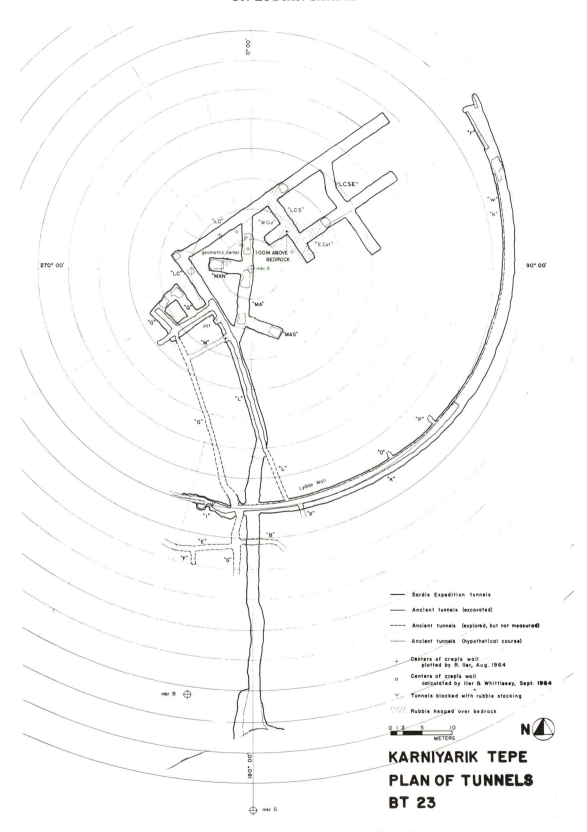

Figure 5. Sardis: mound of Gyges (BT 63.1). Plan.

Figure 6*a*. Sardis: mound of Gyges (BT 63.1). Wall (inner mound crepis). View looking west toward entrance tunnel.

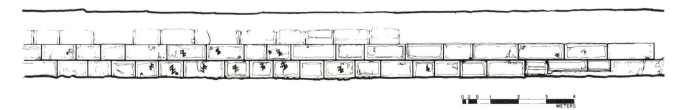

Figure 6*b*. Sardis: mound of Gyges (BT 63.1). Section-elevation of wall (inner mound crepis) showing monograms.

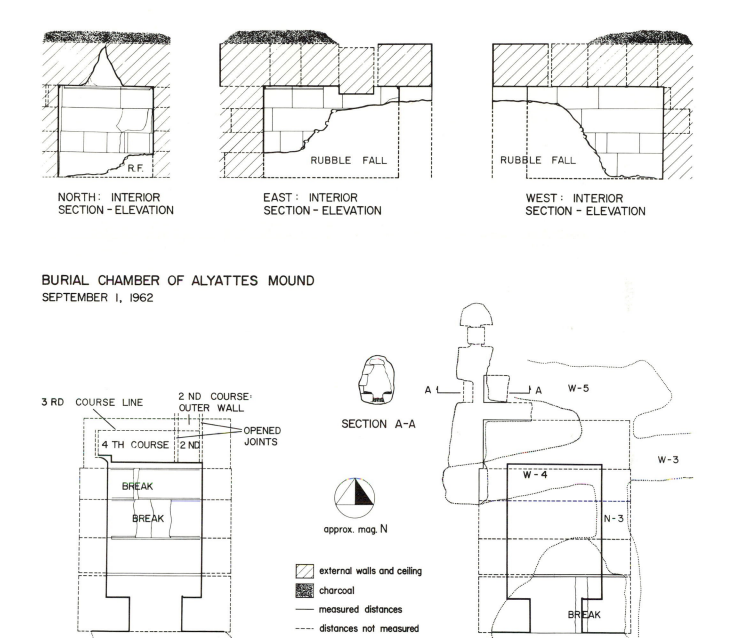

Figure 7. Sardis: mound of Alyattes. Drawings of chamber.

Figure 8. Sardis: the great western mound and the small excavated mound (BT 63.3) at Bin Tepe cemetery. View looking southeast across Hermus plain toward Sardis.

Figure 9. Gordion: air view with city mound in foreground, Great Tumulus upper right

Figure 10. Sardis: view from acropolis over part of Sardis plain and east-west high-way. Foreground, Byzantine tower; background, partly restored Roman gymnasium.

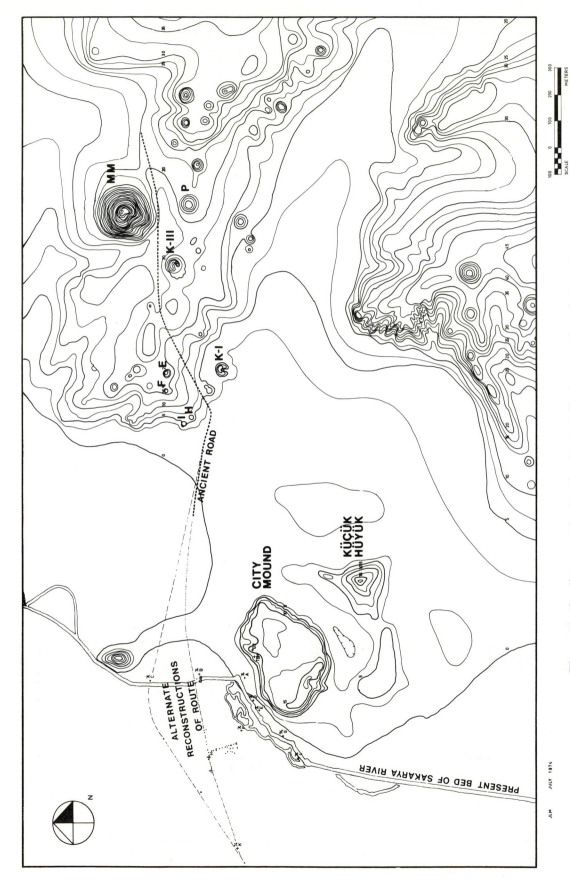

Figure 11. Gordion: overall plan showing tumuli, city mound, and alternate courses of Royal Road

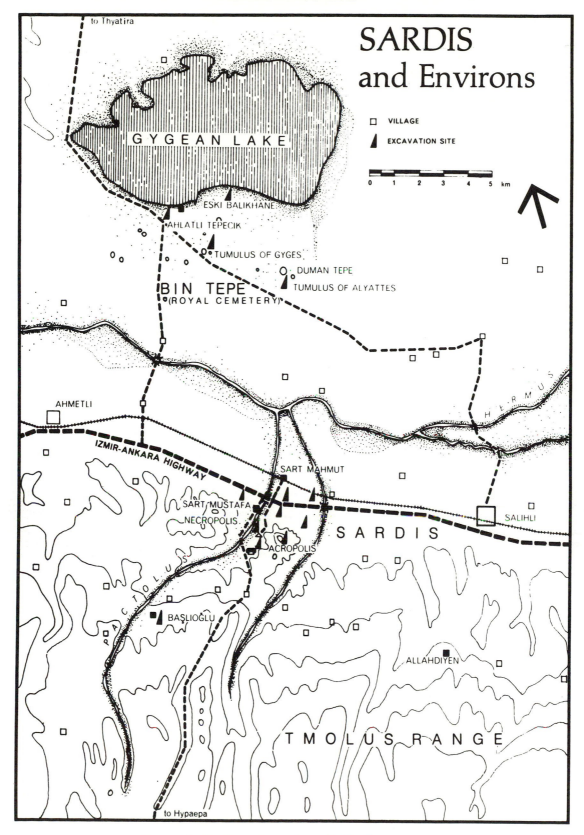

Figure 12. Sardis: regional plan with Bin Tepe cemetery

117

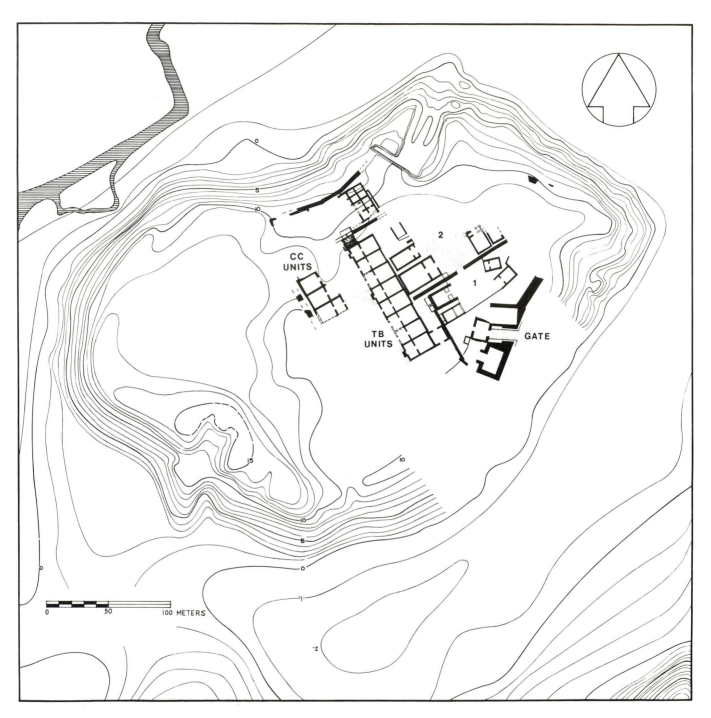

Figure 13. Gordion: plan of city mound at destruction level, ca. 700 B.C.
1, area with Megarons 1, 2, 9, 10
2, area with Megarons 3, 4, 5, 11, 12

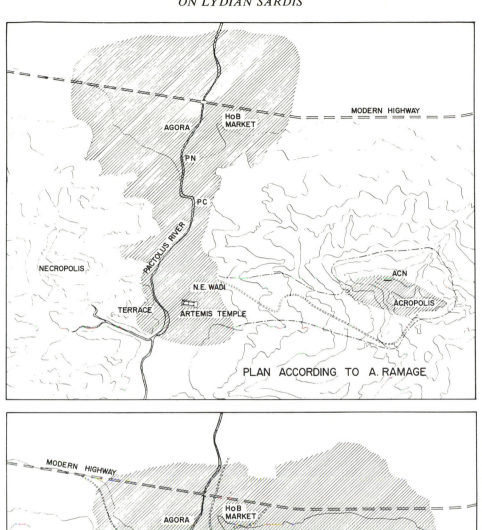

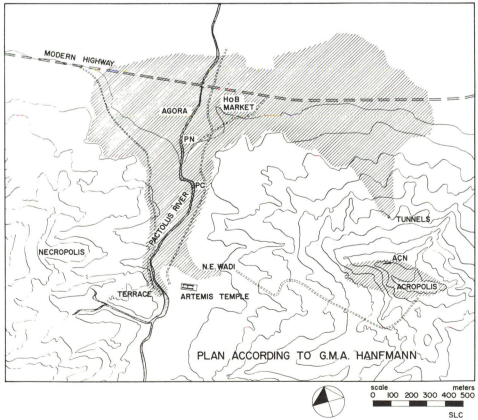

Figure 14. Sardis: two hypothetical plans of area of Lydian city

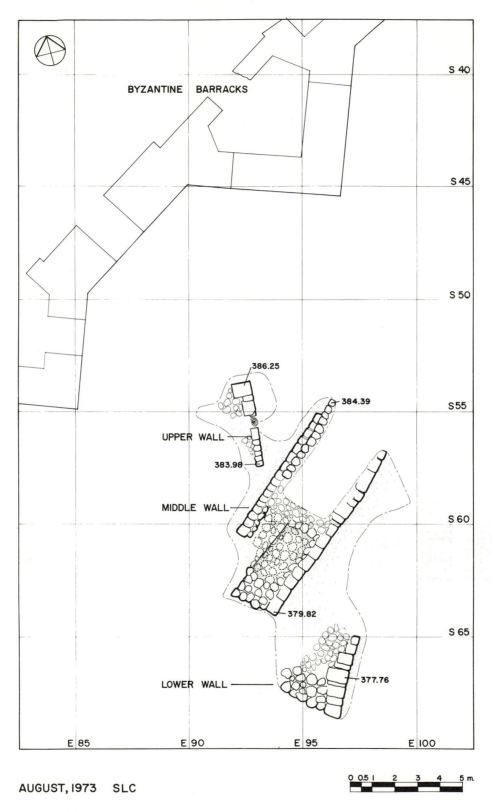

BYZANTINE BARRACKS

386.25

384.39

UPPER WALL

383.98

MIDDLE WALL

S 40

S 45

S 50

S 55

S 60

379.82

S 65

LOWER WALL

377.76

E 85

E 90

E 95

E 100

AUGUST, 1973   SLC

0 0.5 1   2   3   4   5 m.

Figure 15. Sardis: Acropolis South, pre-Hellenistic walls. Plan.

Figure 16. Gordion: Phrygian city gate from east

Figure 17. Sardis: Acropolis South, middle and lower walls

Figure 18. Sardis: Acropolis North, terracing walls of palace and view east over the
Hermus valley

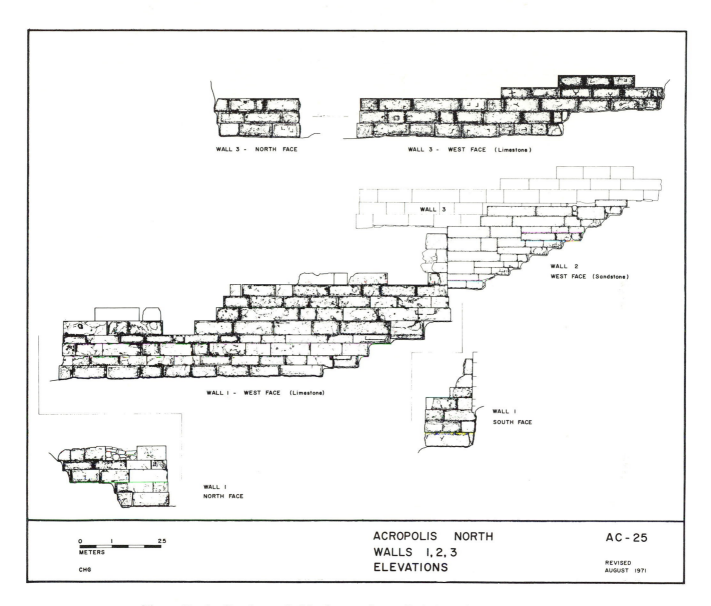

WALL 3 - NORTH FACE

WALL 3 - WEST FACE (Limestone)

WALL 3

WALL 2
WEST FACE (Sandstone)

WALL 1 - WEST FACE (Limestone)

WALL 1
SOUTH FACE

WALL 1
NORTH FACE

0   1   25
METERS

CHG

ACROPOLIS   NORTH
WALLS 1, 2, 3
ELEVATIONS

AC - 25

REVISED
AUGUST 1971

Figure 19. Sardis: Acropolis North, terracing walls 1, 2, 3 of palace. Elevations.

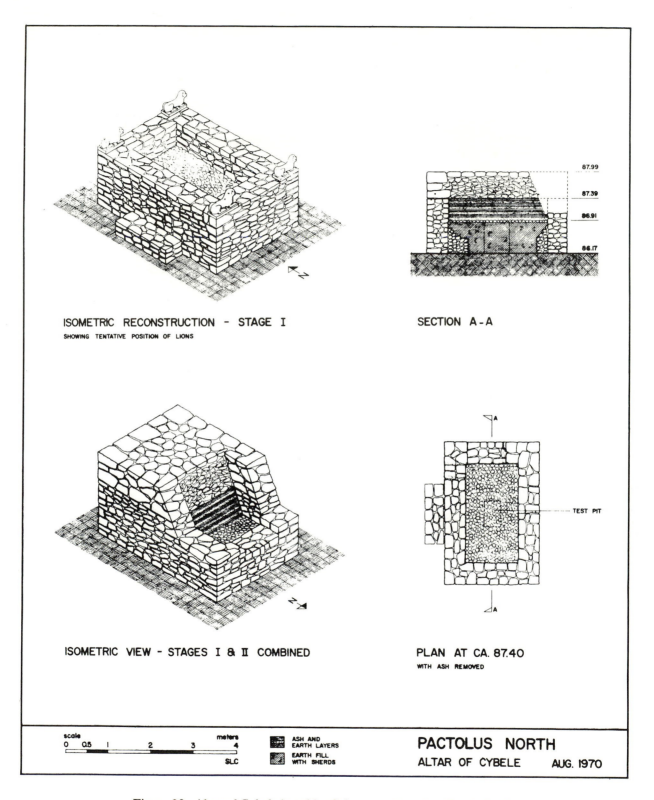

ISOMETRIC RECONSTRUCTION - STAGE I
SHOWING TENTATIVE POSITION OF LIONS

SECTION A-A

ISOMETRIC VIEW - STAGES I & II COMBINED

PLAN AT CA. 87.40
WITH ASH REMOVED

scale
0 0.5 1 2 3 meters 4

SLC

ASH AND
EARTH LAYERS

EARTH FILL
WITH SHERDS

PACTOLUS NORTH
ALTAR OF CYBELE   AUG. 1970

Figure 20. Altar of Cybele in gold-refining area, Pactolus North, Sardis

Figure 21. Archaic Lydian altar of Artemis (LA 1), Sardis

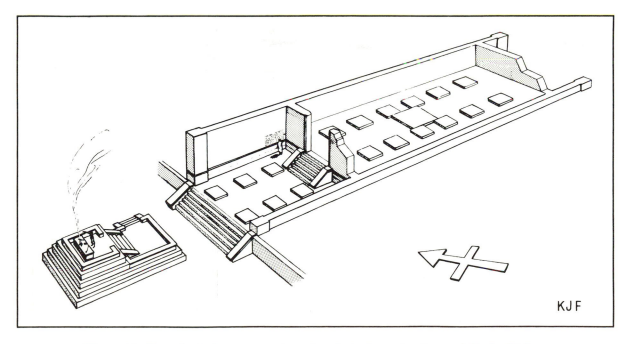

Figure 22. Hypothetical reconstruction of archaic Artemis altar and Early Hellenistic temple by K. J. Frazer. Altar as restored: 7.6 m. (north-south) × 14 m. (east-west).

Figure 23. Reconstruction of model of Cybele shrine (S 63.51), Sardis, by F. K. Yegül

Figure 24. Model of Cybele shrine, right side: lions and procession of priestesses. Drawing by F. K. Yegül.

Figure 25. Model of Cybele shrine with image
and reliefs of left side: priestesses,
komasts, dancers

Figure 26. Archaic Lydian lion (S 73.1), Sardis

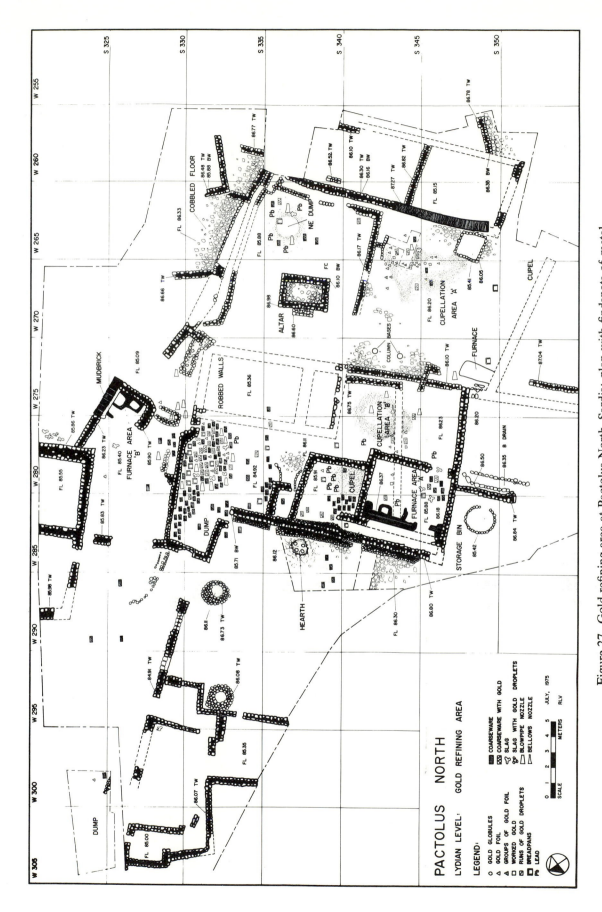

Figure 27. Gold-refining area at Pactolus North, Sardis: plan with findspots of metal-lurgical material of Lydian level. Data by S. M. Goldstein, drawn by R. L. Vann.

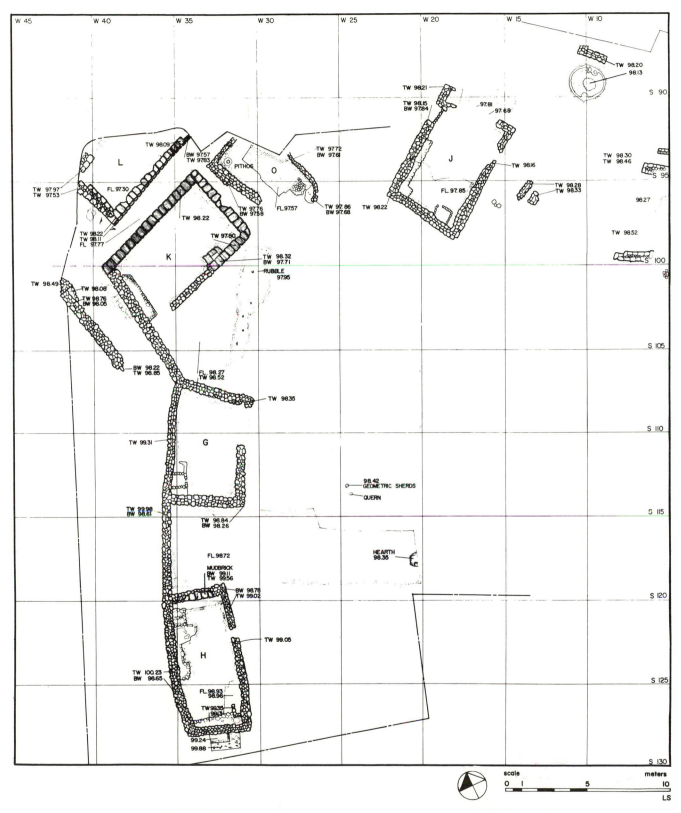

Figure 28. Lydian Market area (HoB), Sardis: plan of second Lydian level, western part (HoB 72), late seventh century B.C.

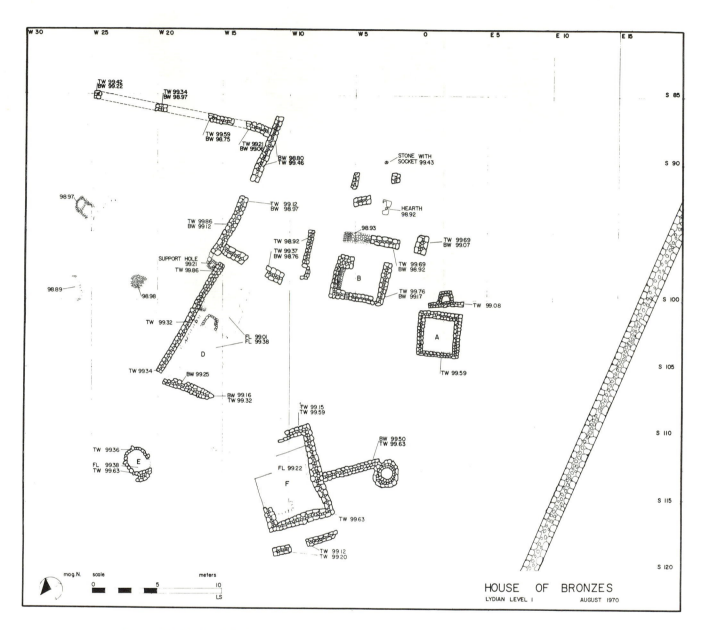

Figure 29. Lydian Market area (HoB): plan of first Lydian level, sixth century B.C.

Figure 30. Unused Lydian lamps found in Lydian Market area (1:3)

Figure 31. Gold ram, J 67.3, found in gold-refining area at Pactolus
North. L. ca. 1 cm.

IX. LYDIAN TEXTILES*

Crawford H. Greenewalt, Jr.
Lawrence J. Majewski

Among the most exotic archaeological discoveries of this century is the pile carpet from Pazyryk in Siberia: 2,500 years old and remarkable for sheer size and well-preserved condition as well as for high technical and artistic quality.

The notion that the Pazyryk carpet may have been made in Asia Minor[1] probably owes more to contemporary ignorance of ancient Near Eastern textile centers than to positive evidence for technique and style; nevertheless it is welcome grist to the mill of all Anatolian chauvinists, like Rodney Young in the wisdom of his later years, and several of the symposiasts who pay homage in this volume to his scholarly and humanitarian achievement.

One region of Asia Minor which has been specifically named in connection with the carpet's place of origin is Phrygia,[2] romantic highland setting of the spectacular discoveries which crowned Professor Young's career. His excavations at the Phrygian capital, Gordion, have furnished impressive documentation for local industry and expertise in textile arts during the eighth century B.C.[3] and fundamental evidence for the diffusion and influence of Phrygian textiles abroad.[4] The tradition current in Roman times (when western Phrygia still produced popular woolen goods and dyes[5]) that credited Phrygians with the invention of embroidery[6] may be an encapsulation of earlier achievement.

---

*Crawford Greenewalt spoke at the symposium; for this volume Lawrence Majewski has supplemented Greenewalt's contribution with the detailed publication of the relevant material from the Bin Tepe tumulus B.T. 2.

[1]R. D. Barnett, W. Watson, "The World's Oldest Persian Carpet, Preserved for 2400 Years in Perpetual Ice in Central Siberia; Astonishing New Discoveries from the Scythian Tombs of Pazyryk," *ILN* 223 no. 5960 (July 11, 1953) 69 (Sardis); C. Roebuck, *Ionian Trade and Colonization* (Monographs on Archaeology and Fine Arts 9; New York 1959) 57 (Sardis); J. Zick-Nissen, "Knüpfteppich von Pazyrik und die Frage seiner Datierung," *AA* (1966) 581, cf. 576-579 (between Susa and Phrygia); R. G. Hubel, *The Book of Carpets* (New York 1970) 15 (Armenia); cf. S. I. Rudenko, *Frozen Tombs of Siberia: the Pazyryk Burials of Iron-Age Horsemen* (Berkeley & Los Angeles 1970) 299, 302-303; *idem, Dr'evn'ejshie v mira Khudozhestvennye Kovry i Tkani* (Moscow 1968).

[2]Zick-Nissen (*supra* n. 1) 557-578, 581.

[3]L. Bellinger, "Textiles from Gordion," *The Bulletin of the Needle and Bobbin Club* 46 (1962) 5-33. The thousands of loom weights recovered from buildings in the eighth century B.C. level of the citadel at Gordion provide important indirect evidence for Phrygian textile activity; cf. R. S. Young, "The Gordion Campaign of 1959: Preliminary Report," *AJA* 64 (1960) 242; *idem,* "The 1961 Campaign at Gordion," *AJA* 66 (1962) 165; G. R. Edwards, "Gordion: 1962," *Expedition* 5, 3 (1963) 45; R. S. Young, "The Gordion Campaign of 1965," *AJA* 70 (1966) 270; "Recent Archaeological Research in Turkey," *AnatSt* 24 (1974) 32.

[4]R. M. Boehmer, "Phrygische Prunkgewänder des 8. Jahrhunderts v. Chr., Herkunft und Export," *AA* (1973) 149-172.

[5]Strabo XII, 6, 16 (578; wool of Laodicaea); XIII, 4, 14 (630; wool dyes of Hierapolis); Pliny, *Historia Naturalis* XXI, 27, 51 (dye of Colossae).

[6]Pliny, *Historia Naturalis* VIII, 74, 196, *pictae vestes iam apud Homerum sunt . . . acu facere id Phryges invenerunt, ideoque Phrygioniae appellatae sunt.* That *acu facere* refers to embroidery rather than to tapestry weave is suggested by the sentence which follows (and evidently refers to tapestry weave), *colores diversos picturae intextere Babylon maxume celebravit . . .* cf. A. J. B. Wace, "Weaving or Embroidery," *AJA* 52 (1948) 51-52. For an actual example of ancient embroidery, J. Beckwith, "Textile Fragments from Classical

The distinctive geometric idiom of Phrygian art—expressed in various media, including textiles, at Gordion and other culturally related sites[7] —however, is absent in the decoration of the Pazyryk carpet; conversely, the carpet's stylistically distinctive motifs are fundamentally alien to Phrygian artistic vocabulary.[8]

A more plausible case may be made for the carpet's manufacture in Lydia, specifically in the Lydian capital, Sardis. That city's promotion of both Achaemenian and Hellenizing artistic styles and its reputation for opulence make it an appropriate source for sumptuary art that combines Achaemenid and Greek iconographic ideas, such as may be combined in the Pazyryk carpet. The carpet's Achaemenid features are obvious and have received suitable comment elsewhere. The presence of Hellenizing ideas, hardly assured, might be detected in the deer, to whose polychromy and abstract contour borders parallels in Eastern Greek vase painting have been remarked,[9] and in the star-rosette motif (fig. 1):

although usually compared to the Assyrian palmetto and palm-bud quatrefoils on the threshold slab from the Palace of Assurbanipal at Nineveh (fig. 2), this motif more closely resembles the star-rosette of Greek and Hellenized art (an adaptation of the Assyrian?).[10] The star-rosette was favored at Sardis in terracotta revetment tiles (fig. 3) and occurs there also in a diaper scheme, like that of the Pazyryk carpet's central zone, carved on mable blocks whose worn (decorated) surfaces suggest that the blocks had served as floor paving and that their carved decoration simulated carpet design (as proposed for the Assyrian thresholds; fig. 5).[11]

The fine quality, polychromy, and Achaemenid associations of the Pazyryk carpet, furthermore, correspond to particulars of a variety of carpet called Sardian that is attested in Greek and Roman literature. Sardian carpets were used in Persia (exclusively by the Persian king) according to the *Persica* of a Greek ethnohistorian who lived in the fourth century B.C. and should therefore have been a contemporary of the last Achaemenid rulers. The fine quality and poly-

---

Antiquity: An Important Find at Koropi, near Athens," *ILN* no. 5988 (January 23, 1954) 114-115.

For Pliny's *Phrygioniae*, cf. Servius, *Commentarii ad Aeneidem* III, 484 (. . . *et artifices talium vestium phrygiones appellati sunt*), Isidorus Hispalensis, *Origines sive Etymologiae* XIX, 22, 22 (. . . *unde et artifices, qui id faciunt, Phrygiones dicuntur*); these two references were kindly supplied by C. E. Murgia.

[7]For the Phrygian geometric style in architecture (rupestral façades, revetment plaques), pottery, furniture, bronze belts, and textiles, E. Akurgal, *Phrygische Kunst* (Ankara Üniversitesi Dil ve Tarih-Coğrafya Fakültesi Yayımları 95, Arkeoloji Enstitüsü 5; Ankara 1955); *idem, Die Kunst Anatoliens* (Berlin 1961) 70-121; Å. Åkerström, *Die Architektonischen Terrakotten Kleinasiens* (Skrifter Utgivna av Svenska Institutet i Athen, 4° XI; Lund 1966) 142, 146-148, 156-157, pls. 72, 80, 82, 84; N. Thomas, "Recent Acquisitions by Birmingham City Museum," *Archaeological Reports for 1964-65* (London 1965) 64-70; R. S. Young, "Phrygian Furniture from Gordion," *Expedition* 16, 3 (1974) 2-13; *idem,* "Gordion on the Royal Road," *ProcPhilSoc* 107 (1963) 360; Bellinger (*supra* n. 3); Boehmer (*supra* n. 4).

[8]The Phrygian comparanda to the carpet's griffin motive which Zick-Nissen has proposed (*supra* n. 1 577-578) do not seem significant to this writer; for griffins in Achaemenid carpets, Hipparchus Ἀνασῳζόμενοι fr. 1 (ed. Kock) apud Athenaeus XI, 477F.

[9]For the clearest illustration of the deer in the Pazyryk carpet, Rudenko, *Dr'evn'ejshie* (*supra* n. 1) 41 fig. 42. For comparison with "Rhodian" vase painting, Zick-Nissen (*supra* n. 1) 576-577. The same vocabulary may have existed in Iranian art, however; cf. O. W. Musca-

rella, "A Bronze Vase from Iran and its Greek Connections," *Metropolitan Museum Journal* 5 (1972) 25-50.

[10]For the clearest illustrations of the star-rosette motive in the Pazyryk carpet, Rudenko, *Dr'evn'ejshie* (*supra* n. 1) opp. p. 41, 45 fig. 33, 53 fig. 42. For the motive in terracotta revetment plaques of Greek and Greek-influenced Asia Minor, Å. Åkerström (*supra* n. 7) 75-76, 92-93, 148, 150, pls. 44-45 (Sardis), 83 (Gordion). For the Near Eastern model (carved on stone paving slabs of the palace of Sennacherib at Nineveh), A. H. Layard, *A Second Series of the Monuments of Nineveh* (London 1853) pl. 56.

R. Ghirshman, *Persia from the Origins to Alexander the Great* (The Arts of Mankind; London 1964) 360, has noted the occurrence of the motive on Luristan bronzes.

[11]These marble fragments were recovered from the Late Antique synagogue at Sardis, where they and some sculpture of demonstrably sixth century B.C. date had been re-used; G. M. A. Hanfmann, "The Sixth Campaign at Sardis (1963)," *BASOR* 174 (1964) 38.

R. Ghirshman (*supra* n. 10) has noted that the saddle cloths with borders scalloped in narrow triangles which appear in the Pazyryk carpet's frieze of horsemen also are represented in Graeco-Persian gems; for fifteen of these (two belonging to or associated with a distinctive group, the "Court Style," which may have been made in Lydia; others with prominent Greek stylistic features, J. Boardman, *Greek Gems and Finger Rings* (London 1970) 303-327. Cf. R. Ghirshman, "La selle en Iran," *Iranica Antiqua* 10 (1973) 94-107.

chromy of Sardian carpets are implied in two other sources, one also of the fourth century B.C.[12]

In most of these sources, however, the term for carpet suggests flat-woven rather than pile construction. The two fourth-century sources give the Greek compound noun ψιλόταπις; τάπις alone evidently might designate pile construction, as in a verse of the *Palatine Anthology* (VI, 250) where the qualifying adjectives are μνιαρός, "mossy," and βαθύρρηνος, "deep-wooled," but the compound with ψιλός, "bare," "smooth" should signify a flat-woven or embroidered covering, a *kilim* or *cicim*.[13] Similarly in the one Latin source carpet is designated by the generic *tapete,* although Latin evidently could distinguish pile fabric (as Greek did not) by use of the adjective *tonsilis,* "clipped." Had Sardian carpets, like the Pazyryk carpet, featured pile construction, ought they not to have been regularly termed ταπίδες and *tonsilia tapetia* or the like in the Greek and Latin sources?[14]

The implied difference in construction if not the tenuousness of Greek stylistic features (and the possibility that such features might merely reflect the Ionian element in Achaemenid expression[15]) and the dominant Achaemenid aspect of the Pazyryk carpet may caution the predatory Lydianist. Until there be good reason to reject the candidacy of other textile centers, documented or anonymous, in the Persian Empire and eastern periphery,[16] it probably were rash

to claim this glittering prize as testimony to the looms of Arachne.[17]

Sardian carpets are only one of several Lydian textile products reported in Greek written documents. Most of the others are garments of exotic character ("for the Lydians . . . encasing their beauty in such garments, pride themselves on these weavings, when they might pride themselves on their natural form"[18]).

"Gold-woven chitons (χρυσοστήμοναι χιτῶνες) made by Lydians" in their palmy days were re-

---

Historia Naturalis VIII, 74, 196; Silius Italicus XIV, 658; Josephus, *De Bello Judaico* V, 5, 4 (212-214) and cf. J. G. Frazer, *Pausanias's Description of Greece* III (London 1913) 545-546 (commentary on Pausanias V, 12, 4). For the tradition of fine textiles in Mesopotamia, J. V. Canby, "Decorated Garments in Ashurnasirpal's Sculpture," *Iraq* 33 (1971) 31-53.

The fine textiles attested for the Achaemenid court in ancient literature (e.g., *Esther* 1, 6; Athenaeus V, 197 B; Curtius, *Historiae Alexandri* III, 3, 13, 17-18) and in Achaemenid art cannot all have been imported from outside Iran; there must have been several if not many important Iranian textile centers. Cf. the texts concerning Elamite textiles of the Achaemenid period from Susa, V. Scheil, "Textes Elamites-Anaznites," *Délégation en Perse, Mémoires* IX (Paris 1907). For representations of fine textiles in Achaemenid art, J. A. Lerner, "A Painted Relief from Persepolis," *Archaeology* 26 (1973) 116-122 and references (particularly to the research of A. Britt Tilia); glazed tile figures of "Immortals" from Susa.

Might the Pazyryk carpet have been created on the eastern periphery or east of the Persian Empire? Cf. E. D. Phillips, *The Royal Hordes; Nomad Peoples of the Steppes* (Library of the Early Civilizations; New York 1965) 85; K. Jettmar, *Art of the Steppes* (Art of the World; New York 1964) 118.

---

[12]Heracleides Cumanus, *Persica* I fr. 1 (ed. Jacoby, *FGrHist* 3C 689) ap. Athenaeus XII, 514 B-C; Clearchus Solensis, *Gergithius* fr. 25 (ed. Müller, *FHG*) ap. Athenaeus VI, 255 E; Varro ap. Nonius Marcellus, *De Genere Vestimentorum* (*De Conpendiosa Doctrina* 20) 542, 13. For another reference, without (surviving) qualification, P. Oxy., 2804 fr. 2 (a), R. Carden, *The Papyrus Fragments of Sophocles* (Texte und Kommentare 7; Berlin 1974) 246, 249.

[13]Like those made in recent times at Gördes, Kula, and Uşak in the territory of ancient Lydia. Cf. also K. Erdmann, *Seven Hundred Years of Oriental Carpets* (Berkeley and Los Angeles 1970) 47-49.

[14]Cf. A. Wace, "Tappeto," *AJA* 76 (1972) 438; Athenaeus V, 197 B (ψιλαὶ . . . Περσικαὶ).

[15]For Greek influence in Achaemenid art, C. Nylander, *Ionians in Pasargadae* (Boreas, Uppsala Studies in Ancient Mediterranean and Near Eastern Civilizations 1; Uppsala 1970).

[16]For Babylonian textiles, Lucretius VI, 1029; Martial XIV, 150; Philostratus, *Vita Apollonii* I, 25; Pliny,

[17]For Arachne (a Colophonian wool dyer's daughter, whose fateful contest with Athena took place at Hypaepa) and the commemoration of Lydian textile art in mythology, Ovid *Metamorphoses* VI, 5-145. Her story, like those of Midas's Golden Touch (cf. Hyginus, *Fabulae* 191) and Philemon and Baucis (cf. Persius IV, 21-22), is known chiefly from Ovid, who evidently had special interest in or access to Anatolian legends; cf. L. Malten, "Motivgeschichtliche Untersuchungen zur Sagenforschung, I. Philemon und Baukis," *Hermes* 74 (1939) 205. Vergil and Pliny also knew of Arachne, *Georgics* IV, 246-247 (*invisa Minervae . . . aranea*), Historia Naturalis VII, 56, 196 (Arachne's son Closter). For representations of Arachne, see G. D. Weinberg and S. S. Weinberg, "Arachne of Lydia at Corinth," *The Aegean and the Near East, Studies Presented to Hetty Goldman on the Occasion of her Seventy-Fifth Birthday* (Locust Valley, N.Y., 1956) 262-267; J. G. Szilagyi, "Une Fausse Gemme de Pyrgotélès," *Bulletin du Musée Hongrois des Beaux-Arts (Szépmuveszeti Museum)* 24 (1964) 97-100.

[18]Philostratus, *Imagines* I, 30, 22-25 (translation by A. Fairbanks, Loeb ed.).

ported by an Early Byzantine native of Lydia, Johannes Laurentius, who cited as authority the reference of a much earlier writer to "Lydian gold chitons" (Λυδοὶ χρυσοχίτωνες).[19] The defined part of the compound adjective *chrysostemonai* shows that the gold of these chitons took the form of thread,[20] and the names suggest the show and richness of cloth-of-gold (although the proportion of gold in the total fabric is not specified). The gold woven *Attalica* or *Attalicae vestes* of later antiquity (named for a territorial legatee of the Lydian kings) probably attest the survival or revival of Lydian gold-weaving tradition.[21]

Johannes Lydus also is the source for another Lydian garment, the σάνδυξ. "Sandykes were chitons devised by the Lydians, which were made of linen and very transparent, but dyed in the juice of the plant *sandyx,* whose color is flesh-like. With these to cover their naked bodies Lydian women seemed to wear nothing but air and attracted observers by a loveliness impure

and unchaste. With such a chiton Omphale enveloped Herakles when she shamefully 'effeminized' her lover."[22]

An inventory of garments dedicated at the Heraion on Samos (recorded in an inscription of the fourth century B.C.) lists several Lydian chitons with ἔξαστες, selvages or fringes, specified as either white, "hyacinthine," ἀλουργοῦς or of ἰσάτις.[23] That these garments were genuine products of Lydia,[24] not merely representatives of a type initiated or popularized by the Lydians,[25] is suggested by the quantities of Near Eastern and Anatolian manufactured goods which were dedicated at the Heraion and have been recovered there in excavation.[26] The precise color values of

---

[19]Johannes Laurentius Lydus, *De Magistratibus Populi Romani* III, 64. Johannes' source, Peisander, might have been the poet of Kameiros in Rhodes who flourished in the seventh or sixth century B.C. or the poet of Laranda in Lycaonia who flourished in the third century A.D.; R. Keydell, *RE* 19, 1 (1937) 144-146.

Chiton, conventionally translated "tunic" or "smock," probably designated a general kind of garment. The word, originally Semitic, was used in the Greek world already in the second millennium B.C. (attested in Linear B): M. Ventris, J. Chadwick, *Documents in Mycenaean Greek,* 2nd ed. (Cambridge 1973) 319-320, 554-555; T. J. Dunbabin, *The Greeks and their Eastern Neighbours* (London 1957) 58.

[20]Not as foil appliques, an alternative possibility if the form of gold in textile decoration is unspecified, e.g., cf. the *thorakes* sent by Amasis to the Lacedaemonians and to Lindos in Rhodes, Herodotus III, 47; C. Blinkenberg, *Inscriptions* (Lindos, Fouilles de l'Acropole 1902-1904 II; Berlin 1941) 174-175 no. XXIX (Lindian Temple Chronicle). Cf. A. L. Oppenheim, "The Golden Garments of the Gods," *JNES* 8 (1949) 172-193.

[21]Pliny, *Historia Naturalis* VIII, 74, 196, *aurum intextere in eadem Asia invenit Attalus rex* (Attalus II according to Servius, *Commentarii ad Aeneidem* I, 697). For use of the name, Cicero, *In Verrem* IV, 12, 27; Propertius II, 13, 22; II, 32, 12; III, 18, 19; IV, 5, 24; Silius Italicus XIV, 659. For a Lydian origin of Pergamon's gold-woven textiles, M. Rostovtzeff, "Notes on the Economic Policy of the Pergamene Kings," *Anatolian Studies Presented to Sir William Mitchell Ramsay* (Manchester 1923) 380-381; for possible representation on the Great Frieze of the Altar of Zeus, E. V. Hansen, *The Attalids of Pergamon,* 2nd ed. (Cornell University Studies in Classical Philology 36; Ithaca 1971) 333-334.

[22]Johannes Lydus (*supra* n. 19). For the plant *sandyx,* Hesychius, s.v. J. Bostock, H. T. Riley, *The Natural History of Pliny* (London 1858) 240 n. 6, have suggested identification with madder, *Rubia tinctorum* L., which would have been available to the Lydians; for the plant (ἐρυθρόδανον) in Dioscurides, *De Materia Medica* III, 143 (ed. Wellmann), E. Bonnet, "Essai d'identification des plantes médicinales mentionnées par Dioscoride, d'après les peintures d'un manuscrit de la Bibliothèque Nationale de Paris (Ms Grec No. 2179)," *Janus* 8 (1903) 229; K. J. Basmadjian, "L'identification des noms des plantes du Codex Constantinopolitanus de Dioscoride," *Journal Asiatique* 230 (1938) 592; H. Gerstinger, *Dioscurides; Codex Vindobonensis Med. Gr. 1 der österreichischen Nationalbibliothek* (Kommentarband zu der Faksimileausgabe; Graz 1970) 15. H. G. Liddell, R. Scott, H. S. Jones, *A Greek-English Lexicon,* 9th ed. (Oxford 1953) have suggested red sandalwood, *Pterocarpus santalinus* (now native to Southeast Asia; less likely to have been available to the Lydians?).

[23]H. Collitz, F. Bechtel, *Sammlung der griechischen Dialekt-Inschriften* III, 2 (Göttingen 1905) 733-734, no. 5702; D. Ohly, "Die Göttin und ihre Basis," *AthMitt* 68 (1953) 46-49.

[24]The fine quality of Lydian fabrics and the use of Sardian carpets in Persia, which are alleged in other sources, would suggest that exportation of Lydian textiles is not inherently implausible; cf. also the reputation of the Lydian μάσλης and μίτρα, Sappho, fr. 20² (ed. Edmonds), Alcman, fr. 1, 67-68 (ed. Edmonds), Pindar, *Nemean* VIII, 15.

[25]Cf. the "Phrygionae" and "Attalices" of Pliny VIII, 74, 196; Pollux, *Onomasticum* VII, 77.

[26]U. Jantzen, *Ägyptische und Orientalische Bronzen aus dem Heraion von Samos* (Samos VIII; Bonn 1972); E. Diehl, "Fragmente aus Samos II," *AA* (1965) 823-850; H. Walter, "Orientalische Kultgeräte," *AthMitt* 74 (1959) 69-74; B. Freyer-Schauenburg, *Elfenbeine aus dem samischen Heraion; Figürliches, Gefässe und Siegel* (Universität Hamburg, Abhandlungen aus dem Gebiet der Auslandkunde 70 B, 40; Hamburg 1966) 51-116. Jantzen, 53, for the hypothesis that the Phrygian belts and fibulae recovered from the Heraion are the surviving components of Phrygian garments dedicated in the

the *exastes* are hard to identify, as is so often the case with Greek terms designating colors in the blue-red range.[27] *Isatis* evidently signifies a dye made from the plant of that name, probably the most famous species, *Isatis tinctoria,* woad (which grows in Lydia today and whose form matches the graphic illustrations of *isatis* in early manuscripts of Dioscurides' *De Materia Medica*[28]). "Hyacinthine" likewise must refer to the plant hyacinth, whose botanical identity has troubled modern scholarship.[29] *Halourgous,* literally the color of the wine-dark sea, was likened in antiquity to the purple of murex dye, a ripening grape, and the interval between red and blue in a rainbow.[30]

Bloody red, if Aristophanes' metaphor is to be trusted,[31] was the color of the Lydians' most famous textile dye, proverbial in the fifth century B.C., φοῖνιξ Σαρδιανικός or βάμμα Σαρδιανικόν, whose only attested application is to coverlets for ivory-footed dining couches, the epitomy of luxurious dining accommodation according to Aristophanes'

contemporary, Plato the comic poet.[32] The reputation of Sardian red and Lydian dyes persisted in Roman times (when the Lydians of Sardis were credited with the discovery of wool-dyeing),[33] perhaps chiefly maintained at Thyateira, the home of prominent dyers' and wool-dealers' guilds and of the lady purple-seller (πορφυρόπωλις) baptised by St. Paul.[34]

The glamorous image of Lydian textiles which written testimonia evoke has yet to receive appropriate archaeological complement.

The only direct evidence for gold-woven fabrics in Lydia is a small assemblage of loose gold threads which were retrieved from the bottom of a Roman sarcophagus (of "garland" type) unearthed in 1972 at the site of Philadelphia (modern Alaşehir).[35] The context indicates that these, while possibly the remnants of a genuine *Attalicum,* probably are too recent to have formed a gold chiton of the age of Croesus. All threads are flat strips, ca. 2-3 mm. wide, of thin gold sheet (*aurum battutum*); although considerably twisted and bent they do not appear to have been wrapped around a core or to have been backed with another medium (fig. 4).[36]

sanctuary; cf. J. Boardman, "Ionian Bronze Belts," *Anatolia* 6 (1961-1962) 189.

That the dedicant of one of the Lydian chitons had a Greek name (Diogenes) need not, of course, affect the question of the chitons' origin.

[27]R. J. Forbes, *Studies in Ancient Technology* IV (Leiden 1956) 119.

[28]For *isatis* and identification with *Isatis tinctoria* L., Dioscurides, *De Materia Medica* II, 184 (ed. Wellmann); Bonnet (*supra* n. 21) 177; Gerstinger (*supra* n. 21) 27; naturalistic rendering of flowering *isatis* in the Pierpont Morgan Library, New York, Dioscurides Ms. no. 652.

The Arabic name added to the illustration of *isatis* in the Vienna Juliana Anicia codex (160 v) suggested identification as *Isatis sativa* to Basmadjian (*supra* n. 21) 594.

Isatis tinctoria grows today in the region of ancient Lydia; P. H. Davis, ed., *Flora of Turkey* I (Edinburgh 1965) 301-302 (middle regions of Mt. Sipylus above Manisa [Magnesia ad Sipylum]).

[29]Cf. Pliny, *Historia Naturalis* XXI, 97, 170. For proposed identifications of ancient hyacinth.

Stadler, "Ὑάκινος," *RE* 9, 1 (1914) 4-7; Bostock, Riley (*supra* n. 22) 337 n. 47; Bonnet (*supra* n. 22) 232.

[30]Aristotle, *De Coloribus* II, 792B; IV, 794A; Plutarch, *Moralia* 894D (*De Placitis Philosophorum* 3, 5). For the colors of murex dye, J. T. Baker, "Tyrian Purple: an Ancient Dye, a Modern Problem," *Endeavour* 33 (1974) 11-17.

[31]Aristophanes, *Acharnenses* 112; *Pax* 1174 and scholium.

[32]Plato Comicus fr. 208 (ed. Kock) ap. Athenaeus II, 48A-B. Cf. Horace, *Satirae* II, 6, 102-103; Catullus LXIV, 48-49.

[33]Aelian, *De Natura Animalium* IV, 46; Clemens Alexandrinus, *Paedogogus* II, 10, 108; Pliny *Historia Naturalis* VII, 56, 196 (*inficere lanas Sardibus Lydi*); Hyginus, *Fabulae* 274, 17 (ed. Rose).

[34]G. Lafaye, *Inscriptiones Graecae ad Res Romanas Pertinentes* IV (Paris 1927) nos. 1213, 1239, 1242, 1250, 1265 (dyers); 1252 (wool-dealers); *Novum Testamentum*, Acts 16, 14, for which cf. F. J. F. Jackson, K. Lake, *The Beginnings of Christianity, Part I: The Acts of the Apostles* IV (London 1933) 191.

[35]The sarcophagus was excavated by the then Director of the Museum in Manisa, K. Z. Polatkan, and, like the gold threads, is now part of the Museum collection (the sarcophagus situated just outside the west entrance of the former *medresse* building which houses the Museum's ethnographic collection).

[36]Cf. Pliny, *Historia Naturalis* XXXIII, 19, 62, *superque netur ac texitur lanae modo vel sine lana.* For techniques of making gold thread, M. Braun-Ronsdorf, "Gold and Silver Fabrics from Mediaeval to Modern Times," *Ciba Review* (1961:3) 2-16; H. W. Wulff, *The Traditional Crafts of Persia* (Cambridge, Mass., 1966) 175-177.

For a suggestion by the writer that dilute-glaze "marbling" on an anthropomorphic ceramic vase of the sixth century B.C. may have been intended to represent cloth-of-gold, "An Exhibitionist from Sardis," *Studies*

The only direct evidence for textile technique in Lydia before the Hellenistic period comes from a small tumulus burial at Bin Tepe, the cemetery patronized by Lydian royalty, situated some five miles distant from Sardis, on the north side of the Hermus valley and near the shores of the Gygaean Lake.

(C. H. G., Jr.)

This tumulus, BT 63.2, situated ca. 300 m. southeast of the large Karnıyarık Tepe, BT 63.1, had been the subject of resistivity tests made by D. Greenewalt, who detected an anomaly and suggested the location of the burial; it was excavated by J. G. Pedley and G. M. A. Hanfmann in August 1963.[37] A hollow space on the top of the mound indicated that the grave had been robbed in antiquity. A trench soon revealed that the grave robbers had gained entrance to the tomb by breaking off an edge of a ceiling block and that they apparently removed all objects of value. However, the robbers left fragments of pottery, the remains of a wooden coffin, and some fragments of iron plates which are of particular interest for this paper. The pottery fragments found on the floor were a streaked skyphos and two squat lekythoi which could date the tomb anywhere from the seventh to the beginning of the fifth century B.C.[38]

The tomb was oriented east-west and measures 2.87 m. in length, 1.35 m. in width, and 1.36 m. in height. On the floor was found the remains of a wooden coffin in four major pieces of Mediterranean cypress: a side board, an end board, an upper side fragment, and a corner join or leg.[39] The long side measures 0.92 m. in length, 0.24 m. in height, 0.018 m. in thickness; the end board 0.76 m. in length, 0.30 m. in height, 0.018 m. in thickness; a small board with a rounded "moulding" which could be the top part of the side measures 0.36 m. in length, 0.24 m. in height, 0.18 m. in thickness on the flat part, 0.021 m. in thickness for the rounded "moulding"; and the leg section measures 0.42 m. in length, 0.09 m. in width, and 0.08 m. in thickness. The tomb plan (fig. 6) indicates the location of the find spots of the wooden pieces as well as holes cut into the floor for the legs of the coffin. Although all wooden fragments are badly deteriorated, the leg has evidence for joining with rather sophisticated carpentry and the side boards were joined to each other with flat dowels approximately 0.10 m. by 0.035 m. by 0.004 m. (fig. 7). The wooden fragments suggest a coffin of some elegance, perhaps similar to that from south Russia near Anapa and now in the Hermitage in Leningrad.[40]

Some twenty-odd pieces of iron plates and nails and other fragments were found almost entirely corroded into yellow, red, and black iron minerals. These proved to be the most interesting finds in the tomb in that one side of the iron plates was partially covered with iron salts that had replaced textile attachments or wrappings, creating a nearly exact replica of the textile structure and making it possible to study the twist of thread and the weave and even to suggest the fiber.

Our knowledge of many ancient textiles depends on transformations of mineral deposits on metal objects where textile fibers in contact with metal surfaces have been replaced by metal salts during burial in the soil. Very few ancient textiles survive unless burial conditions are conducive to preservation of organic materials as in the arid conditions of Egypt or the deep-freeze at-

---

Presented to George M. A. Hanfmann (Fogg Art Museum, Harvard University, Monographs in Art and Archaeology 2; Cambridge, Mass., 1971) 41.

For remains of ancient gold and silver thread and weaving, Greenewalt, *ibid.* n. 34 (examples of the fourth and third centuries B.C. from South Russia and the Mausoleum at Halikarnassos); Beckwith (*supra* n. 6); W. Helbig, *Führer durch die öffentlichen Sammlungen klassischer Altertümer in Rom* (H. Speier, ed.) I (Tübingen 1963) 605 no. 825 (cloth-of-gold garment on Late Antique doll); *The Hamilton Collection, A Bicentenary Exhibit* (London 1972) no. 88 (British Museum Gem 4028; cloth-of-gold contained in a rock-crystal vase dated to the second century A.D.).

[37] For a preliminary report on this burial, G. M. A. Hanfmann, "The Sixth Campaign at Sardis (1963)," *BASOR* 174 (1964) 55, 57, fig. 35.

[38] *Ibid.*

[39] The wood was identified by R. C. Koeppen of the Forest Products Laboratory, Madison, Wisconsin as *Cupressus sempervirens*; the tree still grows today in western Asia Minor: Davis (*supra* n. 28) 76-78, map 11 on p. 77. A sample of the wood was given a C-14 date by Isotopes, Inc., 123 Woodland Avenue, Westwood, New Jersey, as 1100±250 years, giving a minimum date of 850 B.C. Of course the wood could be older than the date of construction of the coffin.

[40] D. C. Kurtz, J. Boardman, *Greek Burial Customs* (Aspects of Greek and Roman Life; London 1971) 255, pl. 71.

mosphere of the Pazyryk of Siberia.[41] The author has observed other examples of such impressions in mineral deposits on a silver vessel in the shape of an anthropomorphic bull from the ancient Near East, dated about 3000 B.C., now in the Metropolitan Museum of Art in New York, and on a foundation figure from an excavation in Iraq of the third millennium B.C. On both of these objects there remained impressions of textiles in a simple tabby weave and apparently of woolen or hair fibers.[42]

Our iron objects from BT 63.2 were apparently used in the construction of the coffin, probably as ornaments on the upper corners as well as for strengthening the carpentry. There is no evidence that nails were used in the side boards; only doweling and mortice-and-tenon joining seem to have been employed. The long nails could only have been used in the corners where the wood was ca. 0.08 to 0.09 m. thick, although there are no nail holes in the fragment of "leg" that is preserved. Of the twenty-odd pieces of iron, the two large pieces are of particular interest as they reveal in their mineral incrustations evidence of their application over wood on one side and considerable information about Lydian textile techniques on the other.

The large pieces are designated as *Plaque A* (L. 0.092 m.; W. 0.080 m.; Th. 0.004 m.) and *Plaque B* (L. 0.090 m.; W. 0.080 m.; Th. 0.004 m.). Both pieces are finished on three sides and broken on the fourth, and they were probably joined at approximately a right angle, although they do not fit securely together at this time. Each plaque has the remains of two nailheads located about 0.020 m. in from the corners (fig. 10). At 0.050 m. in from the edge opposite the broken edge are what appear to be two additional nailheads with the remains of four superimposed layers of textile; however, when the backs of the plaques are examined it is clear that only two nails were used for attaching the pieces of iron to the coffin. The reinforcement angle irons were apparently decorated in part with textiles that were folded and arranged in layers and perhaps embroidered in bright colors.

On Plaque A there is a short section of selvage (fig. 8) which indicates that the weave is a weft-faced plain weave for the most part with nine to twelve warp threads per centimeter and twenty-eight to forty-two weft per centimeter. The threads are loosely spun in the S direction and the individual fibers have a slightly "fuzzy" appearance that suggests that the material is a hair fiber, perhaps wool or mohair. Nearly all threads are single ply, but there are a few that are S spun with two threads Z plied. It is suggested that the two plaques joined to make a corner decoration and reinforcement for an upper corner of the coffin and that the iron was covered at least in part with fine textiles perhaps in combination with other materials such as precious metals, somewhat like the textile belts from Pazyryk.[43]

The back of each plaque presents a textured surface indicating that the iron was applied over other materials in addition to wood. Along the outer edge of the back of each plaque is a series of fine raised lines in groups of three; there are eight such groupings spaced about 0.004 m. apart (fig. 10). These suggest that there was a material between the iron and the wood that could be worked in thin sheets in fine detail, perhaps a precious metal in repoussé, although no such material was recovered from the tomb. If it were a precious metal band around the top of the coffin, it would have been taken by the grave robbers in antiquity. In the central part of the back of each plaque is a heavily corroded area about 0.030 m. wide where a second type of material inlaid into the wood was overlaid by the iron—perhaps leather or an inlay of some other type of material in an ornament extending down the leg as on the Anapa coffin.[44] The backs of the iron plaques and some of the other iron pieces also have bits of wood from the part of the coffin to which they were attached (fig. 10).

The individual fragments of textile in iron salts indicate weaving of fine fabrics with rather

[41]M. Griaznov, A. Boulgakov, *L'Art ancien de l'Altai* (Leningrad 1958).

[42]D. P. Hansen, "A Proto-Elamite Silver Figurine in the Metropolitan Museum of Art," and K. C. Lefferts, "Technical Examination," *Metropolitan Museum of Art Journal* 3 (1970) 5ff.

[43]Griaznov, Boulgakov (*supra* n. 41). For remains of a painted funeral coverlet from a wooden sarcophagus in a tumulus in South Russia, D. Gerziger, "Eine Decke aus dem sechsten Grab der «Sieben Brüder,»" *AntK* 18 (1975) 51-55.

[44]Kurtz, Boardman (*supra* n. 40).

widely spaced warp threads. There is evidence of embroidery on Plaque A near the larger "rosette" of four layers of textile. In this same area there are threads indicating sewing of parts together. In the four-layered structure the warp threads are nine to ten per centimeter and the weft threads about forty per centimeter in all layers. The section with selvage on Plaque A is laid almost at a 45° angle, indicating that the application of the direction of the weave and the manner of folding the textile over the iron were important. The section with selvage has ten warp threads per centimeter and ten weft.

A few warp threads are exposed on both plaques where weft has been worn away or broken off. The warp threads are about half the thickness of the weft in those places and are of a tighter spin, but appear to be of the same type of fiber as the weft, *viz.,* perhaps wool or mohair.

In both plaques the textiles seem to have been worked over the edge of part of the iron plate and in Plaque B there are the remains of a fringe attached to the largest piece of textile imprint on that plaque. The fringe appears to be the ends of warp threads, woven into a selvage and perhaps tied with knots. Also in Plaque B alongside the fringe is a small section that could be called pattern weaving where warp and weft threads are about equal in size and about twenty threads per centimeter in both directions. The fragment is too small to determine a pattern, but some threads float over as many as seven and the weave is quite complicated (figs. 9, 10). In this section there are three threads that are two-thread Z plied and S spun which could also be part of a fringe. In a corner of the broken edge of B (fig. 10) is an area of stitching and possible embroidery.

The magnificence of Lydian textiles reported in Greek literature cannot be found in these humble fragments of iron salts, but it is surprising how much information can be gained regarding technique if not aesthetic significance.

(L. J. M.)

Figure 1. Pazyryk carpet: star-rosette motif. From S. I. Rudenko, *Dr'evn'ejshie v mira Khudozhestvennye Kovry i Tkani* (Moscow 1968) 45, fig. 33.

Figure 2. Threshold block from Palace of Assurbanipal, Nineveh. From A. H. Layard, *A Second Series of the Monuments of Nineveh* (London 1853) pl. 56.

Figure 3. Revetment tile from Sardis. H. 0.186 m. From T. L. Shear, *Terra-Cottas, Part One, Architectural Terra-Cottas* (Sardis X; Cambridge 1926) fig. 20.

Figure 4. Gold thread retrieved from sarcophagus excavated at Philadelphia (Alaşehir), with millimeter scale

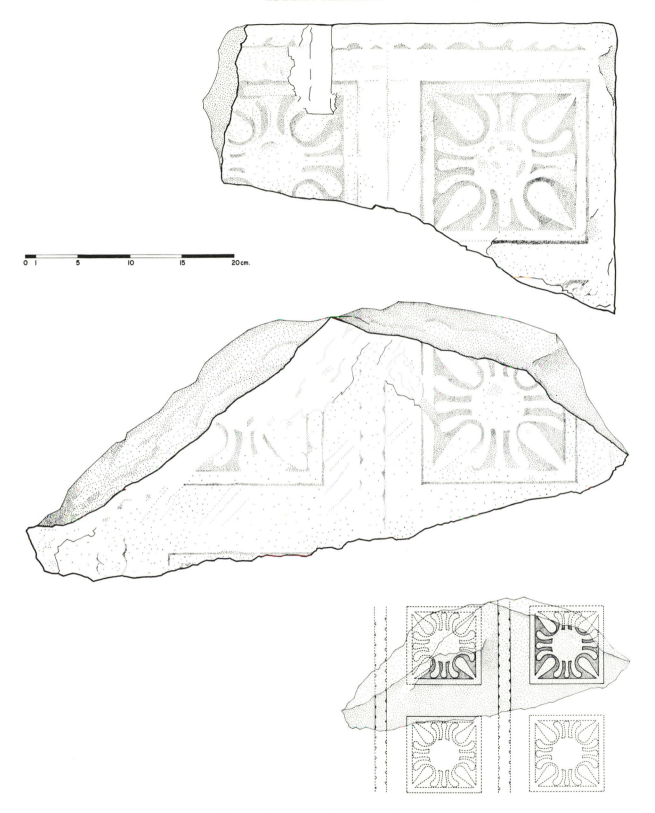

Figure 5. Carved marble blocks from Sardis; *lower right*, restoration of pattern on larger piece. Drawn by Elizabeth Wahle.

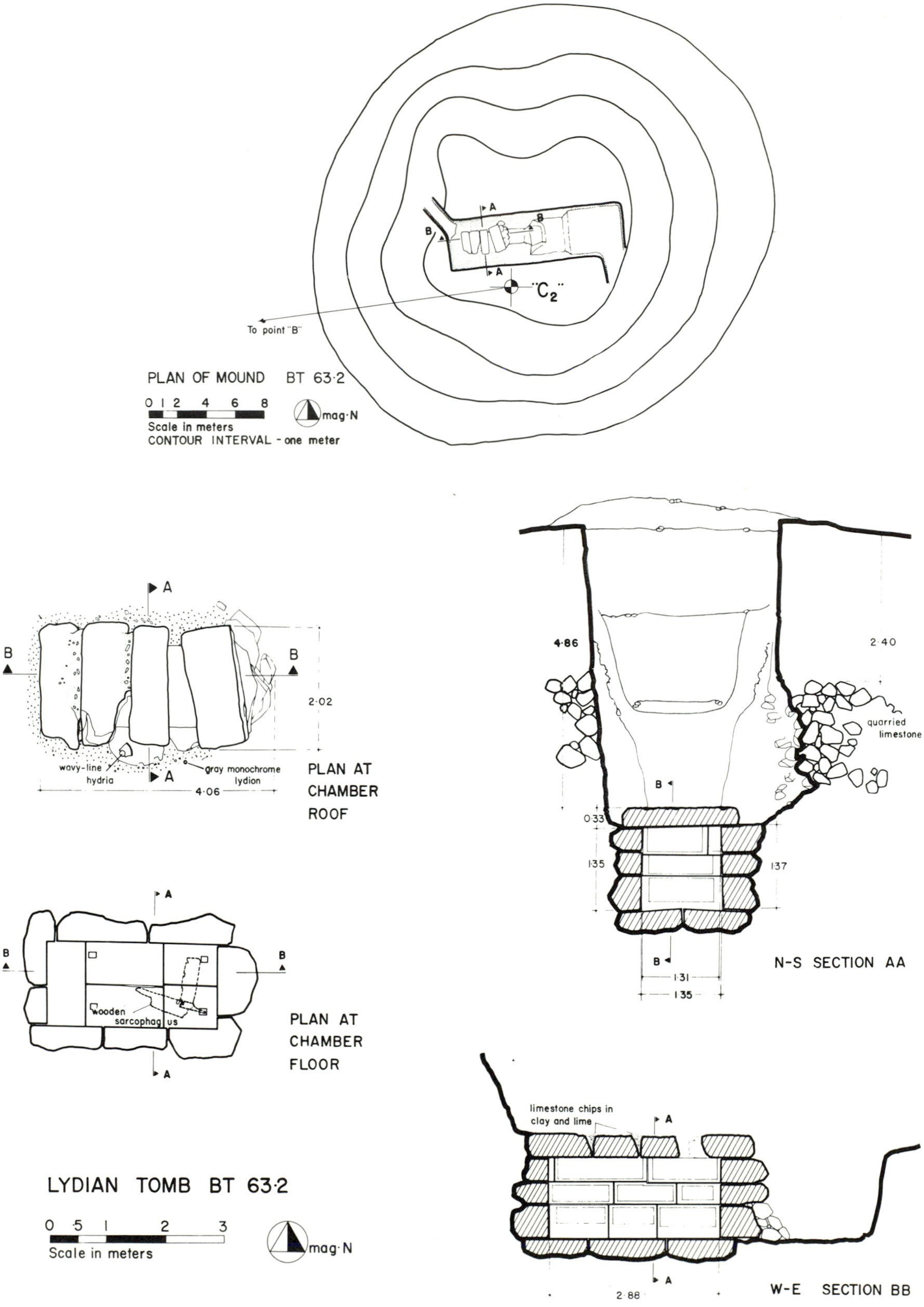

Figure 6. Plans and sections of tumulus grave at Bin Tepe near Sardis (BT 63.2)

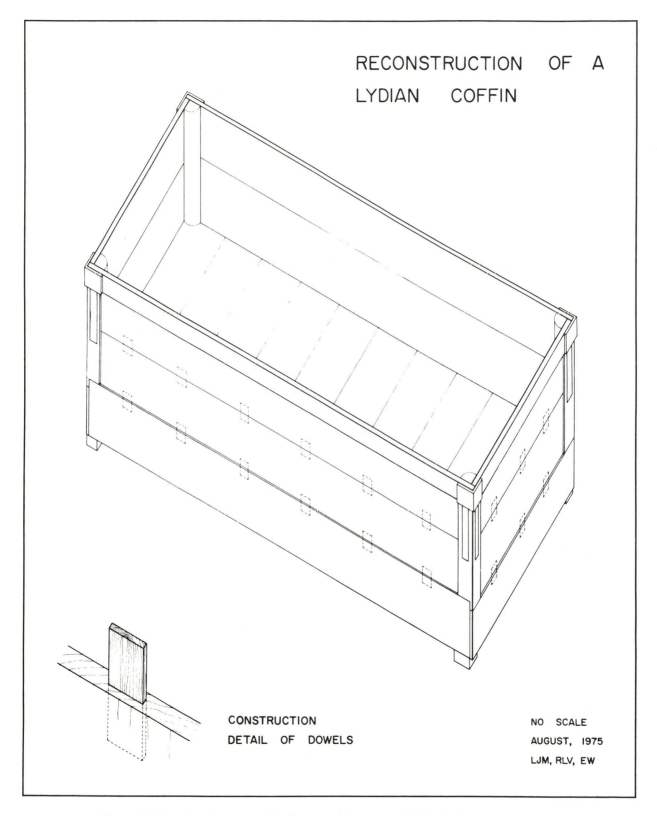

RECONSTRUCTION OF A
LYDIAN COFFIN

CONSTRUCTION
DETAIL OF DOWELS

NO SCALE
AUGUST, 1975
LJM, RLV, EW

Figure 7. Wooden chest from Bin Tepe tumulus grave (BT 63.2). Reconstruction by
Lawrence J. Majewski.

Figure 8. Detail of Plaque A, showing edge of textile form which appears to preserve a selvage

Figure 9. Detail of Plaque B, showing textile form which appears to preserve pattern weave

PLAQUE A

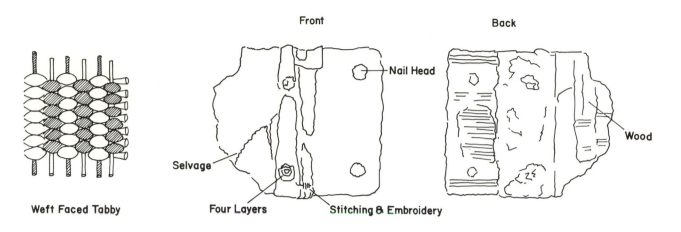

Front   Back

Nail Head

Wood

Selvage

Weft Faced Tabby

Four Layers

Stitching & Embroidery

PLAQUE B

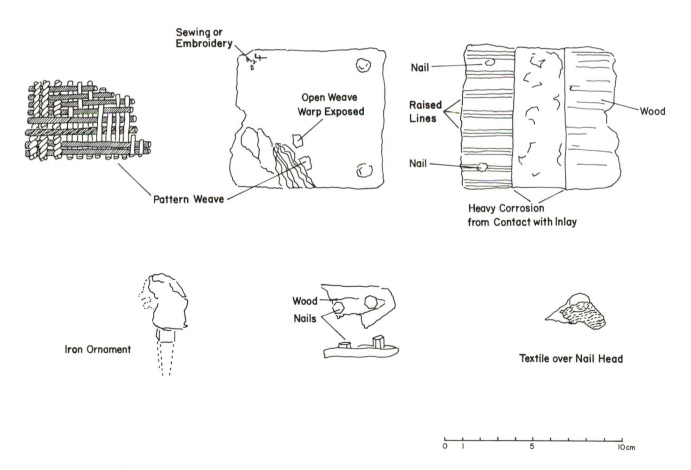

Sewing or Embroidery

Nail

Open Weave Warp Exposed

Raised Lines

Wood

Nail

Pattern Weave

Heavy Corrosion from Contact with Inlay

Iron Ornament

Wood

Nails

Textile over Nail Head

0   1   5   10cm

Figure 10. Iron plaques preserving textile forms. Drawn by Lawrence J. Majewski.

X. THE QUESTION OF BALCONIES AT HASANLU

Robert H. Dyson, Jr.

One of the important buildings excavated by Rodney Young at Gordion was Megaron 3 (fig. 1). The Gordion guidebook prepared by Dr. Young gives a succinct description of the plan:

> This was divided by two rows of four posts into a central nave with aisles at either side. The posts—three in each row in the inner room, one in the anteroom—were bedded on cross timbers set below floor level; at floor level and resting on these, lengthwise timbers were socketed to receive a tenon at the bottom of each post. Two of these sockets were found in good preservation and were able to suggest the measurements of the posts—about 40 by 40 centimeters. A series of holes left by smaller posts in front of the faces of the side and back walls suggested a wooden gallery running around three sides of the megaron room, probably at about half its height.[1]

The posts along the central lines were spaced at about 3 m. while those along the side walls were 2.5 m. apart. The central rows of posts were 3.5 m. out from the side walls. The spans involved thus are those easily crossed by ordinary building beams such as those used in modern village houses, which have a normal span of about 3 m. The suggested reconstruction of the evidence (fig. 2) shows the main hall and balcony with the central columns rising to the gabled roof. The spacing of the aisles and central nave were such that the side aisles (each 3.5 m. wide)

were about half as wide as the nave itself (which measured 7 m.). The pattern was thus of a broad central open area flanked by narrow areas on both sides with the whole balcony forming a free-standing inner shell within the outer shell of the building.

It is not surprising, therefore, that when the plans of the columned halls at Hasanlu appeared (fig. 3), with buildings dating to the centuries just preceding the one in which Megaron 3 was built, the speculative suggestion was made by some observers that the Hasanlu buildings too might in fact have contained balconies. Now that several such buildings are available for examination it is useful to examine their structural characteristics in order to see this question more clearly.

In the southwest quadrant of the Citadel the building which closes the Lower Court on the eastern side in period IV faces north. This building, BB V, was constructed by the standard technique of erecting freestanding uncut stone foundations a meter in height, topping them with walls of square mud brick, and then covering the surfaces with mud plaster. The basic plan of BB V is common to all columned-hall buildings at Hasanlu and apparently originates from simpler structures of the late second millennium at the site.[2] It consists of entry hall, stairway,

---

[1] R. S. Young, *Gordion: A Guide to the Excavations and Museum,* 1st ed. (Ankara 1968) 25-26. For a more detailed presentation, see R. S. Young, "Gordion: Phrygian Construction and Architecture II," *Expedition* 4, 4 (1962) 9-10.

[2] R. H. Dyson, Jr., "Further Excavations at Tepe Hasanlu, Iran," *Archaeology* 26 (1973) 303-304. R. H. Dyson, Jr., "Architecture of the Iron I Period at Hasanlu in Western Iran and its Implications for Theories of Migration on the Iranian Plateau," *Le plateau iranien et l'Asie centrale des origines à la conquête islamique* (Colloques internationaux de la recherche scientifique 567; Paris 1977) 155-169.

main hall with columns,[3] and storerooms. Building V has one extraordinary feature in its original form—a section of the east wall with four pairs of small wooden columns opening eastward onto an area subsequently built over by an adjacent building. This opening was filled in with a secondary brick wall, leaving only a narrow door when the building was rebuilt after an early fire. The columned hall measured approximately 13 by 15 m. inside and was entered by a small door off center at the north end. Around the walls ran a plastered bench with a platform at the rear and a higher section fronted by a pavement in the northwest corner of the room. In the center stood a meter-high hearth with a square column of clay on its southwest corner. The whole hearth structure (including the column) had been burned and replastered over a hundred times. An area of floor paved with mud brick suggests that the hearth in some way may have been centered on the opening in the east wall as well as being placed on the central axis of the room. Four rows of columns occupy the hall with four columns in each of the central rows but only two on the east side and three on the west. The northern column of the two on the east was clearly set in place following the closing of the wall opening which it helps to block, raising the question whether in fact the other column might also be a later addition. Since the building was rebuilt after an earlier fire, it is possible that the columns on the west side are also secondary additions, but this point requires further field study. No columns were set in the corners of the rooms. The columns in the two central rows are spaced 3.5, 4.5, and 5.5 m. apart from north to south. The side columns do not align with the central columns from east to west. The eastern aisle measures 4 m., the western 3.5 m., and the central nave 5 m. In other words, there is no significant difference in proportion between the nave and the side aisles comparable with that found in Megaron 3 at Gordion. Furthermore, the distances to be spanned at the sides—3.5 to 4 m.— are already longer than the normal span for pop-

lar wood beams such as would be used for balconies in present-day houses—that is, about 3 m.— much larger and very heavy timbers being needed for greater spans. Another difficulty in visualizing the reconstructed structure lies in the fact that the side columns are not aligned with the central columns. This means that crosspieces from the side columns would land at the weakest point on the beam lying between two central columns—a system hardly recommending itself for structural stability. No burned beams were found to indicate the presence of such crosspieces although parts of the columns themselves were evidenced as masses of charcoal. Thus we may conclude that at a very minimum beams no doubt ran longitudinally along the rows of columns, but we cannot indicate the nature of the cross connections. It is evident, however, that in a manner similar to the Gordion building, the columns taken together provide a support structure of some sort set up so that the weight of the superstructure rests not directly on the walls but on the columns themselves to a large extent.

Building IV East was built just to the north of BB V but faced west rather than north. This building also went through an early fire and was reconstructed with changes. The structure is not fully excavated, but its general plan can be predicted fairly easily. It follows the basic plan with entry hall, stairway, main hall, and storeroom. It too has a unique feature—a wide internal doorway with three pairs of wooden columns leading from the entry hall to the main hall, in the center of which lay a paved area and hearth. This wide doorway was subsequently blocked up, leaving only a narrow entrance. The main hall is nearly equal in size to that of BB V with a calculated measurement of 12 by about 16 m. While side benches are present, the raised bench with stone pavement at the front of the hall is missing. The layout of the four rows of columns in this room is unique in that they formed aligned rows from side to side as well as from front to back. In no other excavated structure of this period at Hasanlu is this the case. The central nave measures about 4.5 m. across, while the side aisles measure 3.5 m. Thus again there is no significant difference in the proportion of the nave to the side aisles on a scale comparable with the Gordion megaron. In this hall we see for the first time

---

[3]The word "column" is used at Hasanlu to designate vertical round wooden structural elements 30 or more centimeters in diameter. Those with smaller diameters or square elements are referred to as "posts."

columns set in corners of the room (at least in the front corners, the rear wall remaining at present unexcavated). The columns are spaced 5.5 m. apart from front to back, indicating that the longitudinal beams resting upon them must have been of very heavy proportions. This plan of columns was that used in the reconstruction of the building. The two columns marking the western end of the two central rows have clearly been set in place following the blocking of the doorway which they in part mask. The initial floor plan may therefore have been somewhat different, but cannot be reconstructed at this time.

The largest structure excavated so far in period IV is BB II which stood to the west of BB V and, like it, faced north. Its original plan also consisted of entry hall, stairway, main hall, and storerooms. The central hearth is here raised as a rectangular mud-brick platform but without the multiple plasterings seen in BB V. Special sections of high bench fronted by stone paving flanked the main door on the north end of the main hall, while lower benches ran along the walls to the central platform at the back. The unique feature of the hall, apart from its large size (18 by 23.5 m.), is the cella-like room at the back with stepped-in doorway frame—both features which raise the question of a possible religious function for the structure as a whole. The superstructure of the hall was supported on four rows of columns with six columns in each central row and five in each side row. The side columns are not aligned with the central columns. These latter were 50 cm. in diameter, while those on the side were only 30 (as is the case in BB V where the diameters were also preserved in the burned mud plaster around the bases). The arrangement of the side columns (as in BB V) places any crosspieces from the side columns to the central rows at the weakest point of the longitudinal beams between the central columns. The central nave is here approximately 7 m. wide, while the side aisles measure 5 m. (measuring from approximate centers of columns from row to row). The columns in the two central rows are set 3.5, 4, 4.5, and 5 m. apart from front to back. The side columns are set 4.5 to 5.5 m. apart with the left rear column being 6.5 and the right rear corner column 7.5 m. back from the nearest side column. This extra distance

spans the side doorways at the back of the hall and would seem to indicate that these columns could have functioned as part of the support structure for a beam running along the back wall rather than as part of the side-line beam system. In any event, once again the distances to be spanned indicate the use of very heavy structural timbers and not the sort of lighter construction one would expect for side balconies. Nor does the proportion of side aisle to nave suggest such an arrangement.

From the evidence of these buildings we are able to see that there is considerable variation in the important structural details of the arrangement of the halls. At the same time there are also certain general principles being followed in the construction methods. Among these is the construction of a network of large wooden columns within a main hall set both against the side walls and in the open space of the room as in the case of the Gordion megaron. In both types of column emplacements the function would appear to be to relieve the side walls of the weight of some kind of superstructure. The scale of the columns themselves and the fact that they are aligned from front to back but not as a rule from side to side suggest that the next primary element in the structure would have been four longitudinal rows of wooden beams (probably but not necessarily of the poplar wood that has been identified as having composed the columns). The long spans to be crossed further suggest that these beams were massive in size and very heavy. Such an amount of wood and such weight may well help to explain the intensity of the heat which burned sections of the walls which were 1.20 m. thick bright red throughout when the site was sacked around 800 B.C. It would also help to account for the suddenness of the collapse of the rooms where whole walls were dragged down laterally. These factors plus the total lack of any broad nave proportional to the side aisles on the Gordion model suggest strongly that we are not dealing with balconies at Hasanlu.

What then are we dealing with? We know that there were second-floor rooms over the entry halls and storerooms. We know in the case of the central hall of BB II that the side wall rose at least 7 m. in height from the fallen and standing brickwork. The conclusion would seem inevitable that we are dealing with a heavy roof structure rising high above the floor of the room. Although admittedly the relief representation of the temple at Musasir,[4] located somewhere west of the Hasanlu area in the mountains and slightly later in date, provides a possible model for a gabled roof (fig. 4), it seems more probable given other cultural connections that in fact we have in hand one of the prototypes for the type of roof structures reconstructed for similar halls at Godin Tepe,[5] Pasargadae,[6] and Persepolis (fig. 5).[7] In these reconstructions massive timbers ran in one direction along tall columns while lighter materials lay at right angles forming the actual roofing resting on the timbers. If this was in fact the system used at Hasanlu, which seems highly probable, the roof of each building would have

been flat with its weight resting primarily upon the inner structure of columns leaving the side walls free to bear the weight of the surrounding second-floor rooms. This, given the evidence at hand, would appear to be a more suitable reconstruction than the suggested interior balconies drawn from the Gordion model.

---

[4]P. E. Botta, *Monument de Ninive* II (Paris 1849) pl. 141. M. Van Loon, *Urartian Art* (Istanbul 1966) fig. 5b.

[5]T. Cuyler Young, Jr., *Excavations at Godin Tepe: First Progress Report* (Royal Ontario Museum, Art and Archaeology Occasional Paper 17; Toronto 1969) 117.

[6]H. H. von der Osten, *Die Welt der Perser* (Stuttgart 1956) 40.

[7]F. Krefter, *Persepolis Rekonstruktionen* (Teheraner Forschungen 3; Berlin 1971).

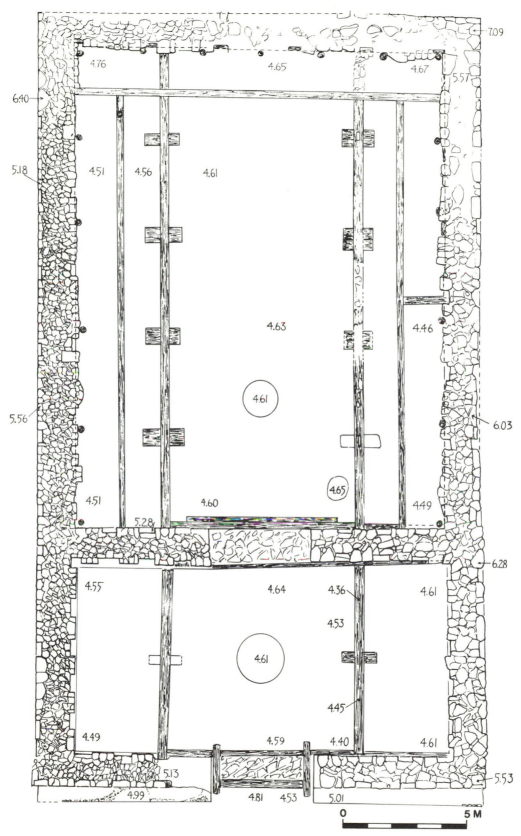

Figure 1. Gordion: plan of Megaron 3

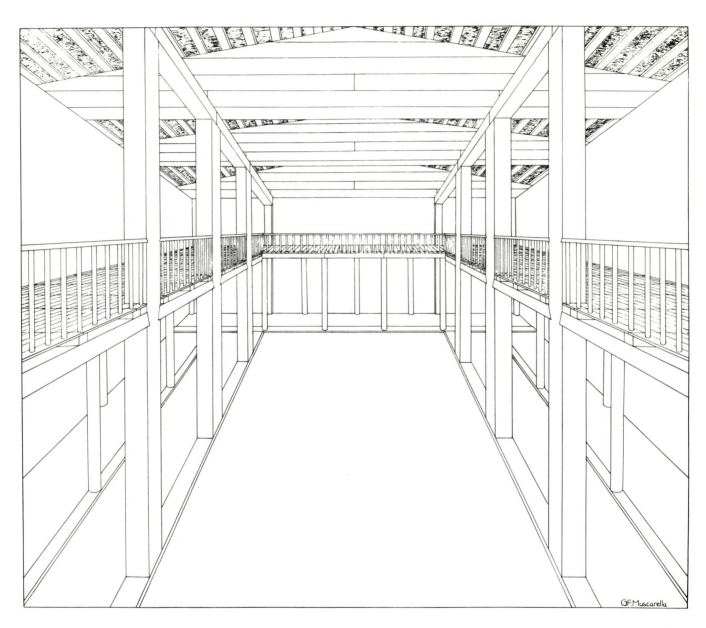

Figure 2. Gordion: reconstruction of Megaron 3

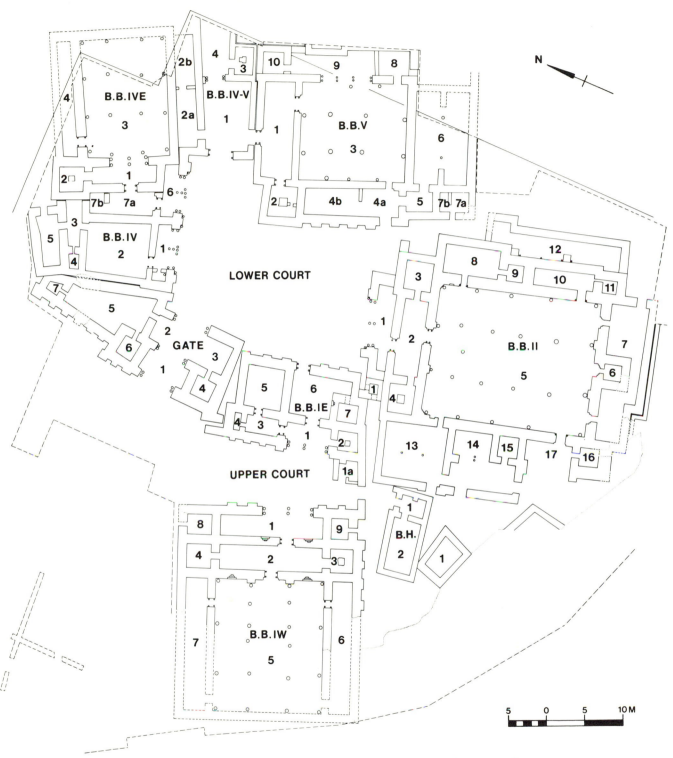

Figure 3. Hasanlu: plan of period IV columned halls, southwest quadrant, citadel mound

Figure 4. Musasir: relief depicting the temple of Haldi. From P. E. Botta *et al.*, *Monument de Ninive II* (Paris 1849) pl. 141.

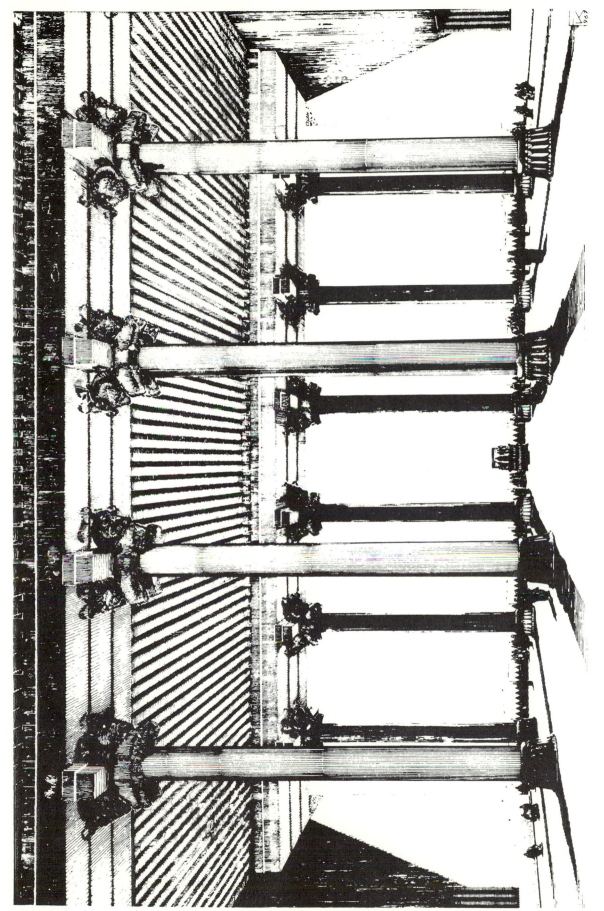

Figure 5. Persepolis: Apadana. Reconstruction of main hall. Reprinted, by permission of Gebr. Mann Verlag, from F. Krefter, *Persepolis Rekonstruktionen* (Teheraner Forschungen 3; Berlin 1971) Beilage 28.

XI. POSTSCRIPT

G. Roger Edwards

A postscript can be defined in various ways. Usually it is something short, something additional to the content of the main part of the communication, something which grows out of the communication and contributes something other. We have heard much communication today of kinds which Rodney would have enjoyed and reacted to with gusto, reflections of some of his many interests and activities. What I would like to add in a postscript to all this are words of his own which, since they are embodied in various of his letters, provide some of the special flavor for which he was known and beloved. They are from letters written from Gordion, which was the predominant interest and joy of his later years. They were written on two occasions, after the first day of excavation there and seven years later when he had finally succeeded in accomplishing his most important piece of excavation, that of the famous Midas Mound, an undertaking which had tantalized us all from the start. Many other letters exist. They will form an important part of the Gordion archives.

The first letter is headed "Sunday 1 April" and in parentheses "(no fooling though)." The year was 1950.

Dear G. Roger:
  Gold the first day; also (for Ellen)[1] carved ivory, but in horrible shape. We opened a tumulus already dug to ground level by the villagers (to get earth for mud bricks) and only 60 cm. below the present level we found a big cremation: late seventh or early sixth cent., apparently a young damsel (perhaps K.M.'s golden daughter),[2] pottery, lydions [fig. 1], an amphora, a bowl; bronzes, all melted together by the fire; carved ivory, burned and in bad shape, but apparently once very nice; gold, bracelet with lions' heads [fig. 2], earrings [fig. 3], pendants, brooch, beads from necklace (some particularly nice ones little acorns [fig. 4]—and not so very little either) and various round beads of gold and electrum from the necklace; also two large boxlike pendants.[3] All very satisfactory. We want ELLEN and we want YOU, not a second later than the first of May. If it will be any temptation, I suspect that I know where to look for Hellenistic graves—but will leave them for you, unless temptation becomes too great to make a trench and see. We haven't yet got our things from Philadelphia-Istanbul (but should have them tomorrow or Tuesday) so we have been working under difficulties—no boxes, no envelopes, no tickets, no films, no sheets, no good lamps (which makes this typing so queer no doubt) and I am sure Lucy would be shocked at our state. We have got however

---

[1]The people referred to in the present letters are Ellen L. Kohler of the University Museum, Lucy Talcott, John L. Caskey of the University of Cincinnati, Piet de Jong. The glues are Miss Talcott and Alison Frantz of the Agora Excavations in Athens.

[2]K. M.'s golden daughter: K. M. meaning King Midas. The story of his daughter, turned to gold by the King's touch, is not ancient but rather nineteenth century, invented by Nathaniel Hawthorne in a story entitled "The Golden Touch" in *A Wonder Book*.

[3]Some of the tomb objects not illustrated here are pictured in E. L. Kohler, "Cremations of the Middle Phrygian Period at Gordion," *supra:* the amphora, fig. 29; the bowl, fig. 30; the smaller pendants, fig. 25; the boxlike pendants, fig. 24. The tomb is Tumulus A.

two houses and will be quite comfortable when the amentities arrive. Mehmet Ali Bey tries to hold us up over his big house, so we simply left him in the lurch and found another, smaller, but new and clean; since we expect more people, and our finds are already starting to crowd us out of our present one I have decided to take a second, for catalogues, mending, storage, and ladies' quarters upstairs. . . . So far we have eaten (or rather bought) 312 eggs for 25.59 liras; they seem to come out at about 2¢ each; I hope nobody hatches chicks in the night.

Really can't see so must stop; this just to let you know we are still alive and enthusiastic, and to remind you to come, bringing your photographic skill and equipment. My best to the Caskeys, to glues and other girls.

RSY

This was an auspicious beginning for his long career at Gordion. And typical too, in his undertaking first an opportunity which might well have escaped the eyes of others, one which produced immediate results of the highest quality with little effort and expense.

The excavation of the Midas Mound came finally in 1957. The problem of its excavation was by no means simple. It was the most prominent feature of the landscape and it had exercised the imagination of all over the years, for the difficulties it presented for excavation were as enormous as was its bulk. Finally the problem of the location of the tomb it covered was solved by drilling (Hanfmann, *supra,* fig. 1) and in 1957 a mining tunnel technique was employed for reaching it and entering it. Rodney's letter of July 1, 1957, reads in part as follows:

Tomb well preserved [fig. 5], barring a bad crack in the cross beams which hold up the roof half-way, and bulges in both end walls. Wooden (pine?) chamber 5 m. wide by 6.30 long; peaked roof, height from floor to ceiling along sides 3.30 m., at center 3.70 m. Heavy double cross beams across width at center; over it and at end gables, heavy timbers filling triangles. Orientation about north-south. Wood very well finished as if with sand or sandpaper; effect of not-too-knotty pine. Floor likewise of heavy beams. Our door, sawn through wall, at north end of west side.

In NW corner four-poster bed-like arrangement along north wall, foot against west wall. About 1.90 wide by 2.90 long. Big cubical

blocks at each corner for it to rest on; a round hole in upper face of each block—purpose not clear. Headboard and footboard curved with cut-out scroll at either end; both fallen—very Victorian. The flat part of the bed fallen and now resting on floor. Heavy bed cover of many layers of cloth, linen and wool; now all broken into chunks but we rescued some stratified chunks and dissected others; Ellen says about 25 layers. Some bright pink. On top, skeleton, head to east, feet to west—the proprietor [fig. 6]. Seems to have a big fibula at each shoulder (bronze, not gold). What if anything was under the bed we do not yet know. Behind end of bed (head) a wooden table with spindly legs, collapsed; and on the floor a linen bag full of bronze (not gold) fibulae [fig. 7], some of which have spilled out on the floor. Some are very big and elaborate, a few with double pins (have always wondered how they work). Beyond these on floor in NE corner a mess of collapsed wooden furniture; have not yet tried to unravel it. Against middle of east wall and leaning, two huge inlaid wood throne backs [fig. 8], if that is what they are, like the one from last year but bigger, handsomer, and more complete. Behind them, between them and the wall, a lot of fragments of inlaid wood, which may mean something when fitted together. Also a lot of bronze pots, among them a handsome lion-headed object of which we cannot as yet tell the shape or purpose [fig. 9]. In the SE corner a mass of bronze pots that once stood on at least two tables: one of these must have been intricate and handsome to a degree, with inlaid panels in the faces of its frame and openwork finials sticking up and elaborately turned legs. It is now collapsed and in pieces, but when put together it will be very original and queer. Along west half of south wall three huge cauldrons standing on iron tripod rings, all very handsome though of bronze (not gold). One has two bulls-head handles looking out (Urartu type); the other two [fig. 10] have four handles each, sirens on one, looking in, with wings spread along below the rim and arms with hands over the wings; the other the same, but two of the sirens are bearded (Assyrian type). These may offer an outside dating for the whole. All the cauldrons full of pots (the only ones visible in the tomb) which don't look very exciting— mostly black polished deep bowls, but there may be something more interesting underneath. There is also a lot of unknown substance in the cauldrons, perhaps the remains of food. Along west wall to foot of bed again, large round-bodied trefoil jugs (have counted ten) like the pottery ones found in the burned layers on the huyuk. Also plaques with bronze studs in designs; some are round, some oblong. Have not tried to lift any; do not know what the backing material is—perhaps wood or leather, perhaps bronze. In the middle four maybe five tables, now collapsed, which bore omphalos bowls (bronze not gold) now scattered over floor; accurate count impossible as some lie under others or parts of the tables; estimate between 70 and 80. These are the things seen up to the present, and some of them very handsome too; but in substance a repetition of tumulus P on a larger scale and with better preservation. Should be quite exciting. Prognosis: bronzes in general in good condition; wood less so. There will be a long battle to dry, clean and preserve the wood; I think the things made of harder woods will survive all right and be very presentable, while the softer wood (pine and the like) may become hopeless through warping, shredding, and shrinking. We are going to try the alcohol treatment for drying and the gasoline and paraffin method for preserving. Needless to say the water came from our own drilling and has done the wooden things no good at all. But at least they were not squashed first by inrushing rubble as in tumulus P; and without the drilling we never would have found anything anyway. The wooden things will probably be left inside the grave as long as possible to dry very slowly; but Piet has agreed to stay for another month (until the end of July) and I would like him to try his hand at one of the throne backs. Up to the moment we have removed nothing except for the footboard of the bed and the cloth over it, which we had to take away to get in.

If one were to suggest a monument for him suitable to his ability and to his achievement one might well suggest the Midas Mound (fig. 11), whose excavation was his greatest and most difficult achievement. It still dominates the Gordion landscape. As indeed will his memory dominate the archaeological landscape and ours for long to come.

Figure 1. Lydion from Tumulus A.   H. 11.6 cm.

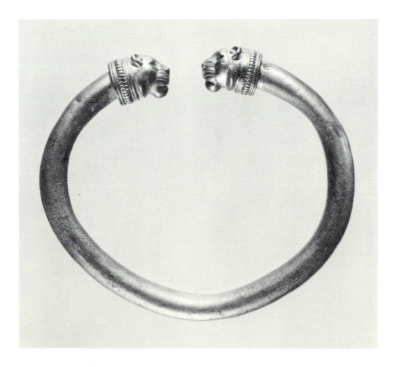

Figure 2. Gold bracelet from Tumulus A.   W. 7.4 cm.

163

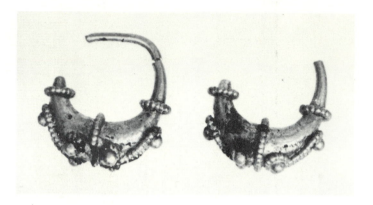

Figure 3. Gold earrings from Tumulus A.   W. of each 1.2 cm.

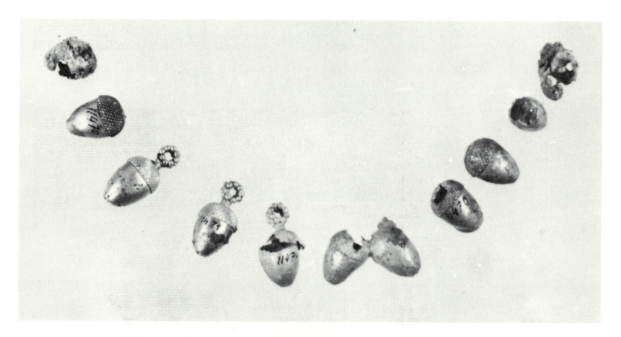

Figure 4. Gold acorn pendants from Tumulus A.   Max. H. 1.9 cm.

Figure 5. Tomb chamber of Midas Mound

Figure 6. Skeleton in tomb chamber of Midas Mound

Figure 7. Bag of bronze fibulae beside bier in Midas Mound

Figure 8. Wooden screens or throne backs in tomb chamber of Midas Mound

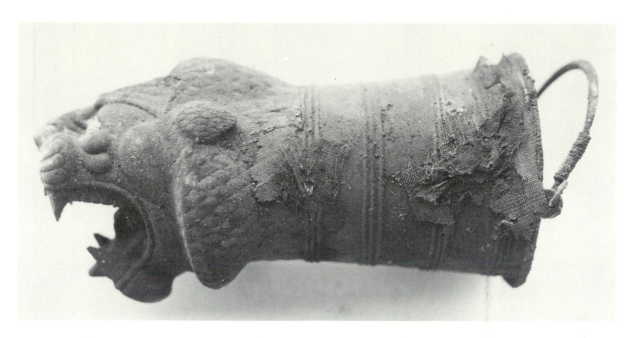

Figure 9. Bronze lion-head situla in tomb chamber of Midas Mound. L. without handle   22.5 cm.

Figure 10. Bronze cauldrons in tomb chamber of Midas Mound

Figure 11. View of Midas Mound

UNIVERSITY MUSEUM MONOGRAPHS

Francis R. Steele
1 THE CODE OF LIPIT-ISHTAR
1949.   28 pp.   7 pls.

Samuel Noah Kramer
2 SCHOOLDAYS: A SUMERIAN COMPOSITION RELATING TO
THE EDUCATION OF A SCRIBE
1949.   19 pp.   4 pls.

J. Alden Mason
3 THE LANGUAGE OF THE PAPAGO OF ARIZONA
1950.   84 pp.

Arthur J. Tobler
4 EXCAVATIONS AT TEPE GAWRA, VOLUME 11
1950.   ii + 260 pp.   182 pls.

Carleton S. Coon
5 CAVE EXPLORATIONS IN IRAN 1949
1951.   ii + 125 pp.   33 illus. in text.   15 pls.

John H. Moss, in collaboration with Kirk Bryan, G. William
Holmes, Linton Satterthwaite, Henry P. Hansen, C. Bertrand
Schultz, W. D. Frankforter
6 EARLY MAN IN THE EDEN VALLEY
1951.   vi + 124 pp.   32 figs. in text.   9 pls.

Samuel Noah Kramer
7 ENMERKAR AND THE LORD OF ARATTA: A SUMERIAN EPIC
TALE OF IRAQ AND IRAN
1952.   iv + 55 pp.   28 pls.

J. L. Giddings, Jr.
8 THE ARCTIC WOODLAND CULTURE OF THE KOBUK RIVER
1952.   x + 144 pp.   43 figs. in text.   46 pls.

Dorothy Hannah Cox
9 A THIRD CENTURY HOARD OF TETRADRACHMS FROM
GORDION
1953.   v + 20 pp.   1 map in text.   8 pls.

Ward H. Goodenough
10 NATIVE ASTRONOMY IN THE CENTRAL CAROLINES
1953.   46 pp.   4 figs. in text.   1 map.

John Howard Young and Suzanna Halstead Young
11 TERRACOTTA FIGURINES FROM KOURION IN CYPRUS
1955.   x + 260 pp.   3 plans.   17 figs. in text.   75 pls.

Daris Ray Swindler
12 A STUDY OF THE CRANIAL AND SKELETAL MATERIAL
FROM NIPPUR
1956.   v + 40 pp.   8 pls.

Machteld J. Mellink
13 A HITTITE CEMETERY AT GORDION
1956.   xii + 60 pp.   30 pls.

Linton Satterthwaite
14 STONE ARTIFACTS AT AND NEAR THE FINLEY SITE, NEAR
EDEN, WYOMING
1957.   iv + 22 pp.   5 figs.

Edwin M. Shook, William R. Coe and Vivian L. Broman, Linton
Satterthwaite
15 TIKAL REPORTS, NUMBERS 1 - 4
1958.   vi + 150 pp.   26 figs.

Rudolf Anthes, with contributions by Hasan S. K. Bakry, John
Dimick, Henry G. Fischer, Labib Habachi, Jean Jacquet
16 MIT RAHINEH 1955
1958.   vi + 93 pp.   18 figs. in text.   45 pls.   Map.

James B. Pritchard
17 HEBREW INSCRIPTIONS AND STAMPS FROM GIBEON
1959.   vi + 32 pp.   12 figs.

William R. Coe
18 PIEDRAS NEGRAS ARCHAEOLOGY: ARTIFACTS, CACHES
AND BURIALS
1959.   x + 245 pp.   69 figs.

Edmund I. Gordon, with a chapter by Thorkild Jacobsen
19 SUMERIAN PROVERBS: GLIMPSES OF EVERYDAY LIFE IN
ANCIENT MESOPOTAMIA
1959.   xxvi + 556 pp.   79 pls.

Richard E. W. Adams, Vivian L. Broman, William R. Coe,
William A. Haviland, Ruben E. Reina, Linton Satterthwaite,
Edwin M. Shook, Aubrey S. Trik
20 TIKAL REPORTS, NUMBERS 5-10
1961.   iv + 225 pp.   73 pls.

Robert F. Carr and James E. Hazard
21 TIKAL REPORTS, NUMBER 11
1961.   Portfolio of 10 maps and iv + 24 pp.

James B. Pritchard
22 THE WATER SYSTEM OF GIBEON
1961.   viii + 34 pp.   48 figs.

J. L. Benson, with contributions by Edith Porada and E. A. and
H. W. Catling

34 THE NECROPOLIS OF KALORIZIKI: EXCAVATED BY J. F.
DANIEL AND G. H. McFADDEN FOR THE UNIVERSITY
MUSEUM, UNIVERSITY OF PENNSYLVANIA, PHILADELPHIA
(published at Göteborg as volume XXVI of Studies in Mediterranean
Archaeology)
1973.   202 pp.   63 pls.

James B. Pritchard, with contributions by William P. Anderson,
Ellen Herscher, Javier Teixidor

35 SAREPTA: A PRELIMINARY REPORT ON THE IRON AGE
1975.   ix + 114 pp.   63 figs.

Robert J. Sharer (General Editor)

36 THE PREHISTORY OF CHALCHUAPA, EL SALVADOR
(published by the University of Pennsylvania Press)
1978. 3 volumes.
VOLUME I xv + 194 pp.   26 tables,   87 figs. (8 maps in pocket).
VOLUME II: xx + 211 pp.   12 tables,   38 figs.
VOLUME III: xvii + 226 pp.   9 tables,   39 figs.

Robert J. Sharer (General Editor) and Wendy Ashmore (Volume
Editor)

37 QUIRIGUA REPORTS, VOLUME I: PAPERS 1-5
1979.   ix + 73 pp.   4 tables.   24 figs.   Site map.

John Bockstoce

38 THE ARCHAEOLOGY OF CAPE NOME, ALASKA
1979.   xiii + 133 pp.   3 maps.   3 tables.   Frontispiece.   28 figs.
9 pls.

Irene J. Winter

39 A DECORATED BREASTPLATE FROM HASANLU, IRAN: TYPE,
STYLE, AND CONTEXT OF AN EQUESTRIAN ORNAMENT
Hasanlu Special Studies, volume I
1980.   xiv + 105 pp.   1 map.   Frontispiece (color). 79 figs.
Folding plate.

Oscar White Muscarella

40 THE CATALOGUE OF IVORIES FROM HASANLU, IRAN
Hasanlu Special Studies, volume II
1980.   xi + 231 pp.   2 plans.   Frontispiece.   293 figs.

James B. Pritchard

41 THE CEMETERY AT TELL ES-SA'IDIYEH, JORDAN
1980.   xii + 103 pp.   2 tables.   Frontispiece.
46 pls.   29 figs. in text.

Saul S. Weinberg

42 BAMBOULA AT KOURION: THE ARCHITECTURE
(In preparation)